23

SELECTED POEMS OF HENRY WADSWORTH LONGFELLOW

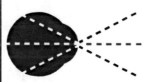 This Large Print Book carries the
Seal of Approval of N.A.V.H.

SELECTED POEMS OF HENRY WADSWORTH LONGFELLOW

HENRY WADSWORTH LONGFELLOW

KENNEBEC LARGE PRINT

A part of Gale, Cengage Learning

GALE
CENGAGE Learning

Detroit • New York • San Francisco • New Haven, Conn • Waterville, Maine • London

Kennebec Large Print, a part of Gale, Cengage Learning.
Kennebec Large Print® Perennial Favorites Collection.
The text of this Large Print edition is unabridged.
Other aspects of the book may vary from the original edition.
Set in 16 pt. Plantin.
Printed on permanent paper.

LIBRARY OF CONGRESS CATALOGING-IN-PUBLICATION DATA

Longfellow, Henry Wadsworth, 1807–1882.
  [Poems. Selections]
  Selected poems of Henry Wadsworth Longfellow / by Henry Wadsworth Longfellow.
    p. cm. — (Kennebec Large Print perennial favorites collection)
  ISBN-13: 978-1-4104-2478-5 (softcover : alk. paper)
  ISBN-10: 1-4104-2478-2 (softcover : alk. paper)
  1. Large type books. I. Title.
  PS2252 2010
  811'.3—dc22
                                    2009048400

Printed in the United States of America
  1 2 3 4 5   14 13 12 11 10
ED067

CONTENTS

6

FROM

THE VOICES OF THE NIGHT

THE SPIRIT OF POETRY

There is a quiet spirit in these woods,
That dwells where'er the gentle south-wind
 blows;
Where, underneath the white-thorn, in the
 glade,
The wild flowers bloom, or, kissing the soft
 air,
The leaves above their sunny palms out-
 spread.
With what a tender and impassioned voice
It fills the nice and delicate ear of thought,
When the fast ushering star of morning
 comes
O'er-riding the gray hills with golden scarf;
Or when the cowled and dusky-sandalled
 Eve,
In mourning weeds, from out the western
 gate,
Departs with silent pace! That spirit moves
In the green valley, where the silver brook,

11

From its full laver, pours the white cascade;
And, babbling low amid the tangled woods,
Slips down through moss-grown stones with
    endless laughter.
And frequent, on the everlasting hills,
Its feet go forth, when it doth wrap itself
In all the dark embroidery of the storm,
And shouts the stern, strong wind. And here,
    amid
The silent majesty of these deep woods,
Its presence shall uplift thy thoughts from
    earth,
As to the sunshine and the pure, bright air
Their tops the green trees lift. Hence gifted
    bards
Have ever loved the calm and quiet shades.
For them there was an eloquent voice in all
The sylvan pomp of woods, the golden sun,
The flowers, the leaves, the river on its way,
Blue skies, and silver clouds, and gentle
    winds,
The swelling upland, where the sidelong sun
Aslant the wooded slope, at evening, goes,
Groves, through whose broken roof the sky
    looks in,
Mountain, and shattered cliff, and sunny
    vale,
The distant lake, fountains, and mighty trees,
In many a lazy syllable, repeating
Their old poetic legends to the wind.

And this is the sweet spirit, that doth fill
The world; and, in these wayward days of
   youth,
My busy fancy oft embodies it,
As a bright image of the light and beauty
That dwell in nature; of the heavenly forms
We worship in our dreams, and the soft hues
That stain the wild bird's wing, and flush the
   clouds
When the sun sets. Within her tender eye
The heaven of April, with its changing light,
And when it wears the blue of May, is hung,
And on her lip the rich, red rose. Her hair
Is like the summer tresses of the trees,
When twilight makes them brown, and on
   her cheek
Blushes the richness of an autumn sky,
With ever-shifting beauty. Then her breath,
It is so like the gentle air of Spring,
As, from the morning's dewy flowers, it
   comes
Full of their fragrance, that it is a joy
To have it round us, and her silver voice
Is the rich music of a summer bird,
Heard in the still night, with its passionate
   cadence.

HYMN TO THE NIGHT
'Ασπασίη, τρίλλιστος.

I heard the trailing garments of the Night
   Sweep through her marble halls!
I saw her sable skirts all fringed with light
   From the celestial walls!

I felt her presence, by its spell of might,
   Stoop o'er me from above;
The calm, majestic presence of the Night,
   As of the one I love.

I heard the sounds of sorrow and delight,
   The manifold, soft chimes,
That fill the haunted chambers of the Night,
   Like some old poet's rhymes.

From the cool cisterns of the midnight air
   My spirit drank repose;
The fountain of perpetual peace flows
   there, —
   From those deep cisterns flows.

O holy Night! from thee I learn to bear
   What man has borne before!
Thou layest thy finger on the lips of Care,
   And they complain no more.

Peace! Peace! Orestes-like I breathe this
   prayer!

14

Descend with broad-winged flight,
The welcome, the thrice-prayed for, the most
   fair,
  The best-beloved Night!

A PSALM OF LIFE

Tell me not, in mournful numbers,
  Life is but an empty dream! —
For the soul is dead that slumbers,
  And things are not what they seem.

Life is real! Life is earnest!
  And the grave is not its goal;
Dust thou art, to dust returnest,
  Was not spoken of the soul.

Not enjoyment, and not sorrow,
  Is our destined end or way;
But to act, that each to-morrow
  Find us farther than to-day.

Art is long, and Time is fleeting,
  And our hearts, though stout and brave,
Still, like muffled drums, are beating
  Funeral marches to the grave.

In the world's broad field of battle,
  In the bivouac of Life,
Be not like dumb, driven cattle!
  Be a hero in the strife!

Trust no Future, howe'er pleasant!
  Let the dead Past bury its dead!
Act, — act in the living Present!
  Heart within, and God o'erhead!

Lives of great men all remind us
  We can make our lives sublime,
And, departing, leave behind us
  Footprints on the sands of time;

Footprints, that perhaps another,
  Sailing o'er life's solemn main,
A forlorn and shipwrecked brother,
  Seeing, shall take heart again.

Let us, then, be up and doing,
  With a heart for any fate;
Still achieving, still pursuing,
  Learn to labor and to wait.

THE LIGHT OF STARS

The night is come, but not too soon;
  And sinking silently,
All silently, the little moon
  Drops down behind the sky.

There is no light in earth or heaven
  But the cold light of stars;
And the first watch of night is given
  To the red planet Mars.

Is it the tender star of love?
　The star of love and dreams?
Oh no! from that blue tent above
　A hero's armor gleams.

And earnest thoughts within me rise,
　When I behold afar,
Suspended in the evening skies,
　The shield of that red star.

O star of strength! I see thee stand
　And smile upon my pain;
Thou beckonest with thy mailed hand,
　And I am strong again.

Within my breast there is no light
　But the cold light of stars;
I give the first watch of the night
　To the red planet Mars.

The star of the unconquered will,
　He rises in my breast,
Serene, and resolute, and still,
　And calm, and self-possessed.

And thou, too, whosoe'er thou art,
　That readest this brief psalm,
As one by one thy hopes depart,
　Be resolute and calm.

Oh, fear not in a world like this,

And thou shalt know erelong,
Know how sublime a thing it is
  To suffer and be strong.

FOOTSTEPS OF ANGELS

When the hours of Day are numbered,
  And the voices of the Night
Wake the better soul, that slumbered,
  To a holy, calm delight;

Ere the evening lamps are lighted,
  And, like phantoms grim and tall,
Shadows from the fitful firelight
  Dance upon the parlor wall;

Then the forms of the departed
  Enter at the open door;
The beloved, the true-hearted,
  Come to visit me once more;

He, the young and strong, who cherished
  Noble longings for the strife,
By the roadside fell and perished,
  Weary with the march of life!

They, the holy ones and weakly,
  Who the cross of suffering bore,
Folded their pale hands so meekly,
  Spake with us on earth no more!

And with them the Being Beauteous,
   Who unto my youth was given,
More than all things else to love me,
   And is now a saint in heaven.

With a slow and noiseless footstep
   Comes that messenger divine,
Takes the vacant chair beside me,
   Lays her gentle hand in mine.

And she sits and gazes at me
   With those deep and tender eyes,
Like the stars, so still and saint-like,
   Looking downward from the skies.

Uttered not, yet comprehended,
   Is the spirit's voiceless prayer,
Soft rebukes, in blessings ended,
   Breathing from her lips of air.

Oh, though oft depressed and lonely,
   All my fears are laid aside,
If I but remember only
   Such as these have lived and died!

BALLADS AND OTHER POEMS

THE SKELETON IN ARMOR

"Speak! speak! thou fearful guest!
Who, with thy hollow breast
Still in rude armor drest,
  Comest to daunt me!
Wrapt not in Eastern balms,
But with thy fleshless palms
Stretched, as if asking alms,
  Why dost thou haunt me?"

Then, from those cavernous eyes
Pale flashes seemed to rise,
As when the Northern skies
  Gleam in December;
And, like the water's flow
Under December's snow,
Came a dull voice of woe
  From the heart's chamber.

"I was a Viking old!
My deeds, though manifold,

No Skald in song has told,
  No Saga taught thee!
Take heed, that in thy verse
Thou dost the tale rehearse,
Else dread a dead man's curse;
  For this I sought thee.

"Far in the Northern Land,
By the wild Baltic's strand,
I, with my childish hand,
  Tamed the gerfalcon;
And, with my skates fast-bound,
Skimmed the half-frozen Sound,
That the poor whimpering hound
  Trembled to walk on.

"Oft to his frozen lair
Tracked I the grisly bear,
While from my path the hare
  Fled like a shadow;
Oft through the forest dark
Followed the were-wolf's bark,
Until the soaring lark
  Sang from the meadow.

"But when I older grew,
Joining a corsair's crew,
O'er the dark sea I flew
  With the marauders.
Wild was the life we led;
Many the souls that sped,

Many the hearts that bled,
  By our stern orders.

"Many a wassail-bout
Wore the long Winter out;
Often our midnight shout
  Set the cocks crowing,
As we the Berserk's tale
Measured in cups of ale,
Draining the oaken pail,
  Filled to o'erflowing.

"Once as I told in glee
Tales of the stormy sea,
Soft eyes did gaze on me,
  Burning yet tender;
And as the white stars shine
On the dark Norway pine,
On that dark heart of mine
  Fell their soft splendor.

"I wooed the blue-eyed maid,
Yielding, yet half afraid,
And in the forest's shade
  Our vows were plighted.
Under its loosened vest
Fluttered her little breast,
Like birds within their nest
  By the hawk frighted.

"Bright in her father's hall
Shields gleamed upon the wall,

Loud sang the minstrels all,
   Chanting his glory;
When of old Hildebrand
I asked his daughter's hand,
Mute did the minstrels stand
   To hear my story.

"While the brown ale he quaffed,
Loud then the champion laughed,
And as the wind-gusts waft
   The sea-foam brightly,
So the loud laugh of scorn,
Out of those lips unshorn,
From the deep drinking-horn
   Blew the foam lightly.

"She was a Prince's child,
I but a Viking wild,
And though she blushed and smiled,
   I was discarded!
Should not the dove so white
Follow the sea-mew's flight,
Why did they leave that night
   Her nest unguarded?

"Scarce had I put to sea,
Bearing the maid with me,
Fairest of all was she
   Among the Norsemen!
When on the white sea-strand,
Waving his armed hand,
Saw we old Hildebrand,

With twenty horsemen.

"Then launched they to the blast,
Bent like a reed each mast,
Yet we were gaining fast,
  When the wind failed us;
And with a sudden flaw
Came round the gusty Skaw,
So that our foe we saw
  Laugh as he hailed us.

"And as to catch the gale
Round veered the flapping sail,
'Death!' was the helmsman's hail,
  'Death without quarter!'
Mid-ships with iron keel
Struck we her ribs of steel;
Down her black hulk did reel
  Through the black water!

"As with his wings aslant,
Sails the fierce cormorant,
Seeking some rocky haunt,
  With his prey laden, —
So toward the open main,
Beating to sea again,
Through the wild hurricane,
  Bore I the maiden.

"Three weeks we westward bore,
And when the storm was o'er,
Cloud-like we saw the shore

Stretching to leeward;
There for my lady's bower
Built I the lofty tower,
Which, to this very hour,
   Stands looking seaward.

"There lived we many years;
Time dried the maiden's tears;
She had forgot her fears,
   She was a mother;
Death closed her mild blue eyes,
Under that tower she lies;
Ne'er shall the sun arise
   On such another!

"Still grew my bosom then,
Still as a stagnant fen!
Hateful to me were men,
   The sunlight hateful!
In the vast forest here,
Clad in my warlike gear,
Fell I upon my spear,
   Oh, death was grateful!

"Thus, seamed with many scars,
Bursting these prison bars,
Up to its native stars
   My soul ascended!
There from the flowing bowl
Deep drinks the warrior's soul,
Skoal! to the Northland! *skoal!*"
   Thus the tale ended.

THE WRECK OF THE HESPERUS

It was the schooner Hesperus,
  That sailed the wintry sea;
And the skipper had taken his little daugh-
    tèr,
  To bear him company.

Blue were her eyes as the fairy-flax,
  Her cheeks like the dawn of day,
And her bosom white as the hawthorn buds,
  That ope in the month of May.

The skipper he stood beside the helm,
  His pipe was in his mouth,
And he watched how the veering flaw did
    blow
  The smoke now West, now South.

Then up and spake an old Sailòr,
  Had sailed to the Spanish Main,
"I pray thee, put into yonder port,
  For I fear a hurricane.

"Last night, the moon had a golden ring,
  And to-night no moon we see!"
The skipper, he blew a whiff from his pipe,
  And a scornful laugh laughed he.

Colder and louder blew the wind,
  A gale from the Northeast,

The snow fell hissing in the brine,
    And the billows frothed like yeast.

Down came the storm, and smote amain
    The vessel in its strength;
She shuddered and paused, like a frighted
        steed,
    Then leaped her cable's length.

"Come hither! come hither! my little daugh-
        tèr,
    And do not tremble so;
For I can weather the roughest gale
    That ever wind did blow."

He wrapped her warm in his seaman's coat
    Against the stinging blast;
He cut a rope from a broken spar,
    And bound her to the mast.

"O father! I hear the church-bells ring,
    Oh say, what may it be?"
" 'T is a fog-bell on a rock-bound coast!" —
    And he steered for the open sea.

"O father! I hear the sound of guns,
    Oh say, what may it be?"
"Some ship in distress, that cannot live
    In such an angry sea!"

"O father! I see a gleaming light,
    Oh say, what may it be?"

But the father answered never a word,
   A frozen corpse was he.

Lashed to the helm, all stiff and stark,
   With his face turned to the skies,
The lantern gleamed through the gleaming
   snow
   On his fixed and glassy eyes.

Then the maiden clasped her hands and
   prayed
   That savèd she might be;
And she thought of Christ, who stilled the
   wave,
   On the Lake of Galilee.

And fast through the midnight dark and
   drear,
   Through the whistling sleet and snow,
Like a sheeted ghost, the vessel swept
   Tow'rds the reef of Norman's Woe.

And ever the fitful gusts between
   A sound came from the land;
It was the sound of the trampling surf
   On the rocks and the hard sea-sand.

The breakers were right beneath her bows,
   She drifted a dreary wreck,
And a whooping billow swept the crew
   Like icicles from her deck.

She struck where the white and fleecy waves
  Looked soft as carded wool,
But the cruel rocks, they gored her side
  Like the horns of an angry bull.

Her rattling shrouds, all sheathed in ice,
  With the masts went by the board;
Like a vessel of glass, she stove and sank,
  Ho! ho! the breakers roared!

At daybreak, on the bleak sea-beach,
  A fisherman stood aghast,
To see the form of a maiden fair,
  Lashed close to a drifting mast.

The salt sea was frozen on her breast,
  The salt tears in her eyes;
And he saw her hair, like the brown sea-
    weed,
  On the billows fall and rise.

Such was the wreck of the Hesperus,
  In the midnight and the snow!
Christ save us all from a death like this,
  On the reef of Norman's Woe!

THE VILLAGE BLACKSMITH

Under a spreading chestnut-tree
  The village smithy stands;
The smith, a mighty man is he,
  With large and sinewy hands;
And the muscles of his brawny arms
  Are strong as iron bands.

His hair is crisp, and black, and long,
  His face is like the tan;
His brow is wet with honest sweat,
  He earns whate'er he can,
And looks the whole world in the face,
  For he owes not any man.

Week in, week out, from morn till night,
  You can hear his bellows blow;
You can hear him swing his heavy sledge,
  With measured beat and slow,
Like a sexton ringing the village bell,
  When the evening sun is low.

And children coming home from school
  Look in at the open door;
They love to see the flaming forge,
  And hear the bellows roar,
And catch the burning sparks that fly
  Like chaff from a threshing-floor.

He goes on Sunday to the church,

And sits among his boys;
He hears the parson pray and preach,
  He hears his daughter's voice,
Singing in the village choir,
  And it makes his heart rejoice.

It sounds to him like her mother's voice,
  Singing in Paradise!
He needs must think of her once more,
  How in the grave she lies;
And with his hard, rough hand he wipes
  A tear out of his eyes.

Toiling, — rejoicing, — sorrowing,
  Onward through life he goes;
Each morning sees some task begin,
  Each evening sees it close;
Something attempted, something done,
  Has earned a night's repose.

Thanks, thanks to thee, my worthy friend,
  For the lesson thou hast taught!
Thus at the flaming forge of life
  Our fortunes must be wrought;
Thus on its sounding anvil shaped
  Each burning deed and thought.

IT IS NOT ALWAYS MAY

No hay pájaros en los nidos de antaño.
                                    Spanish Proverb.

The sun is bright, — the air is clear,
  The darting swallows soar and sing,
And from the stately elms I hear
  The bluebird prophesying Spring.

So blue yon winding river flows,
  It seems an outlet from the sky,
Where, waiting till the west wind blows,
  The freighted clouds at anchor lie.

All things are new; — the buds, the leaves,
  That gild the elm-tree's nodding crest,
And even the nest beneath the eaves; —
  There are no birds in last year's nest!

All things rejoice in youth and love,
  The fulness of their first delight!
And learn from the soft heavens above
  The melting tenderness of night.

Maiden, that read'st this simple rhyme,
  Enjoy thy youth, it will not stay;
Enjoy the fragrance of thy prime,
  For oh, it is not always May!

Enjoy the Spring of Love and Youth,
  To some good angel leave the rest;
For Time will teach thee soon the truth,
  There are no birds in last year's nest!

THE RAINY DAY

The day is cold, and dark, and dreary;
It rains, and the wind is never weary;
The vine still clings to the mouldering wall,
But at every gust the dead leaves fall,
  And the day is dark and dreary.

My life is cold, and dark, and dreary;
It rains, and the wind is never weary;
My thoughts still cling to the mouldering
    Past,
But the hopes of youth fall thick in the blast,
  And the days are dark and dreary.

Be still, sad heart! and cease repining;
Behind the clouds is the sun still shining;
Thy fate is the common fate of all,
Into each life some rain must fall,
  Some days must be dark and dreary.

GOD'S-ACRE

I like that ancient Saxon phrase, which calls
  The burial-ground God's-Acre! It is just;
It consecrates each grave within its walls,
  And breathes a benison o'er the sleeping
  dust.

God's-Acre! Yes, that blessed name imparts

Comfort to those who in the grave have
    sown
The seed that they had garnered in their
    hearts,
    Their bread of life, alas! no more their own.

Into its furrows shall we all be cast,
    In the sure faith, that we shall rise again
At the great harvest, when the archangel's
    blast
    Shall winnow, like a fan, the chaff and
    grain.

Then shall the good stand in immortal
    bloom,
    In the fair gardens of that second birth;
And each bright blossom mingle its perfume
    With that of flowers, which never bloomed
    on earth.

With thy rude ploughshare, Death, turn up
    the sod,
    And spread the furrow for the seed we sow;
This is the field and Acre of our God,
    This is the place where human harvests
    grow.

TO THE RIVER CHARLES

River! that in silence windest
    Through the meadows, bright and free,

Till at length thy rest thou findest
  In the bosom of the sea!

Four long years of mingled feeling,
  Half in rest, and half in strife,
I have seen thy waters stealing
  Onward, like the stream of life.

Thou hast taught me, Silent River!
  Many a lesson, deep and long;
Thou hast been a generous giver;
  I can give thee but a song.

Oft in sadness and in illness,
  I have watched thy current glide,
Till the beauty of its stillness
  Overflowed me, like a tide.

And in better hours and brighter,
  When I saw thy waters gleam,
I have felt my heart beat lighter,
  And leap onward with thy stream.

Not for this alone I love thee,
  Nor because thy waves of blue
From celestial seas above thee
  Take their own celestial hue.

Where yon shadowy woodlands hide thee,
  And thy waters disappear,
Friends I love have dwelt beside thee,

And have made thy margin dear.

More than this; — thy name reminds me
  Of three friends, all true and tried;
And that name, like magic, binds me
  Closer, closer to thy side.

Friends my soul with joy remembers!
  How like quivering flames they start,
When I fan the living embers
  On the hearth-stone of my heart!

'T is for this, thou Silent River!
  That my spirit leans to thee;
Thou hast been a generous giver,
  Take this idle song from me.

THE GOBLET OF LIFE

Filled is Life's goblet to the brim;
And though my eyes with tears are dim,
I see its sparkling bubbles swim,
And chant a melancholy hymn
  With solemn voice and slow.

No purple flowers, — no garlands green,
Conceal the goblet's shade or sheen,
Nor maddening draughts of Hippocrene,
Like gleams of sunshine, flash between
  Thick leaves of mistletoe.

This goblet, wrought with curious art,
Is filled with waters, that upstart,
When the deep fountains of the heart,
By strong convulsions rent apart,
  Are running all to waste.

And as it mantling passes round,
With fennel is it wreathed and crowned,
Whose seed and foliage sun-imbrowned
Are in its waters steeped and drowned,
  And give a bitter taste.

Above the lowly plants it towers,
The fennel, with its yellow flowers,
And in an earlier age than ours
Was gifted with the wondrous powers,
  Lost vision to restore.

It gave new strength, and fearless mood;
And gladiators, fierce and rude,
Mingled it in their daily food;
And he who battled and subdued,
  A wreath of fennel wore.

Then in Life's goblet freely press,
The leaves that give it bitterness,
Nor prize the colored waters less,
For in thy darkness and distress
  New light and strength they give!

And he who has not learned to know

How false its sparkling bubbles show,
How bitter are the drops of woe,
With which its brim may overflow,
   He has not learned to live.

The prayer of Ajax was for light;
Through all that dark and desperate fight,
The blackness of that noonday night,
He asked but the return of sight,
   To see his foeman's face.

Let our unceasing, earnest prayer
Be, too, for light, — for strength to bear
Our portion of the weight of care,
That crushes into dumb despair
   One half the human race.

O suffering, sad humanity!
O ye afflicted ones, who lie
Steeped to the lips in misery,
Longing, and yet afraid to die,
   Patient, though sorely tried!

I pledge you in this cup of grief,
Where floats the fennel's bitter leaf!
The Battle of our Life is brief,
The alarm, — the struggle, — the relief,
   Then sleep we side by side.

EXCELSIOR

The shades of night were falling fast,
As through an Alpine village passed
A youth, who bore, 'mid snow and ice,
A banner with the strange device,
  Excelsior!

His brow was sad; his eye beneath,
Flashed like a falchion from its sheath,
And like a silver clarion rung
The accents of that unknown tongue,
  Excelsior!

In happy homes he saw the light
Of household fires gleam warm and bright;
Above, the spectral glaciers shone,
And from his lips escaped a groan,
  Excelsior!

"Try not the Pass!" the old man said;
"Dark lowers the tempest overhead,
The roaring torrent is deep and wide!"
And loud that clarion voice replied,
  Excelsior!

"Oh stay," the maiden said, "and rest
Thy weary head upon this breast!"
A tear stood in his bright blue eye,
But still he answered, with a sigh,
  Excelsior!

"Beware the pine-tree's withered branch!
Beware the awful avalanche!"
This was the peasant's last Good-night,
A voice replied, far up the height,
   Excelsior!

At break of day, as heavenward
The pious monks of Saint Bernard
Uttered the oft-repeated prayer,
A voice cried through the startled air,
   Excelsior!

A traveller, by the faithful hound,
Half-buried in the snow was found,
Still grasping in his hand of ice
That banner with the strange device,
   Excelsior!

There in the twilight cold and gray,
Lifeless, but beautiful, he lay,
And from the sky, serene and far,
A voice fell, like a falling star,
   Excelsior!

POEMS ON SLAVERY

THE SLAVE'S DREAM

Beside the ungathered rice he lay,
  His sickle in his hand;
His breast was bare, his matted hair
  Was buried in the sand.
Again, in the mist and shadow of sleep,
  He saw his Native Land.

Wide through the landscape of his dreams
  The lordly Niger flowed;
Beneath the palm-trees on the plain
  Once more a king he strode;
And heard the tinkling caravans
  Descend the mountain road.

He saw once more his dark-eyed queen
  Among her children stand;
They clasped his neck, they kissed his cheeks,
  They held him by the hand! —
A tear burst from the sleeper's lids
  And fell into the sand.

41

And then at furious speed he rode
    Along the Niger's bank;
His bridle-reins were golden chains,
    And, with a martial clank,
At each leap he could feel his scabbard of
        steel
    Smiting his stallion's flank.

Before him, like a blood-red flag,
    The bright flamingoes flew;
From morn till night he followed their flight,
    O'er plains where the tamarind grew,
Till he saw the roofs of Caffre huts,
    And the ocean rose to view.

At night he heard the lion roar,
    And the hyena scream,
And the river-horse, as he crushed the reeds
    Beside some hidden stream;
And it passed, like a glorious roll of drums,
    Through the triumph of his dream.

The forests, with their myriad tongues,
    Shouted of liberty;
And the Blast of the Desert cried aloud,
    With a voice so wild and free,
That he started in his sleep and smiled
    At their tempestuous glee.

He did not feel the driver's whip,
    Nor the burning heat of day;

For Death had illumined the Land of Sleep,
  And his lifeless body lay
A worn-out fetter, that the soul
  Had broken and thrown away!

THE SLAVE SINGING AT MIDNIGHT

Loud he sang the psalm of David!
He, a Negro and enslaved,
Sang of Israel's victory,
Sang of Zion, bright and free.

In that hour, when night is calmest,
Sang he from the Hebrew Psalmist,
In a voice so sweet and clear
That I could not choose but hear,

Songs of triumph, and ascriptions,
Such as reached the swart Egyptians,
When upon the Red Sea coast
Perished Pharaoh and his host.

And the voice of his devotion
Filled my soul with strange emotion;
For its tones by turns were glad,
Sweetly solemn, wildly sad.

Paul and Silas, in their prison,
Sang of Christ, the Lord arisen.
And an earthquake's arm of might
Broke their dungeon-gates at night.

But, alas! what holy angel
Brings the Slave this glad evangel?
And what earthquake's arm of might
Breaks his dungeon-gates at night?

THE WITNESSES

In Ocean's wide domains,
  Half buried in the sands,
Lie skeletons in chains,
  With shackled feet and hands.

Beyond the fall of dews,
  Deeper than plummet lies,
Float ships, with all their crews,
  No more to sink nor rise.

There the black Slave-ship swims,
  Freighted with human forms,
Whose fettered, fleshless limbs
  Are not the sport of storms.

These are the bones of Slaves;
  They gleam from the abyss;
They cry, from yawning waves,
  "We are the Witnesses!"

Within Earth's wide domains
  Are markets for men's lives;
Their necks are galled with chains,
  Their wrists are cramped with gyves.

Dead bodies, that the kite
    In deserts makes its prey;
Murders, that with affright
    Scare school-boys from their play!

All evil thoughts and deeds;
    Anger, and lust, and pride;
The foulest, rankest weeds,
    That choke Life's groaning tide!

These are the woes of Slaves;
    They glare from the abyss;
They cry, from unknown graves,
    "We are the Witnesses!"

THE WARNING

Beware! The Israelite of old, who tore
    The lion in his path, — when, poor and
    blind,
He saw the blessed light of heaven no more,
    Shorn of his noble strength and forced to
    grind
In prison, and at last led forth to be
A pander to Philistine revelry, —

Upon the pillars of the temple laid
    His desperate hands, and in its overthrow
Destroyed himself, and with him those who
    made
    A cruel mockery of his sightless woe;

45

The poor, blind Slave, the scoff and jest of
    all,
Expired, and thousands perished in the fall!

There is a poor, blind Samson in this land,
    Shorn of his strength and bound in bonds
    of steel,
Who may, in some grim revel, raise his hand,
    And shake the pillars of this Commonweal,
Till the vast Temple of our liberties
A shapeless mass of wreck and rubbish lies.

FROM

THE BELFRY OF BRUGES AND OTHER POEMS

THE BELFRY OF BRUGES

In the market-place of Bruges stands the
    belfry old and brown;
Thrice consumed and thrice rebuilded, still
    it watches o'er the town.

As the summer morn was breaking, on that
    lofty tower I stood,
And the world threw off the darkness, like
    the weeds of widowhood.

Thick with towns and hamlets studded, and
    with streams and vapors gray,
Like a shield embossed with silver, round
    and vast the landscape lay.

At my feet the city slumbered. From its
    chimneys, here and there,
Wreaths of snow-white smoke, ascending,
    vanished, ghost-like, into air.

Not a sound rose from the city at that early
    morning hour,
But I heard a heart of iron beating in the
    ancient tower.

From their nests beneath the rafters sang the
    swallows wild and high;
And the world, beneath me sleeping, seemed
    more distant than the sky.

Then most musical and solemn, bringing
    back the olden times,
With their strange, unearthly changes rang
    the melancholy chimes,

Like the psalms from some old cloister, when
    the nuns sing in the choir;
And the great bell tolled among them, like
    the chanting of a friar.

Visions of the days departed, shadowy phan-
    toms filled my brain;
They who live in history only seemed to walk
    the earth again;

All the Foresters of Flanders, — mighty
    Baldwin Bras de Fer,
Lyderick du Bucq and Cressy, Philip, Guy
    de Dampierre.

I beheld the pageants splendid that adorned

those days of old;
Stately dames, like queens attended, knights
who bore the Fleece of Gold;

Lombard and Venetian merchants with deep-
laden argosies;
Ministers from twenty nations; more than
royal pomp and ease.

I beheld proud Maximilian, kneeling humbly
on the ground;
I beheld the gentle Mary, hunting with her
hawk and hound;

And her lighted bridal-chamber, where a
duke slept with the queen,
And the armed guard around them, and the
sword unsheathed between.

I beheld the Flemish weavers, with Namur
and Juliers bold,
Marching homeward from the bloody battle
of the Spurs of Gold;

Saw the fight at Minnewater, saw the White
Hoods moving west,
Saw great Artevelde victorious scale the
Golden Dragon's nest.

And again the whiskered Spaniard all the
land with terror smote;
And again the wild alarum sounded from the

tocsin's throat;

Till the bell of Ghent responded o'er lagoon
  and dike of sand,
"I am Roland! I am Roland! there is victory
  in the land!"

Then the sound of drums aroused me. The
  awakened city's roar
Chased the phantoms I had summoned back
  into their graves once more.

Hours had passed away like minutes; and,
  before I was aware,
Lo! the shadow of the belfry crossed the sun-
  illumined square.

A GLEAM OF SUNSHINE

This is the place. Stand still, my steed,
  Let me review the scene,
And summon from the shadowy Past
  The forms that once have been.

The Past and Present here unite
  Beneath Time's flowing tide,
Like footprints hidden by a brook,
  But seen on either side.

Here runs the highway to the town;
  There the green lane descends,

Through which I walked to church with thee,
   O gentlest of my friends!

The shadow of the linden trees
   Lay moving on the grass;
Between them and the moving boughs,
   A shadow, thou didst pass.

Thy dress was like the lilies,
   And thy heart as pure as they:
One of God's holy messengers
   Did walk with me that day.

I saw the branches of the trees
   Bend down thy touch to meet,
The clover-blossoms in the grass
   Rise up to kiss thy feet.

"Sleep, sleep to-day, tormenting cares,
   Of earth and folly born!"
Solemnly sang the village choir
   On that sweet Sabbath morn.

Through the closed blinds the golden sun
   Poured in a dusty beam,
Like the celestial ladder seen
   By Jacob in his dream.

And ever and anon, the wind
   Sweet-scented with the hay,

Turned o'er the hymn-book's fluttering
 leaves
  That on the window lay.

Long was the good man's sermon,
  Yet it seemed not so to me;
For he spake of Ruth the beautiful,
  And still I thought of thee.

Long was the prayer he uttered,
  Yet it seemed not so to me;
For in my heart I prayed with him,
  And still I thought of thee.

But now, alas! the place seems changed;
  Thou art no longer here:
Part of the sunshine of the scene
  With thee did disappear.

Though thoughts, deep-rooted in my heart,
  Like pine trees dark and high,
Subdue the light of noon, and breathe
  A low and ceaseless sigh;

This memory brightens o'er the past,
  As when the sun, concealed
Behind some cloud that near us hangs,
  Shines on a distant field.

THE ARSENAL AT SPRINGFIELD

This is the Arsenal. From floor to ceiling,
  Like a huge organ, rise the burnished arms;
But from their silent pipes no anthem peal-
    ing
  Startles the villages with strange alarms.

Ah! what a sound will rise, how wild and
    dreary,
  When the death-angel touches those swift
    keys!
What loud lament and dismal Miserere
  Will mingle with their awful symphonies!

I hear even now the infinite fierce chorus,
  The cries of agony, the endless groan,
Which, through the ages that have gone
    before us,
  In long reverberations reach our own.

On helm and harness rings the Saxon ham-
    mer,
  Through Cimbric forest roars the Norse-
    man's song,
And loud, amid the universal clamor,
  O'er distant deserts sounds the Tartar gong.

I hear the Florentine, who from his palace
  Wheels out his battle-bell with dreadful din,
And Aztec priests upon their teocallis

Beat the wild war-drums made of serpent's
  skin;

The tumult of each sacked and burning vil-
    lage;
  The shout that every prayer for mercy
    drowns;
The soldiers' revels in the midst of pillage;
  The wail of famine in beleaguered towns;

The bursting shell, the gateway wrenched
    asunder,
  The rattling musketry, the clashing blade;
And ever and anon, in tones of thunder
  The diapason of the cannonade.

Is it, O man, with such discordant noises,
  With such accursed instruments as these,
Thou drownest Nature's sweet and kindly
    voices,
  And jarrest the celestial harmonies?

Were half the power, that fills the world with
    terror,
  Were half the wealth bestowed on camps
    and courts,
Given to redeem the human mind from er-
    ror,
  There were no need of arsenals or forts:

The warrior's name would be a name ab-
  horred!

And every nation, that should lift again
Its hand against a brother, on its forehead
  Would wear forevermore the curse of Cain!

Down the dark future, through long genera-
    tions,
  The echoing sounds grow fainter and then
    cease;
And like a bell, with solemn, sweet vibra-
    tions,
  I hear once more the voice of Christ say,
    "Peace!"

Peace! and no longer from its brazen portals
  The blast of War's great organ shakes the
    skies!
But beautiful as songs of the immortals,
  The holy melodies of love arise.

RAIN IN SUMMER

How beautiful is the rain!
After the dust and heat,
In the broad and fiery street,
In the narrow lane,
How beautiful is the rain!

How it clatters along the roofs,
Like the tramp of hoofs!
How it gushes and struggles out
From the throat of the overflowing spout!

Across the window-pane
It pours and pours;
And swift and wide,
With a muddy tide,
Like a river down the gutter roars
The rain, the welcome rain!

The sick man from his chamber looks
At the twisted brooks;
He can feel the cool
Breath of each little pool;
His fevered brain
Grows calm again,
And he breathes a blessing on the rain.

From the neighboring school
Come the boys,
With more than their wonted noise
And commotion;
And down the wet streets
Sail their mimic fleets,
Till the treacherous pool
Ingulfs them in its whirling
And turbulent ocean.

In the country, on every side,
Where far and wide,
Like a leopard's tawny and spotted hide,
Stretches the plain,
To the dry grass and the drier grain
How welcome is the rain!

In the furrowed land
The toilsome and patient oxen stand;
Lifting the yoke-encumbered head,
With their dilated nostrils spread,
They silently inhale
The clover-scented gale,
And the vapors that arise
From the well-watered and smoking soil.
For this rest in the furrow after toil
Their large and lustrous eyes
Seem to thank the Lord,
More than man's spoken word.

Near at hand,
From under the sheltering trees,
The farmer sees
His pastures, and his fields of grain,
As they bend their tops
To the numberless beating drops
Of the incessant rain.
He counts it as no sin
That he sees therein
Only his own thrift and gain.

These, and far more than these,
The Poet sees!
He can behold
Aquarius old
Walking the fenceless fields of air;
And from each ample fold
Of the clouds about him rolled
Scattering everywhere

The showery rain,
As the farmer scatters his grain.

He can behold
Things manifold
That have not yet been wholly told, —
Have not been wholly sung nor said.
For his thought, that never stops,
Follows the water-drops
Down to the graves of the dead,
Down through chasms and gulfs profound,
To the dreary fountain-head
Of lakes and rivers under ground;
And sees them, when the rain is done,
On the bridge of colors seven
Climbing up once more to heaven,
Opposite the setting sun.

Thus the Seer,
With vision clear,
Sees forms appear and disappear,
In the perpetual round of strange,
Mysterious change
From birth to death, from death to birth,
From earth to heaven, from heaven to earth;
Till glimpses more sublime
Of things, unseen before
Unto his wondering eyes reveal
The Universe, as an immeasurable wheel
Turning forevermore
In the rapid and rushing river of Time.

TO A CHILD

Dear child! how radiant on thy mother's
  knee,
With merry-making eyes and jocund smiles,
Thou gazest at the painted tiles,
Whose figures grace,
With many a grotesque form and face,
The ancient chimney of thy nursery!
The lady with the gay macaw,
The dancing girl, the grave bashaw
With bearded lip and chin;
And, leaning idly o'er his gate,
Beneath the imperial fan of state,
The Chinese mandarin.

With what a look of proud command
Thou shakest in thy little hand
The coral rattle with its silver bells,
Making a merry tune!
Thousands of years in Indian seas
That coral grew, by slow degrees,
Until some deadly and wild monsoon
Dashed it on Coromandel's sand!
Those silver bells
Reposed of yore,
As shapeless ore,
Far down in the deep-sunken wells
Of darksome mines,
In some obscure and sunless place,
Beneath huge Chimborazo's base,

Or Potosí's o'erhanging pines!
And thus for thee, O little child,
Through many a danger and escape,
The tall ships passed the stormy cape;
For thee in foreign lands remote,
Beneath a burning, tropic clime,
The Indian peasant, chasing the wild goat,
Himself as swift and wild,
In falling, clutched the frail arbute,
The fibres of whose shallow root,
Uplifted from the soil, betrayed
The silver veins beneath it laid,
The buried treasures of the miser, Time.

But, lo! thy door is left ajar!
Thou hearest footsteps from afar!
And, at the sound,
Thou turnest round
With quick and questioning eyes,
Like one, who, in a foreign land,
Beholds on every hand
Some source of wonder and surprise!
And, restlessly, impatiently,
Thou strivest, strugglest, to be free.

The four walls of thy nursery
Are now like prison walls to thee.
No more thy mother's smiles,
No more the painted tiles,
Delight thee, nor the playthings on the floor,
That won thy little, beating heart before;
Thou strugglest for the open door.

Through these once solitary halls
Thy pattering footstep falls.
The sound of thy merry voice
Makes the old walls
Jubilant, and they rejoice
With the joy of thy young heart,
O'er the light of whose gladness
No shadows of sadness
From the sombre background of memory
    start.

Once, ah, once, within these walls,
One whom memory oft recalls,
The Father of his Country, dwelt.
And yonder meadows broad and damp
The fires of the besieging camp
Encircled with a burning belt.
Up and down these echoing stairs,
Heavy with the weight of cares,
Sounded his majestic tread;
Yes, within this very room
Sat he in those hours of gloom,
Weary both in heart and head.

But what are these grave thoughts to thee?
Out, out! into the open air!
Thy only dream is liberty,
Thou carest little how or where.
I see thee eager at thy play,
Now shouting to the apples on the tree,
With cheeks as round and red as they;
And now among the yellow stalks,

Among the flowering shrubs and plants,
As restless as the bee.
Along the garden walks,
The tracks of thy small carriage-wheels I
    trace;
And see at every turn how they efface
Whole villages of sand-roofed tents,
That rise like golden domes
Above the cavernous and secret homes
Of wandering and nomadic tribes of ants.
Ah, cruel little Tamerlane,
Who, with thy dreadful reign,
Dost persecute and overwhelm
These hapless Troglodytes of thy realm!

What! tired already! with those suppliant
    looks,
And voice more beautiful than a poet's books
Or murmuring sound of water as it flows,
Thou comest back to parley with repose!
This rustic seat in the old apple-tree,
With its o'erhanging golden canopy
Of leaves illuminate with autumnal hues,
And shining with the argent light of dews,
Shall for a season be our place of rest.
Beneath us, like an oriole's pendent nest,
From which the laughing birds have taken
    wing,
By thee abandoned, hangs thy vacant swing.
Dream-like the waters of the river gleam;
A sailless vessel drops adown the stream,
And like it, to a sea as wide and deep,

Thou driftest gently down the tides of sleep.

O child! O new-born denizen
Of life's great city! on thy head
The glory of the morn is shed,
Like a celestial benison!
Here at the portal thou dost stand,
And with thy little hand
Thou openest the mysterious gate
Into the future's undiscovered land.
I see its valves expand,
As at the touch of Fate!
Into those realms of love and hate,
Into that darkness blank and drear,
By some prophetic feeling taught,
I launch the bold, adventurous thought,
Freighted with hope and fear;
As upon subterranean streams,
In caverns unexplored and dark,
Men sometimes launch a fragile bark,
Laden with flickering fire,
And watch its swift-receding beams,
Until at length they disappear,
And in the distant dark expire.

By what astrology of fear or hope
Dare I to cast thy horoscope!
Like the new moon thy life appears;
A little strip of silver light,
And widening outward into night
The shadowy disk of future years;
And yet upon its outer rim,

A luminous circle, faint and dim,
And scarcely visible to us here,
Rounds and completes the perfect sphere;
A prophecy and intimation,
A pale and feeble adumbration,
Of the great world of light, that lies
Behind all human destinies.

Ah! if thy fate, with anguish fraught,
Should be to wet the dusty soil
With the hot tears and sweat of toil, —
To struggle with imperious thought,
Until the overburdened brain,
Weary with labor, faint with pain,
Like a jarred pendulum, retain
Only its motion, not its power, —
Remember, in that perilous hour,
When most afflicted and oppressed,
From labor there shall come forth rest.

And if a more auspicious fate
On thy advancing steps await,
Still let it ever be thy pride
To linger by the laborer's side;
With words of sympathy or song
To cheer the dreary march along
Of the great army of the poor,
O'er desert sand, o'er dangerous moor.
Nor to thyself the task shall be
Without reward; for thou shalt learn
The wisdom early to discern
True beauty in utility;

As great Pythagoras of yore,
Standing beside the blacksmith's door,
And hearing the hammers, as they smote
The anvils with a different note,
Stole from the varying tones, that hung
Vibrant on every iron tongue,
The secret of the sounding wire,
And formed the seven-chorded lyre.

Enough! I will not play the Seer;
I will no longer strive to ope
The mystic volume, where appear
The herald Hope, forerunning Fear,
And Fear, the pursuivant of Hope.
Thy destiny remains untold;
For, like Acestes' shaft of old,
The swift thought kindles as it flies,
And burns to ashes in the skies.

THE OCCULTATION OF ORION

I saw, as in a dream sublime,
The balance in the hand of Time.
O'er East and West its beam impended;
And Day, with all its hours of light,
Was slowly sinking out of sight,
While, opposite, the scale of Night
Silently with the stars ascended.

Like the astrologers of eld,
In that bright vision I beheld

Greater and deeper mysteries.
I saw, with its celestial keys,
Its chords of air, its frets of fire,
The Samian's great Æolian lyre,
Rising through all its sevenfold bars,
From earth unto the fixed stars.
And through the dewy atmosphere,
Not only could I see, but hear,
Its wondrous and harmonious strings,
In sweet vibration, sphere by sphere,
From Dian's circle light and near,
Onward to vaster and wider rings,
Where, chanting through his beard of snows,
Majestic, mournful, Saturn goes,
And down the sunless realms of space
Reverberates the thunder of his bass.

Beneath the sky's triumphal arch
This music sounded like a march,
And with its chorus seemed to be
Preluding some great tragedy.
Sirius was rising in the east;
And, slow ascending one by one,
The kindling constellations shone.
Begirt with many a blazing star,
Stood the great giant Algebar,
Orion, hunter of the beast!
His sword hung gleaming by his side,
And, on his arm, the lion's hide
Scattered across the midnight air
The golden radiance of its hair.

The moon was pallid, but not faint;
And beautiful as some fair saint,
Serenely moving on her way
In hours of trial and dismay.
As if she heard the voice of God,
Unharmed with naked feet she trod
Upon the hot and burning stars,
As on the glowing coals and bars,
That were to prove her strength and try
Her holiness and her purity.

Thus moving on, with silent pace,
And triumph in her sweet, pale face,
She reached the station of Orion.
Aghast he stood in strange alarm!
And suddenly from his outstretched arm
Down fell the red skin of the lion
Into the river at his feet.
His mighty club no longer beat
The forehead of the bull; but he
Reeled as of yore beside the sea,
When, blinded by Œnopion,
He sought the blacksmith at his forge,
And, climbing up the mountain gorge,
Fixed his blank eyes upon the sun.

Then, through the silence overhead,
An angel with a trumpet said,
"Forevermore, forevermore,
The reign of violence is o'er!"
And, like an instrument that flings
Its music on another's strings,

The trumpet of the angel cast
Upon the heavenly lyre its blast,
And on from sphere to sphere the words
Reëchoed down the burning chords, —
"Forevermore, forevermore,
The reign of violence is o'er!"

THE BRIDGE

I stood on the bridge at midnight,
  As the clocks were striking the hour,
And the moon rose o'er the city,
  Behind the dark church-tower.

I saw her bright reflection
  In the waters under me,
Like a golden goblet falling
  And sinking into the sea.

And far in the hazy distance
  Of that lovely night in June,
The blaze of the flaming furnace
  Gleamed redder than the moon.

Among the long, black rafters
  The wavering shadows lay,
And the current that came from the ocean
  Seemed to lift and bear them away;

As, sweeping and eddying through them,
  Rose the belated tide,

And, streaming into the moonlight,
  The seaweed floated wide.

And like those waters rushing
  Among the wooden piers,
A flood of thoughts came o'er me
  That filled my eyes with tears.

How often, oh how often,
  In the days that had gone by,
I had stood on that bridge at midnight
  And gazed on that wave and sky!

How often, oh how often,
  I had wished that the ebbing tide
Would bear me away on its bosom
  O'er the ocean wild and wide!

For my heart was hot and restless,
  And my life was full of care,
And the burden laid upon me
  Seemed greater than I could bear.

But now it has fallen from me,
  It is buried in the sea;
And only the sorrow of others
  Throws its shadow over me.

Yet whenever I cross the river
  On its bridge with wooden piers,
Like the odor of brine from the ocean

Comes the thought of other years.

And I think how many thousands
  Of care-encumbered men,
Each bearing his burden of sorrow,
  Have crossed the bridge since then.

I see the long procession
  Still passing to and fro,
The young heart hot and restless,
  And the old subdued and slow!

And forever and forever,
  As long as the river flows,
As long as the heart has passions,
  As long as life has woes;

The moon and its broken reflection
  And its shadows shall appear,
As the symbol of love in heaven,
  And its wavering image here.

TO THE DRIVING CLOUD

Gloomy and dark art thou, O chief of the
  mighty Omahas;
Gloomy and dark as the driving cloud, whose
  name thou hast taken!
Wrapped in thy scarlet blanket, I see thee
  stalk through the city's
Narrow and populous streets, as once by the

margin of rivers
Stalked those birds unknown, that have left
us only their footprints.
What, in a few short years, will remain of thy
race but the footprints?

How canst thou walk these streets, who hast
trod the green turf of the prairies?
How canst thou breathe this air, who hast
breathed the sweet air of the mountains?
Ah! 'tis in vain that with lordly looks of
disdain thou dost challenge
Looks of disdain in return, and question
these walls and these pavements,
Claiming the soil for thy hunting-grounds,
while down-trodden millions
Starve in the garrets of Europe, and cry from
its caverns that they, too,
Have been created heirs of the earth, and
claim its division!

Back, then, back to thy woods in the regions
west of the Wabash!
There as a monarch thou reignest. In autumn
the leaves of the maple
Pave the floors of thy palace-halls with gold,
and in summer
Pine-trees waft through its chambers the
odorous breath of their branches.
There thou art strong and great, a hero, a
tamer of horses!

There thou chasest the stately stag on the
banks of the Elkhorn,
Or by the roar of the Running-Water, or
where the Omaha
Calls thee, and leaps through the wild ravine
like a brave of the Blackfeet!
Hark! what murmurs arise from the heart of
those mountainous deserts?
Is it the cry of the Foxes and Crows, or the
mighty Behemoth,
Who, unharmed, on his tusks once caught
the bolts of the thunder,
And now lurks in his lair to destroy the race
of the red man?
Far more fatal to thee and thy race than the
Crows and the Foxes,
Far more fatal to thee and thy race than the
tread of Behemoth,
Lo! the big thunder-canoe, that steadily
breasts the Missouri's
Merciless current! and yonder, afar on the
prairies, the camp-fires
Gleam through the night; and the cloud of
dust in the gray of the daybreak
Marks not the buffalo's track, nor the Man-
dan's dexterous horse-race;
It is a caravan, whitening the desert where
dwell the Camanches!
Ha! how the breath of these Saxons and
Celts, like the blast of the east-wind,
Drifts evermore to the west the scanty
smokes of thy wigwams!

The Day Is Done

The day is done, and the darkness
  Falls from the wings of Night,
As a feather is wafted downward
  From an eagle in his flight.

I see the lights of the village
  Gleam through the rain and the mist,
And a feeling of sadness comes o'er me
  That my soul cannot resist:

A feeling of sadness and longing,
  That is not akin to pain,
And resembles sorrow only
  As the mist resembles the rain.

Come, read to me some poem,
  Some simple and heartfelt lay,
That shall soothe this restless feeling,
  And banish the thoughts of day.

Not from the grand old masters,
  Not from the bards sublime,
Whose distant footsteps echo
  Through the corridors of Time.

For, like strains of martial music,
  Their mighty thoughts suggest
Life's endless toil and endeavor;
  And to-night I long for rest.

Read from some humbler poet,
  Whose songs gushed from his heart,
As showers from the clouds of summer,
  Or tears from the eyelids start;

Who, through long days of labor,
  And nights devoid of ease,
Still heard in his soul the music
  Of wonderful melodies.

Such songs have power to quiet
  The restless pulse of care,
And come like the benediction
  That follows after prayer.

Then read from the treasured volume
  The poem of thy choice,
And lend to the rhyme of the poet
  The beauty of thy voice.

And the night shall be filled with music,
  And the cares, that infest the day,
Shall fold their tents, like the Arabs,
  And as silently steal away.

AFTERNOON IN FEBRUARY

The day is ending,
The night is descending;
The marsh is frozen,
  The river dead.

Through clouds like ashes
The red sun flashes
On village windows
  That glimmer red.

The snow recommences;
The buried fences
Mark no longer
  The road o'er the plain;

While through the meadows,
Like fearful shadows,
Slowly passes
  A funeral train.

The bell is pealing,
And every feeling
Within me responds
  To the dismal knell;

Shadows are trailing,
My heart is bewailing
And tolling within
  Like a funeral bell.

THE OLD CLOCK ON THE STAIRS

Somewhat back from the village street
Stands the old-fashioned country-seat.
Across its antique portico
Tall poplar-trees their shadows throw;

And from its station in the hall
An ancient timepiece says to all, —
    "Forever — never!
    Never — forever!"

Half-way up the stairs it stands,
And points and beckons with its hands
From its case of massive oak,
Like a monk, who, under his cloak,
Crosses himself, and sighs, alas!
With sorrowful voice to all who pass, —
    "Forever — never!
    Never — forever!"

By day its voice is low and light;
But in the silent dead of night,
Distinct as a passing footstep's fall,
It echoes along the vacant hall,
Along the ceiling, along the floor,
And seems to say, at each chamber-door, —
    "Forever — never!
    Never — forever!"

Through days of sorrow and of mirth,
Through days of death and days of birth,
Through every swift vicissitude
Of changeful time, unchanged it has stood,
And as if, like God, it all things saw,
It calmly repeats those words of awe, —
    "Forever — never!
    Never — forever!"

In that mansion used to be
Free-hearted Hospitality;
His great fires up the chimney roared;
The stranger feasted at his board;
But, like the skeleton at the feast,
That warning timepiece never ceased, —
    "Forever — never!
    Never — forever!"

There groups of merry children played,
There youths and maidens dreaming strayed;
O precious hours! O golden prime,
And affluence of love and time!
Even as a miser counts his gold,
Those hours the ancient timepiece told, —
    "Forever — never!
    Never — forever!"

From that chamber, clothed in white,
The bride came forth on her wedding night;
There, in that silent room below,
The dead lay in his shroud of snow;
And in the hush that followed the prayer,
Was heard the old clock on the stair, —
    "Forever — never!
    Never — forever!"

All are scattered now and fled,
Some are married, some are dead;
And when I ask, with throbs of pain,
"Ah! when shall they all meet again?"
As in the days long since gone by,

The ancient timepiece makes reply, —
   "Forever — never!
   Never — forever!"

Never here, forever there,
Where all parting, pain, and care,
And death, and time shall disappear, —
Forever there, but never here!
The horologe of Eternity
Sayeth this incessantly, —
   "Forever — never!
   Never — forever!"

THE ARROW AND THE SONG

I shot an arrow into the air,
It fell to earth, I knew not where;
For, so swiftly it flew, the sight
Could not follow it in its flight.

I breathed a song into the air,
It fell to earth, I knew not where;
For who has sight so keen and strong,
That it can follow the flight of song?

Long, long afterward, in an oak
I found the arrow, still unbroke;
And the song, from beginning to end,
I found again in the heart of a friend.

THE EVENING STAR

Lo! in the painted oriel of the West,
  Whose panes the sunken sun incarnadines,
  Like a fair lady at her casement, shines
  The evening star, the star of love and rest!
And then anon she doth herself divest
  Of all her radiant garments, and reclines
  Behind the sombre screen of yonder pines,
  With slumber and soft dreams of love op-
    pressed.
O my beloved, my sweet Hesperus!
  My morning and my evening star of love!
  My best and gentlest lady! even thus,
As that fair planet in the sky above,
  Dost thou retire unto thy rest at night,
  And from thy darkened window fades the
    light.

AUTUMN

Thou comest, Autumn, heralded by the rain,
  With banners, by great gales incessant
    fanned,
  Brighter than brightest silks of Samarcand,
  And stately oxen harnessed to thy wain!
Thou standest, like imperial Charlemagne,
  Upon thy bridge of gold; thy royal hand
  Outstretched with benedictions o'er the
    land,

Blessing the farms through all thy vast domain!
Thy shield is the red harvest moon, suspended
So long beneath the heaven's o'erhanging
eaves;
Thy steps are by the farmer's prayers attended;
Like flames upon an altar shine the sheaves;
And, following thee, in thy ovation splendid,
Thine almoner, the wind, scatters the
golden leaves!

DANTE

Tuscan, that wanderest through the realms
of gloom,
With thoughtful pace, and sad, majestic
eyes,
Stern thoughts and awful from thy soul
arise,
Like Farinata from his fiery tomb.
Thy sacred song is like the trump of doom;
Yet in thy heart what human sympathies,
What soft compassion glows, as in the skies
The tender stars their clouded lamps relume!
Methinks I see thee stand with pallid cheeks
By Fra Hilario in his diocese,
As up the convent-walls, in golden streaks,

The ascending sunbeams mark the day's de-
   crease;
   And, as he asks what there the stranger
   seeks,
   Thy voice along the cloister whispers
   "Peace!"

CURFEW

I.

Solemnly, mournfully,
  Dealing its dole,
The Curfew Bell
  Is beginning to toll.

Cover the embers,
  And put out the light;
Toil comes with the morning,
  And rest with the night.

Dark grow the windows,
  And quenched is the fire;
Sound fades into silence, —
  All footsteps retire.

No voice in the chambers,
  No sound in the hall!
Sleep and oblivion
  Reign over all!

II.

The book is completed,
  And closed, like the day;
And the hand that has written it
  Lays it away.

Dim grow its fancies;
  Forgotten they lie;
Like coals in the ashes,
  They darken and die.

Song sinks into silence,
  The story is told,
The windows are darkened,
  The hearth-stone is cold.

Darker and darker
  The black shadows fall;
Sleep and oblivion
  Reign over all.

EVANGELINE

A Tale of Acadie

This is the forest primeval. The murmuring
    pines and the hemlocks,
Bearded with moss, and in garments green,
    indistinct in the twilight,
Stand like Druids of eld, with voices sad and
    prophetic,
Stand like harpers hoar, with beards that rest
    on their bosoms.
Loud from its rocky caverns, the deep-voiced
    neighboring ocean
Speaks, and in accents disconsolate answers
    the wail of the forest.

  This is the forest primeval; but where are
    the hearts that beneath it
Leaped like the roe, when he hears in the
    woodland the voice of the huntsman?
Where is the thatch-roofed village, the home
    of Acadian farmers, —
Men whose lives glided on like rivers that

water the woodlands,
Darkened by shadows of earth, but reflecting an image of heaven?
Waste are those pleasant farms, and the farmers forever departed!
Scattered like dust and leaves, when the mighty blasts of October
Seize them, and whirl them aloft, and sprinkle them far o'er the ocean.
Naught but tradition remains of the beautiful village of Grand-Pré.

Ye who believe in affection that hopes, and endures, and is patient,
Ye who believe in the beauty and strength of woman's devotion,
List to the mournful tradition, still sung by the pines of the forest;
List to a Tale of Love in Acadie, home of the happy.

Part The First
I.

In the Acadian land, on the shores of the Basin of Minas,
Distant, secluded, still, the little village of Grand-Pré
Lay in the fruitful valley. Vast meadows stretched to the eastward,
Giving the village its name, and pasture to flocks without number.

Dikes, that the hands of the farmers had
  raised with labor incessant,
Shut out the turbulent tides; but at stated
  seasons the floodgates
Opened, and welcomed the sea to wander at
  will o'er the meadows.
West and south there were fields of flax, and
  orchards and cornfields
Spreading afar and unfenced o'er the plain;
  and away to the northward
Blomidon rose, and the forests old, and aloft
  on the mountains
Sea-fogs pitched their tents, and mists from
  the mighty Atlantic
Looked on the happy valley, but ne'er from
  their station descended.
There, in the midst of its farms, reposed the
  Acadian village.
Strongly built were the houses, with frames
  of oak and of hemlock,
Such as the peasants of Normandy built in
  the reign of the Henries.
Thatched were the roofs, with dormer-
  windows; and gables projecting
Over the basement below protected and
  shaded the doorway.
There in the tranquil evenings of summer,
  when brightly the sunset
Lighted the village street, and gilded the
  vanes on the chimneys,
Matrons and maidens sat in snow-white caps
  and in kirtles

Scarlet and blue and green, with distaffs
spinning the golden
Flax for the gossiping looms, whose noisy
shuttles within doors
Mingled their sounds with the whir of the
wheels and the songs of the maidens.
Solemnly down the street came the parish
priest, and the children
Paused in their play to kiss the hand he
extended to bless them.
Reverend walked he among them; and up
rose matrons and maidens,
Hailing his slow approach with words of af-
fectionate welcome.
Then came the laborers home from the field,
and serenely the sun sank
Down to his rest, and twilight prevailed.
Anon from the belfry
Softly the Angelus sounded, and over the
roofs of the village
Columns of pale blue smoke, like clouds of
incense ascending,
Rose from a hundred hearths, the homes of
peace and contentment.
Thus dwelt together in love these simple Aca-
dian farmers, —
Dwelt in the love of God and of man. Alike
were they free from
Fear, that reigns with the tyrant, and envy,
the vice of republics.
Neither locks had they to their doors, nor
bars to their windows;

But their dwellings were open as day and the
hearts of the owners;
There the richest was poor, and the poorest
lived in abundance.

Somewhat apart from the village, and
nearer the Basin of Minas,
Benedict Bellefontaine, the wealthiest farmer
of Grand-Pré,
Dwelt on his goodly acres; and with him,
directing his household,
Gentle Evangeline lived, his child, and the
pride of the village.
Stalworth and stately in form was the man of
seventy winters;
Hearty and hale was he, an oak that is
covered with snowflakes;
White as the snow were his locks, and his
cheeks as brown as the oak-leaves.
Fair was she to behold, that maiden of
seventeen summers.
Black were her eyes as the berry that grows
on the thorn by the wayside,
Black, yet how softly they gleamed beneath
the brown shade of her tresses!
Sweet was her breath as the breath of kine
that feed in the meadows.
When in the harvest heat she bore to the
reapers at noontide
Flagons of home-brewed ale, ah! fair in sooth
was the maiden.
Fairer was she when, on Sunday morn, while

the bell from its turret
Sprinkled with holy sounds the air, as the
priest with his hyssop
Sprinkles the congregation, and scatters
blessings upon them,
Down the long street she passed, with her
chaplet of beads and her missal,
Wearing her Norman cap, and her kirtle of
blue, and the earrings,
Brought in the olden time from France, and
since, as an heirloom,
Handed down from mother to child, through
long generations.
But a celestial brightness — a more ethereal
beauty —
Shone on her face and encircled her form,
when, after confession,
Homeward serenely she walked with God's
benediction upon her.
When she had passed, it seemed like the
ceasing of exquisite music.

Firmly builded with rafters of oak, the
house of the farmer
Stood on the side of a hill commanding the
sea; and a shady
Sycamore grew by the door, with a wood-
bine wreathing around it.
Rudely carved was the porch, with seats
beneath; and a footpath
Led through an orchard wide, and dis-
appeared in the meadow.

Under the sycamore-tree were hives overhung
    by a penthouse,
Such as the traveller sees in regions remote
    by the roadside,
Built o'er a box for the poor, or the blessed
    image of Mary.
Farther down, on the slope of the hill, was
    the well with its moss-grown
Bucket, fastened with iron, and near it a
    trough for the horses.
Shielding the house from storms, on the
    north, were the barns and the farm-yard.
There stood the broad-wheeled wains and
    the antique ploughs and the harrows;
There were the folds for the sheep; and there,
    in his feathered seraglio,
Strutted the lordly turkey, and crowed the
    cock, with the selfsame
Voice that in ages of old had startled the
    penitent Peter.
Bursting with hay were the barns, themselves
    a village. In each one
Far o'er the gable projected a roof of thatch;
    and a staircase,
Under the sheltering eaves, led up to the
    odorous corn-loft.
There too the dove-cot stood, with its meek
    and innocent inmates
Murmuring ever of love; while above in the
    variant breezes
Numberless noisy weathercocks rattled and
    sang of mutation.

Thus, at peace with God and the world, the farmer of Grand-Pré

Lived on his sunny farm, and Evangeline governed his household.

Many a youth, as he knelt in church and opened his missal,

Fixed his eyes upon her as the saint of his deepest devotion;

Happy was he who might touch her hand or the hem of her garment!

Many a suitor came to her door, by the darkness befriended,

And, as he knocked and waited to hear the sound of her footsteps,

Knew not which beat the louder, his heart or the knocker of iron;

Or at the joyous feast of the Patron Saint of the village,

Bolder grew, and pressed her hand in the dance as he whispered

Hurried words of love, that seemed a part of the music.

But, among all who came, young Gabriel only was welcome;

Gabriel Lajeunesse, the son of Basil the blacksmith,

Who was a mighty man in the village, and honored of all men;

For, since the birth of time, throughout all ages and nations,

Has the craft of the smith been held in repute by the people.

Basil was Benedict's friend. Their children
from earliest childhood
Grew up together as brother and sister; and
Father Felician,
Priest and pedagogue both in the village, had
taught them their letters
Out of the selfsame book, with the hymns of
the church and the plain-song.
But when the hymn was sung, and the daily
lesson completed,
Swiftly they hurried away to the forge of Basil
the blacksmith.
There at the door they stood, with wonder-
ing eyes to behold him
Take in his leathern lap the hoof of the horse
as a plaything,
Nailing the shoe in its place; while near him
the tire of the cart-wheel
Lay like a fiery snake, coiled round in a circle
of cinders.
Oft on autumnal eves, when without in the
gathering darkness
Bursting with light seemed the smithy,
through every cranny and crevice,
Warm by the forge within they watched the
laboring bellows,
And as its panting ceased, and the sparks
expired in the ashes,
Merrily laughed, and said they were nuns
going into the chapel.
Oft on sledges in winter, as swift as the swoop
of the eagle,

Down the hillside bounding, they glided
   away o'er the meadow.
Oft in the barns they climbed to the populous
   nests on the rafters,
Seeking with eager eyes that wondrous stone,
   which the swallow
Brings from the shore of the sea to restore
   the sight of its fledglings;
Lucky was he who found that stone in the
   nest of the swallow!
Thus passed a few swift years, and they no
   longer were children.
He was a valiant youth, and his face, like the
   face of the morning,
Gladdened the earth with its light, and
   ripened thought into action.
She was a woman now, with the heart and
   hopes of a woman.
"Sunshine of Saint Eulalie" was she called;
   for that was the sunshine
Which, as the farmers believed, would load
   their orchards with apples;
She, too, would bring to her husband's house
   delight and abundance,
Filling it with love and the ruddy faces of
   children.

II.

Now had the season returned, when the
   nights grow colder and longer,
And the retreating sun the sign of the Scor-

pion enters.

Birds of passage sailed through the leaden
air, from the ice-bound,

Desolate northern bays to the shores of tropi-
cal islands.

Harvests were gathered in; and wild with the
winds of September

Wrestled the trees of the forest, as Jacob of
old with the angel.

All the signs foretold a winter long and in-
clement.

Bees, with prophetic instinct of want, had
hoarded their honey

Till the hives overflowed; and the Indian
hunters asserted

Cold would the winter be, for thick was the
fur of the foxes.

Such was the advent of autumn. Then fol-
lowed that beautiful season,

Called by the pious Acadian peasants the
Summer of All-Saints!

Filled was the air with a dreamy and magical
light; and the landscape

Lay as if new-created in all the freshness of
childhood.

Peace seemed to reign upon earth, and the
restless heart of the ocean

Was for a moment consoled. All sounds were
in harmony blended.

Voices of children at play, the crowing of
cocks in the farm-yards,

Whir of wings in the drowsy air, and the cooing of pigeons,

All were subdued and low as the murmurs of
love, and the great sun

Looked with the eye of love through the
golden vapors around him;

While arrayed in its robes of russet and
scarlet and yellow,

Bright with the sheen of the dew, each glit-
tering tree of the forest

Flashed like the plane-tree the Persian
adorned with mantles and jewels.

Now recommenced the reign of rest and
affection and stillness.

Day with its burden and heat had departed,
and twilight descending

Brought back the evening star to the sky, and
the herds to the homestead.

Pawing the ground they came, and resting
their necks on each other,

And with their nostrils distended inhaling
the freshness of evening.

Foremost, bearing the bell, Evangeline's
beautiful heifer,

Proud of her snow-white hide, and the rib-
bon that waved from her collar,

Quietly paced and slow, as if conscious of
human affection.

Then came the shepherd back with his bleat-
ing flocks from the seaside,

Where was their favorite pasture. Behind
them followed the watch-dog,

Patient, full of importance, and grand in the
    pride of his instinct,
Walking from side to side with a lordly air,
    and superbly
Waving his bushy tail, and urging forward
    the stragglers;
Regent of flocks was he when the shepherd
    slept; their protector,
When from the forest at night, through the
    starry silence the wolves howled.
Late, with the rising moon, returned the
    wains from the marshes,
Laden with briny hay, that filled the air with
    its odor.
Cheerily neighed the steeds, with dew on
    their manes and their fetlocks,
While aloft on their shoulders the wooden
    and ponderous saddles,
Painted with brilliant dyes, and adorned with
    tassels of crimson,
Nodded in bright array, like hollyhocks heavy
    with blossoms.
Patiently stood the cows meanwhile, and
    yielded their udders
Unto the milkmaid's hand; whilst loud and
    in regular cadence
Into the sounding pails the foaming stream-
    lets descended.
Lowing of cattle and peals of laughter were
    heard in the farm-yard,
Echoed back by the barns. Anon they sank
    into stillness;

Heavily closed, with a jarring sound, the valves of the barn-doors,
Rattled the wooden bars, and all for a season was silent.

In-doors, warm by the wide-mouthed fireplace, idly the farmer
Sat in his elbow-chair and watched how the flames and the smoke-wreaths
Struggled together like foes in a burning city. Behind him,
Nodding and mocking along the wall, with gestures fantastic,
Darted his own huge shadow, and vanished away into darkness.
Faces, clumsily carved in oak, on the back of his arm-chair
Laughed in the flickering light; and the pewter plates on the dresser
Caught and reflected the flame, as shields of armies the sunshine.
Fragments of song the old man sang, and carols of Christmas,
Such as at home, in the olden time, his fathers before him
Sang in their Norman orchards and bright Burgundian vineyards.
Close at her father's side was the gentle Evangeline seated,
Spinning flax for the loom, that stood in the corner behind her,
Silent awhile were its treadles, at rest was its

diligent shuttle,
While the monotonous drone of the wheel, like the drone of a bagpipe,
Followed the old man's song and united the fragments together.
As in a church, when the chant of the choir at intervals ceases,
Footfalls are heard in the aisles, or words of the priest at the altar,
So, in each pause of the song, with measured motion the clock clicked.

Thus as they sat, there were footsteps heard, and, suddenly lifted,
Sounded the wooden latch, and the door swung back on its hinges.
Benedict knew by the hob-nailed shoes it was Basil the blacksmith,
And by her beating heart Evangeline knew who was with him.
"Welcome!" the farmer exclaimed, as their footsteps paused on the threshold,
"Welcome, Basil, my friend! Come, take thy place on the settle
Close by the chimney-side, which is always empty without thee;
Take from the shelf overhead thy pipe and the box of tobacco;
Never so much thyself art thou as when through the curling
Smoke of the pipe or the forge thy friendly and jovial face gleams

Round and red as the harvest moon through
the mist of the marshes."
Then, with a smile of content, thus answered
Basil the blacksmith,
Taking with easy air the accustomed seat by
the fireside: —
"Benedict Bellefontaine, thou hast ever thy
jest and thy ballad!
Ever in cheerfullest mood art thou, when
others are filled with
Gloomy forebodings of ill, and see only ruin
before them.
Happy art thou, as if every day thou hadst
picked up a horseshoe."
Pausing a moment, to take the pipe that
Evangeline brought him,
And with a coal from the embers had lighted,
he slowly continued: —
"Four days now are passed since the English
ships at their anchors
Ride in the Gaspereau's mouth, with their
cannon pointed against us.
What their design may be is unknown; but
all are commanded
On the morrow to meet in the church, where
his Majesty's mandate
Will be proclaimed as law in the land. Alas!
in the mean time
Many surmises of evil alarm the hearts of
the people."
Then made answer the farmer: "Perhaps
some friendlier purpose

Brings these ships to our shores. Perhaps the harvests in England
By untimely rains or untimelier heat have been blighted,
And from our bursting barns they would feed their cattle and children."
"Not so thinketh the folk in the village," said, warmly, the blacksmith,
Shaking his head, as in doubt; then, heaving a sigh, he continued: —
"Louisburg is not forgotten, nor Beau Séjour, nor Port Royal.
Many already have fled to the forest, and lurk on its outskirts,
Waiting with anxious hearts the dubious fate of to-morrow.
Arms have been taken from us, and warlike weapons of all kinds;
Nothing is left but the blacksmith's sledge and the scythe of the mower."
Then with a pleasant smile made answer the jovial farmer: —
"Safer are we unarmed, in the midst of our flocks and our cornfields,
Safer within these peaceful dikes, besieged by the ocean,
Than our fathers in forts, besieged by the enemy's cannon.
Fear no evil, my friend, and to-night may no shadow of sorrow
Fall on this house and hearth; for this is the night of the contract.

Built are the house and the barn. The merry
    lads of the village
Strongly have built them and well; and,
    breaking the glebe round about them,
Filled the barn with hay, and the house with
    food for a twelvemonth.
René Leblanc will be here anon, with his
    papers and inkhorn.
Shall we not then be glad, and rejoice in the
    joy of our children?"
As apart by the window she stood, with her
    hand in her lover's,
Blushing Evangeline heard the words that
    her father had spoken,
And, as they died on his lips, the worthy
    notary entered.

III.

Bent like a laboring oar, that toils in the surf
    of the ocean,
Bent, but not broken, by age was the form of
    the notary public;
Shocks of yellow hair, like the silken floss of
    the maize, hung
Over his shoulders; his forehead was high;
    and glasses with horn bows
Sat astride on his nose, with a look of wisdom
    supernal.
Father of twenty children was he, and more
    than a hundred
Children's children rode on his knee, and

heard his great watch tick.

Four long years in the times of the war had
he languished a captive,

Suffering much in an old French fort as the
friend of the English.

Now, though warier grown, without all guile
or suspicion,

Ripe in wisdom was he, but patient, and
simple, and childlike.

He was beloved by all, and most of all by the
children;

For he told them tales of the Loup-garou in
the forest,

And of the goblin that came in the night to
water the horses,

And of the white Létiche, the ghost of a child
who unchristened

Died, and was doomed to haunt unseen the
chambers of children;

And how on Christmas eve the oxen talked
in the stable,

And how the fever was cured by a spider shut
up in a nutshell,

And of the marvellous powers of four-leaved
clover and horseshoes,

With whatsoever else was writ in the lore of
the village.

Then up rose from his seat by the fireside
Basil the blacksmith,

Knocked from his pipe the ashes, and slowly
extending his right hand,

"Father Leblanc," he exclaimed, "thou hast

heard the talk in the village,
And, perchance, canst tell us some news of
these ships and their errand."
Then with modest demeanor made answer
the notary public, —
"Gossip enough have I heard, in sooth, yet
am never the wiser;
And what their errand may be I know not
better than others.
Yet am I not of those who imagine some evil
intention
Brings them here, for we are at peace; and
why then molest us?"
"God's name!" shouted the hasty and some-
what irascible blacksmith;
"Must we in all things look for the how, and
the why, and the wherefore?
Daily injustice is done, and might is the right
of the strongest!"
But without heeding his warmth, continued
the notary public, —
"Man is unjust, but God is just; and finally
justice
Triumphs; and well I remember a story, that
often consoled me,
When as a captive I lay in the old French
fort at Port Royal."
This was the old man's favorite tale, and he
loved to repeat it
When his neighbors complained that any
injustice was done them.
"Once in an ancient city, whose name I no

longer remember,
Raised aloft on a column, a brazen statue of
   Justice
Stood in the public square, upholding the
   scales in its left hand,
And in its right a sword, as an emblem that
   justice presided
Over the laws of the land, and the hearts and
   homes of the people.
Even the birds had built their nests in the
   scales of the balance,
Having no fear of the sword that flashed in
   the sunshine above them.
But in the course of time the laws of the land
   were corrupted;
Might took the place of right, and the weak
   were oppressed, and the mighty
Ruled with an iron rod. Then it chanced in a
   nobleman's palace
That a necklace of pearls was lost, and ere-
   long a suspicion
Fell on an orphan girl who lived as a maid in
   the household.
She, after form of trial condemned to die on
   the scaffold,
Patiently met her doom at the foot of the
   statue of Justice.
As to her Father in heaven her innocent spirit
   ascended,
Lo! o'er the city a tempest rose; and the bolts
   of the thunder
Smote the statue of bronze, and hurled in

wrath from its left hand
Down on the pavement below the clattering
scales of the balance,
And in the hollow thereof was found the nest
of a magpie,
Into whose clay-built walls the necklace of
pearls was inwoven."
Silenced, but not convinced, when the story
was ended, the blacksmith
Stood like a man who fain would speak, but
findeth no language;
All his thoughts were congealed into lines on
his face, as the vapors
Freeze in fantastic shapes on the window-
panes in the winter.

  Then Evangeline lighted the brazen lamp
on the table,
Filled, till it overflowed, the pewter tankard
with home-brewed
Nut-brown ale, that was famed for its
strength in the village of Grand-Pré;
While from his pocket the notary drew his
papers and inkhorn,
Wrote with a steady hand the date and the
age of the parties,
Naming the dower of the bride in flocks of
sheep and in cattle.
Orderly all things proceeded, and duly and
well were completed,
And the great seal of the law was set like a
sun on the margin.

Then from his leathern pouch the farmer
threw on the table
Three times the old man's fee in solid pieces
of silver;
And the notary rising, and blessing the bride
and the bridegroom,
Lifted aloft the tankard of ale and drank to
their welfare.
Wiping the foam from his lip, he solemnly
bowed and departed,
While in silence the others sat and mused by
the fireside,
Till Evangeline brought the draught-board
out of its corner.
Soon was the game begun. In friendly con-
tention the old men
Laughed at each lucky hit, or unsuccessful
manœuvre,
Laughed when a man was crowned, or a
breach was made in the king-row.
Meanwhile apart, in the twilight gloom of a
window's embrasure,
Sat the lovers, and whispered together,
beholding the moon rise
Over the pallid sea, and the silvery mists of
the meadows.
Silently one by one, in the infinite meadows
of heaven,
Blossomed the lovely stars, the forget-me-
nots of the angels.

Thus was the evening passed. Anon the bell

from the belfry
Rang out the hour of nine, the village curfew,
and straightway
Rose the guests and departed; and silence
reigned in the household.
Many a farewell word and sweet good-night
on the doorstep
Lingered long in Evangeline's heart, and
filled it with gladness.
Carefully then were covered the embers that
glowed on the hearth-stone,
And on the oaken stairs resounded the tread
of the farmer.
Soon with a soundless step the foot of
Evangeline followed.
Up the staircase moved a luminous space in
the darkness,
Lighted less by the lamp than the shining
face of the maiden.
Silent she passed the hall, and entered the
door of her chamber.
Simple that chamber was, with its curtains of
white, and its clothes-press
Ample and high, on whose spacious shelves
were carefully folded
Linen and woollen stuffs, by the hand of
Evangeline woven.
This was the precious dower she would bring
to her husband in marriage,
Better than flocks and herds, being proofs of
her skill as a housewife.
Soon she extinguished her lamp, for the mel-

low and radiant moonlight
Streamed through the windows, and lighted
the room, till the heart of the maiden
Swelled and obeyed its power, like the
tremulous tides of the ocean.
Ah! she was fair, exceeding fair to behold, as
she stood with
Naked snow-white feet on the gleaming floor
of her chamber!
Little she dreamed that below, among the
trees of the orchard,
Waited her lover and watched for the gleam
of her lamp and her shadow.
Yet were her thoughts of him, and at times a
feeling of sadness
Passed o'er her soul, as the sailing shade of
clouds in the moonlight
Flitted across the floor and darkened the
room for a moment.
And, as she gazed from the window, she saw
serenely the moon pass
Forth from the folds of a cloud, and one star
follow her footsteps,
As out of Abraham's tent young Ishmael
wandered with Hagar!

IV.

Pleasantly rose next morn the sun on the vil-
lage of Grand-Pré.
Pleasantly gleamed in the soft, sweet air the
Basin of Minas,

Where the ships, with their wavering shadows, were riding at anchor.
Life had long been astir in the village, and clamorous labor
Knocked with its hundred hands at the golden gates of the morning.
Now from the country around, from the farms and neighboring hamlets,
Came in their holiday dresses the blithe Acadian peasants.
Many a glad good-morrow and jocund laugh from the young folk
Made the bright air brighter, as up from the numerous meadows,
Where no path could be seen but the track of wheels in the greensward,
Group after group appeared, and joined, or passed on the highway.
Long ere noon, in the village all sounds of labor were silenced.
Thronged were the streets with people; and noisy groups at the house-doors
Sat in the cheerful sun, and rejoiced and gossiped together.
Every house was an inn, where all were welcomed and feasted;
For with this simple people, who lived like brothers together,
All things were held in common, and what one had was another's.
Yet under Benedict's roof hospitality seemed more abundant:

For Evangeline stood among the guests of
her father;
Bright was her face with smiles, and words
of welcome and gladness
Fell from her beautiful lips, and blessed the
cup as she gave it.

Under the open sky, in the odorous air of
the orchard,
Stript of its golden fruit, was spread the feast
of betrothal.
There in the shade of the porch were the
priest and the notary seated;
There good Benedict sat, and sturdy Basil
the blacksmith.
Not far withdrawn from these, by the cider-
press and the beehives,
Michael the fiddler was placed, with the gay-
est of hearts and of waistcoats.
Shadow and light from the leaves alternately
played on his snow-white
Hair, as it waved in the wind; and the jolly
face of the fiddler
Glowed like a living coal when the ashes are
blown from the embers.
Gayly the old man sang to the vibrant sound
of his fiddle,
Tous les Bourgeois de Chartres, and *Le Caril-
lon de Dunquerque,*
And anon with his wooden shoes beat time
to the music.
Merrily, merrily whirled the wheels of the

dizzying dances
Under the orchard-trees and down the path
to the meadows;
Old folk and young together, and children
mingled among them.
Fairest of all the maids was Evangeline,
Benedict's daughter!
Noblest of all the youths was Gabriel, son of
the blacksmith!

So passed the morning away. And lo! with
a summons sonorous
Sounded the bell from its tower, and over
the meadows a drum beat.
Thronged erelong was the church with men.
Without, in the churchyard,
Waited the women. They stood by the graves,
and hung on the headstones
Garlands of autumn-leaves and evergreens
fresh from the forest.
Then came the guard from the ships, and
marching proudly among them
Entered the sacred portal. With loud and dis-
sonant clangor
Echoed the sound of their brazen drums
from ceiling and casement, —
Echoed a moment only, and slowly the
ponderous portal
Closed, and in silence the crowd awaited the
will of the soldiers.
Then uprose their commander, and spake
from the steps of the altar,

Holding aloft in his hands, with its seals, the
  royal commission.
"You are convened this day," he said, "by his
  Majesty's orders.
Clement and kind has be been; but how you
  have answered his kindness,
Let your own hearts reply! To my natural
  make and my temper
Painful the task is I do, which to you I know
  must be grievous.
Yet must I bow and obey, and deliver the will
  of our monarch;
Namely, that all your lands, and dwellings,
  and cattle of all kinds
Forfeited be to the crown; and that you
  yourselves from this province
Be transported to other lands. God grant you
  may dwell there
Ever as faithful subjects, a happy and peace-
  able people!
Prisoners now I declare you; for such is his
  Majesty's pleasure!"
As, when the air is serene in sultry solstice of
  summer,
Suddenly gathers a storm, and the deadly
  sling of the hailstones
Beats down the farmer's corn in the field and
  shatters his windows,
Hiding the sun, and strewing the ground with
  thatch from the house-roofs,
Bellowing fly the herds, and seek to break
  their enclosures;

So on the hearts of the people descended the
    words of the speaker.
Silent a moment they stood in speechless
    wonder, and then rose
Louder and ever louder a wail of sorrow and
    anger,
And, by one impulse moved, they madly
    rushed to the doorway.
Vain was the hope of escape; and cries and
    fierce imprecations
Rang through the house of prayer; and high
    o'er the heads of the others
Rose, with his arms uplifted, the figure of
    Basil the blacksmith,
As, on a stormy sea, a spar is tossed by the
    billows.
Flushed was his face and distorted with pas-
    sion; and wildly he shouted, —
"Down with the tyrants of England! we never
    have sworn them allegiance!
Death to these foreign soldiers, who seize on
    our homes and our harvests!"
More he fain would have said, but the merci-
    less hand of a soldier
Smote him upon the mouth, and dragged
    him down to the pavement.

  In the midst of the strife and tumult of
    angry contention,
Lo! the door of the chancel opened, and
    Father Felician
Entered, with serious mien, and ascended

the steps of the altar.

Raising his reverend hand, with a gesture he awed into silence

All that clamorous throng; and thus he spake to his people;

Deep were his tones and solemn; in accents measured and mournful

Spake he, as, after the tocsin's alarum, distinctly the clock strikes.

"What is this that ye do, my children? what madness has seized you?

Forty years of my life have I labored among you, and taught you,

Not in word alone, but in deed, to love one another?

Is this the fruit of my toils, of my vigils and prayers and privations?

Have you so soon forgotten all lessons of love and forgiveness?

This is the house of the Prince of Peace, and would you profane it

Thus with violent deeds and hearts overflowing with hatred?

Lo! where the crucified Christ from his cross is gazing upon you!

See! in those sorrowful eyes what meekness and holy compassion!

Hark! how those lips still repeat the prayer, 'O Father, forgive them!'

Let us repeat that prayer in the hour when the wicked assail us,

Let us repeat it now, and say, 'O Father,

forgive them!' "
Few were his words of rebuke, but deep in
the hearts of his people
Sank they, and sobs of contrition succeeded
the passionate outbreak,
While they repeated his prayer, and said, "O
Father, forgive them!"

Then came the evening service. The tapers
gleamed from the altar.
Fervent and deep was the voice of the priest,
and the people responded,
Not with their lips alone, but their hearts;
and the Ave Maria
Sang they, and fell on their knees, and their
souls, with devotion translated,
Rose on the ardor of prayer, like Elijah
ascending to heaven.

Meanwhile had spread in the village the
tidings of ill, and on all sides
Wandered, wailing, from house to house the
women and children.
Long at her father's door Evangeline stood,
with her right hand
Shielding her eyes from the level rays of the
sun, that, descending,
Lighted the village street with mysterious
splendor, and roofed each
Peasant's cottage with golden thatch, and
emblazoned its windows.
Long within had been spread the snow-white

cloth on the table;
There stood the wheaten loaf, and the honey
fragrant with wild-flowers;
There stood the tankard of ale, and the
cheese fresh brought from the dairy,
And, at the head of the board, the great arm-
chair of the farmer.
Thus did Evangeline wait at her father's
door, as the sunset
Threw the long shadows of trees o'er the
broad ambrosial meadows.
Ah! on her spirit within a deeper shadow had
fallen,
And from the fields of her soul a fragrance
celestial ascended, —
Charity, meekness, love, and hope, and
forgiveness, and patience!
Then, all-forgetful of self, she wandered into
the village,
Cheering with looks and words the mournful
hearts of the women,
As o'er the darkening fields with lingering
steps they departed,
Urged by their household cares, and the
weary feet of their children.
Down sank the great red sun, and in golden,
glimmering vapors
Veiled the light of his face, like the Prophet
descending from Sinai.
Sweetly over the village the bell of the
Angelus sounded.

Meanwhile, amid the gloom, by the church
Evangeline lingered.

All was silent within; and in vain at the door
and the windows

Stood she, and listened and looked, till,
overcome by emotion,

"Gabriel!" cried she aloud with tremulous
voice; but no answer

Came from the graves of the dead, nor the
gloomier grave of the living.

Slowly at length she returned to the tenant-
less house of her father.

Smouldered the fire on the hearth, on the
board was the supper untasted,

Empty and drear was each room, and
haunted with phantoms of terror.

Sadly echoed her step on the stair and the
floor of her chamber.

In the dead of the night she heard the
disconsolate rain fall

Loud on the withered leaves of the sycamore-
tree by the window.

Keenly the lightning flashed; and the voice of
the echoing thunder

Told her that God was in heaven, and gov-
erned the world he created!

Then she remembered the tale she had heard
of the justice of Heaven;

Soothed was her troubled soul, and she
peacefully slumbered till morning.

V.

Four times the sun had risen and set; and
  now on the fifth day
Cheerily called the cock to the sleeping
  maids of the farmhouse.
Soon o'er the yellow fields, in silent and
  mournful procession,
Came from the neighboring hamlets and
  farms the Acadian women,
Driving in ponderous wains their household
  goods to the sea-shore,
Pausing and looking back to gaze once more
  on their dwellings,
Ere they were shut from sight by the winding
  road and the woodland.
Close at their sides their children ran, and
  urged on the oxen,
While in their little hands they clasped some
  fragments of playthings.

  Thus to the Gaspereau's mouth they hur-
  ried; and there on the sea-beach
Piled in confusion lay the household goods
  of the peasants.
All day long between the shore and the ships
  did the boats ply;
All day long the wains came laboring down
  from the village.
Late in the afternoon, when the sun was near
  to his setting,
Echoed far o'er the fields came the roll of

drums from the churchyard.
Thither the women and children thronged.
On a sudden the church-doors
Opened, and forth came the guard, and
marching in gloomy procession
Followed the long-imprisoned, but patient,
Acadian farmers.
Even as pilgrims, who journey afar from their
homes and their country,
Sing as they go, and in singing forget they
are weary and wayworn,
So with songs on their lips the Acadian peas-
ants descended
Down from the church to the shore, amid
their wives and their daughters.
Foremost the young men came; and, raising
together their voices,
Sang with tremulous lips a chant of the Cath-
olic Missions: —
"Sacred heart of the Saviour! O inexhaust-
ible fountain!
Fill our hearts this day with strength and
submission and patience!"
Then the old men, as they marched, and the
women that stood by the wayside
Joined in the sacred psalm, and the birds in
the sunshine above them
Mingled their notes therewith, like voices of
spirits departed.

Half-way down to the shore Evangeline
waited in silence,

Not overcome with grief, but strong in the
hour of affliction, —
Calmly and sadly she waited, until the
procession approached her,
And she beheld the face of Gabriel pale with
emotion.
Tears then filled her eyes, and, eagerly run-
ning to meet him,
Clasped she his hands, and laid her head on
his shoulder, and whispered, —
"Gabriel! be of good cheer! for if we love one
another
Nothing, in truth, can harm us, whatever
mischances may happen!"
Smiling she spake these words; then suddenly
paused, for her father
Saw she slowly advancing. Alas! how changed
was his aspect!
Gone was the glow from his cheek, and the
fire from his eye, and his footstep
Heavier seemed with the weight of the heavy
heart in his bosom.
But with a smile and a sigh, she clasped his
neck and embraced him,
Speaking words of endearment where words
of comfort availed not.
Thus to the Gaspereau's mouth moved on
that mournful procession.

There disorder prevailed, and the tumult
and stir of embarking.
Busily plied the freighted boats; and in the

confusion
Wives were torn from their husbands, and
mothers, too late, saw their children
Left on the land, extending their arms, with
wildest entreaties.
So unto separate ships were Basil and Ga-
briel carried,
While in despair on the shore Evangeline
stood with her father.
Half the task was not done when the sun
went down, and the twilight
Deepened and darkened around; and in haste
the refluent ocean
Fled away from the shore, and left the line of
the sand-beach
Covered with waifs of the tide, with kelp and
the slippery seaweed.
Farther back in the midst of the household
goods and the wagons,
Like to a gypsy camp, or a leaguer after a
battle,
All escape cut off by the sea, and the sentinels
near them,
Lay encamped for the night the houseless
Acadian farmers.
Back to its nethermost caves retreated the
bellowing ocean,
Dragging adown the beach the rattling
pebbles, and leaving
Inland and far up the shore the stranded
boats of the sailors.
Then, as the night descended, the herds

returned from their pastures;
Sweet was the moist still air with the odor of
  milk from their udders;
Lowing they waited, and long, at the well-
  known bars of the farm-yard, —
Waited and looked in vain for the voice and
  the hand of the milk-maid.
Silence reigned in the streets; from the
  church no Angelus sounded,
Rose no smoke from the roofs, and gleamed
  no lights from the windows.

But on the shores meanwhile the evening
  fires had been kindled,
Built of the drift-wood thrown on the sands
  from wrecks in the tempest.
Round them shapes of gloom and sorrowful
  faces were gathered,
Voices of women were heard, and of men,
  and the crying of children.
Onward from fire to fire, as from hearth to
  hearth in his parish,
Wandered the faithful priest, consoling and
  blessing and cheering,
Like unto shipwrecked Paul on Melita's
  desolate sea-shore.
Thus he approached the place where Evange-
  line sat with her father,
And in the flickering light beheld the face of
  the old man,
Haggard and hollow and wan, and without
  either thought or emotion,

E'en as the face of a clock from which the
hands have been taken.
Vainly Evangeline strove with words and
caresses to cheer him,
Vainly offered him food; yet he moved not,
he looked not, he spake not,
But, with a vacant stare, ever gazed at the
flickering fire-light.
"Benedicite!" murmured the priest, in tones
of compassion.
More he fain would have said, but his heart
was full, and his accents
Faltered and paused on his lips, as the feet of
a child on the threshold,
Hushed by the scene he beholds, and the aw-
ful presence of sorrow.
Silently, therefore, he laid his hand on the
head of the maiden,
Raising his tearful eyes to the silent stars that
above them
Moved on their way, unperturbed by the
wrongs and sorrows of mortals.
Then sat he down at her side, and they wept
together in silence.

Suddenly rose from the south a light, as in
autumn the blood-red
Moon climbs the crystal walls of heaven, and
o'er the horizon
Titan-like stretches its hundred hands upon
the mountain and meadow,
Seizing the rocks and the rivers, and piling

huge shadows together.
Broader and ever broader it gleamed on the
roofs of the village,
Gleamed on the sky and sea, and the ships
that lay in the roadstead.
Columns of shining smoke uprose, and
flashes of flame were
Thrust through their folds and withdrawn,
like the quivering hands of a martyr.
Then as the wind seized the gleeds and the
burning thatch, and, uplifting,
Whirled them aloft through the air, at once
from a hundred house-tops
Started the sheeted smoke with flashes of
flame intermingled.

These things beheld in dismay the crowd
on the shore and on shipboard.
Speechless at first they stood, then cried
aloud in their anguish,
"We shall behold no more our homes in the
village of Grand-Pré!"
Loud on a sudden the cocks began to crow
in the farm-yards,
Thinking the day had dawned; and anon the
lowing of cattle
Came on the evening breeze, by the barking
of dogs interrupted.
Then rose a sound of dread, such as startles
the sleeping encampments
Far in the western prairies or forests that skirt
the Nebraska,

When the wild horses affrighted sweep by
  with the speed of the whirlwind,
Or the loud bellowing herds of buffaloes rush
  to the river.
Such was the sound that arose on the night,
  as the herds and the horses
Broke through their folds and fences, and
  madly rushed o'er the meadows.

  Overwhelmed with the sight, yet speech-
  less, the priest and the maiden
Gazed on the scene of terror that reddened
  and widened before them;
And as they turned at length to speak to their
  silent companion,
Lo! from his seat he had fallen, and stretched
  abroad on the sea-shore
Motionless lay his form, from which the soul
  had departed.
Slowly the priest uplifted the lifeless head,
  and the maiden
Knelt at her father's side, and wailed aloud
  in her terror.
Then in a swoon she sank, and lay with her
  head on his bosom.
Through the long night she lay in deep,
  oblivious slumber;
And when she awoke from the trance, she
  beheld a multitude near her.
Faces of friends she beheld, that were mourn-
  fully gazing upon her,
Pallid, with tearful eyes, and looks of saddest

compassion.

Still the blaze of the burning village illumined
the landscape,

Reddened the sky overhead, and gleamed on
the faces around her,

And like the day of doom it seemed to her
wavering senses.

Then a familiar voice she heard, as it said to
the people, —

"Let us bury him here by the sea. When a
happier season

Brings us again to our homes from the
unknown land of our exile,

Then shall his sacred dust be piously laid in
the churchyard."

Such were the words of the priest. And there
in haste by the sea-side,

Having the glare of the burning village for
funeral torches,

But without bell or book, they buried the
farmer of Grand-Pré.

And as the voice of the priest repeated the
service of sorrow,

Lo! with a mournful sound, like the voice of
a vast congregation,

Solemnly answered the sea, and mingled its
roar with the dirges.

'T was the returning tide, that afar from the
waste of the ocean,

With the first dawn of the day, came heaving
and hurrying landward.

Then recommenced once more the stir and

noise of embarking;
And with the ebb of the tide the ships sailed
out of the harbor,
Leaving behind them the dead on the shore,
and the village in ruins.

Part The Second
I.

Many a weary year had passed since the
burning of Grand-Pré,
When on the falling tide the freighted vessels
departed,
Bearing a nation, with all its household gods,
into exile,
Exile without an end, and without an ex-
ample in story.
Far asunder, on separate coasts, the Acadi-
ans landed;
Scattered were they, like flakes of snow, when
the wind from the northeast
Strikes aslant through the fogs that darken
the Banks of Newfoundland.
Friendless, homeless, hopeless, they wan-
dered from city to city,
From the cold lakes of the North to sultry
Southern savannas, —
From the bleak shores of the sea to the lands
where the Father of Waters
Seizes the hills in his hands, and drags them
down to the ocean,
Deep in their sands to bury the scattered

bones of the mammoth.
Friends they sought and homes; and many, despairing, heartbroken,
Asked of the earth but a grave, and no longer a friend nor a fireside.
Written their history stands on tablets of stone in the churchyards.
Long among them was seen a maiden who waited and wandered,
Lowly and meek in spirit, and patiently suffering all things.
Fair was she and young: but, alas! before her extended,
Dreary and vast and silent, the desert of life, with its pathway
Marked by the graves of those who had sorrowed and suffered before her,
Passions long extinguished, and hopes long dead and abandoned,
As the emigrant's way o'er the Western desert is marked by
Camp-fires long consumed, and bones that bleach in the sunshine.
Something there was in her life incomplete, imperfect, unfinished;
As if a morning of June, with all its music and sunshine,
Suddenly paused in the sky, and, fading, slowly descended
Into the east again, from whence it late had arisen.
Sometimes she lingered in towns, till, urged

by the fever within her,
Urged by a restless longing, the hunger and
thirst of the spirit,
She would commence again her endless
search and endeavor;
Sometimes in churchyards strayed, and gazed
on the crosses and tombstones,
Sat by some nameless grave, and thought
that perhaps in its bosom
He was already at rest, and she longed to
slumber beside him.
Sometimes a rumor, a hearsay, an inarticulate
whisper,
Came with its airy hand to point and beckon
her forward.
Sometimes she spake with those who had
seen her beloved and known him,
But it was long ago, in some far-off place or
forgotten.
"Gabriel Lajeunesse!" they said; "Oh yes! we
have seen him.
He was with Basil the blacksmith, and both
have gone to the prairies;
Coureurs-des-Bois are they, and famous
hunters and trappers."
"Gabriel Lajeunesse!" said others; "Oh yes!
we have seen him.
He is a Voyageur in the lowlands of Louisi-
ana."
Then would they say, "Dear child! why
dream and wait for him longer?

Are there not other youths as fair as Gabriel?
others

Who have hearts as tender and true, and
spirits as loyal?

Here is Baptiste Leblanc, the notary's son,
who has loved thee

Many a tedious year; come, give him thy
hand and be happy!

Thou art too fair to be left to braid St. Cath-
erine's tresses."

Then would Evangeline answer, serenely but
sadly, "I cannot!

Whither my heart has gone, there follows my
hand, and not elsewhere.

For when the heart goes before, like a lamp,
and illumines the pathway,

Many things are made clear, that else lie hid-
den in darkness."

Thereupon the priest, her friend and father-
confessor,

Said, with a smile, "O daughter! thy God
thus speaketh within thee!

Talk not of wasted affection, affection never
was wasted;

If it enrich not the heart of another, its
waters, returning

Back to their springs, like the rain, shall fill
them full of refreshment;

That which the fountain sends forth returns
again to the fountain.

Patience; accomplish thy labor; accomplish
thy work of affection!

Sorrow and silence are strong, and patient
endurance is godlike.
Therefore accomplish thy labor of love, till
the heart is made godlike,
Purified, strengthened, perfected, and ren-
dered more worthy of heaven!"
Cheered by the good man's words, Evange-
line labored and waited.
Still in her heart she heard the funeral dirge
of the ocean,
But with its sound there was mingled a voice
that whispered, "Despair not!"
Thus did that poor soul wander in want and
cheerless discomfort,
Bleeding, barefooted, over the shards and
thorns of existence.
Let me essay, O Muse! to follow the wander-
er's footsteps; —
Not through each devious path, each change-
ful year of existence,
But as a traveller follows a streamlet's course
through the valley:
Far from its margin at times, and seeing the
gleam of its water
Here and there, in some open space, and at
intervals only;
Then drawing nearer its banks, through
sylvan glooms that conceal it,
Though he behold it not, he can hear its
continuous murmur;
Happy, at length, if he find the spot where it
reaches an outlet.

II.

It was the month of May. Far down the
Beautiful River,

Past the Ohio shore and past the mouth of
the Wabash,

Into the golden stream of the broad and swift
Mississippi,

Floated a cumbrous boat, that was rowed by
Acadian boatmen.

It was a band of exiles: a raft, as it were, from
the shipwrecked

Nation, scattered along the coast, now float-
ing together,

Bound by the bonds of a common belief and
a common misfortune;

Men and women and children, who, guided
by hope or by hearsay,

Sought for their kith and their kin among the
few-acred farmers

On the Acadian coast, and the prairies of fair
Opelousas.

With them Evangeline went, and her guide,
the Father Felician.

Onward o'er sunken sands, through a wilder-
ness sombre with forests,

Day after day they glided adown the turbu-
lent river;

Night after night, by their blazing fires,
encamped on its borders.

Now through rushing chutes, among green
islands, where plumelike

Cotton-trees nodded their shadowy crests,
they swept with the current,
Then emerged into broad lagoons, where
silvery sand-bars
Lay in the stream, and along the wimpling
waves of their margin,
Shining with snow-white plumes, large flocks
of pelicans waded.
Level the landscape grew, and along the
shores of the river,
Shaded by china-trees, in the midst of luxuri-
ant gardens,
Stood the houses of planters, with negro-
cabins and dove-cots.
They were approaching the region where
reigns perpetual summer,
Where through the Golden Coast, and groves
of orange and citron,
Sweeps with majestic curve the river away to
the eastward.
They, too, swerved from their course; and,
entering the Bayou of Plaquemine,
Soon were lost in a maze of sluggish and
devious waters,
Which, like a network of steel, extended in
every direction.
Over their heads the towering and tenebrous
boughs of the cypress
Met in a dusky arch, and trailing mosses in
mid-air
Waved like banners that hang on the walls of
ancient cathedrals.

Deathlike the silence seemed, and unbroken, save by the herons
Home to their roosts in the cedar-trees returning at sunset,
Or by the owl, as he greeted the moon with demoniac laughter.
Lovely the moonlight was as it glanced and gleamed on the water,
Gleamed on the columns of cypress and cedar sustaining the arches,
Down through whose broken vaults it fell as through chinks in a ruin.
Dreamlike, and indistinct, and strange were all things around them;
And o'er their spirits there came a feeling of wonder and sadness, —
Strange forebodings of ill, unseen and that cannot be compassed.
As, at the tramp of a horse's hoof on the turf of the prairies,
Far in advance are closed the leaves of the shrinking mimosa,
So, at the hoof-beats of fate, with sad forebodings of evil,
Shrinks and closes the heart, ere the stroke of doom has attained it.
But Evangeline's heart was sustained by a vision, that faintly
Floated before her eyes, and beckoned her on through the moonlight.
It was the thought of her brain that assumed the shape of a phantom.

Through those shadowy aisles had Gabriel
wandered before her,
And every stroke of the oar now brought him
nearer and nearer.

Then in his place, at the prow of the boat,
rose one of the oarsmen,
And, as a signal sound, if others like them
peradventure
Sailed on those gloomy and midnight
streams, blew a blast on his bugle.
Wild through the dark colonnades and cor-
ridors leafy the blast rang,
Breaking the seal of silence, and giving
tongues to the forest.
Soundless above them the banners of moss
just stirred to the music.
Multitudinous echoes awoke and died in the
distance,
Over the watery floor, and beneath the
reverberant branches;
But not a voice replied; no answer came from
the darkness;
And, when the echoes had ceased, like a
sense of pain was the silence.
Then Evangeline slept; but the boatmen
rowed through the midnight,
Silent at times, then singing familiar Cana-
dian boat-songs,
Such as they sang of old on their own Aca-
dian rivers,
While through the night were heard the

mysterious sounds of the desert,
Far off, — indistinct, — as of wave or wind
in the forest,
Mixed with the whoop of the crane and the
roar of the grim alligator.

Thus ere another noon they emerged from
the shades; and before them
Lay, in the golden sun, the lakes of the Atcha-
falaya.
Water-lilies in myriads rocked on the slight
undulations
Made by the passing oars, and, resplendent
in beauty, the lotus
Lifted her golden crown above the heads of
the boatmen.
Faint was the air with the odorous breath of
magnolia blossoms,
And with the heat of noon; and numberless
sylvan islands,
Fragrant and thickly embowered with blos-
soming hedges of roses,
Near to whose shores they glided along,
invited to slumber.
Soon by the fairest of these their weary oars
were suspended.
Under the boughs of Wachita willows, that
grew by the margin,
Safely their boat was moored; and scattered
about on the greensward,
Tired with their midnight toil, the weary
travellers slumbered.

Over them vast and high extended the cope
of a cedar.
Swinging from its great arms, the trumpet-
flower and the grapevine
Hung their ladder of ropes aloft like the lad-
der of Jacob,
On whose pendulous stairs the angels as-
cending, descending,
Were the swift humming-birds, that flitted
from blossom to blossom.
Such was the vision Evangeline saw as she
slumbered beneath it.
Filled was her heart with love, and the dawn
of an opening heaven
Lighted her soul in sleep with the glory of
regions celestial.

Nearer, and ever nearer, among the num-
berless islands,
Darted a light, swift boat, that sped away o'er
the water,
Urged on its course by the sinewy arms of
hunters and trappers.
Northward its prow was turned, to the land
of the bison and beaver.
At the helm sat a youth, with countenance
thoughtful and careworn.
Dark and neglected locks overshadowed his
brow, and a sadness
Somewhat beyond his years on his face was
legibly written.
Gabriel was it, who, weary with waiting,

unhappy and restless,
Sought in the Western wilds oblivion of self
and of sorrow.
Swiftly they glided along, close under the lee
of the island,
But by the opposite bank, and behind a
screen of palmettos,
So that they saw not the boat, where it lay
concealed in the willows;
All undisturbed by the dash of their oars,
and unseen, were the sleepers.
Angel of God was there none to awaken the
slumbering maiden.
Swiftly they glided away, like the shade of a
cloud on the prairie.
After the sound of their oars on the tholes
had died in the distance,
As from a magic trance the sleepers awoke,
and the maiden
Said with a sigh to the friendly priest, "O
Father Felician!
Something says in my heart that near me Ga-
briel wanders.
Is it a foolish dream, an idle and vague
superstition?
Or has an angel passed, and revealed the
truth to my spirit?"
Then, with a blush, she added, "Alas for my
credulous fancy!
Unto ears like thine such words as these have
no meaning."
But made answer the reverend man, and he

smiled as he answered, —

"Daughter, thy words are not idle; nor are
they to me without meaning.

Feeling is deep and still; and the word that
floats on the surface

Is as the tossing buoy, that betrays where the
anchor is hidden.

Therefore trust to thy heart, and to what the
world calls illusions.

Gabriel truly is near thee; for not far away to
the southward,

On the banks of the Têche, are the towns of
St. Maur and St. Martin.

There the long-wandering bride shall be
given again to her bridegroom,

There the long-absent pastor regain his flock
and his sheepfold.

Beautiful is the land, with its prairies and
forests of fruit-trees;

Under the feet a garden of flowers, and the
bluest of heavens

Bending above, and resting its dome on the
walls of the forest.

They who dwell there have named it the
Eden of Louisiana!"

With these words of cheer they arose and
continued their journey.

Softly the evening came. The sun from the
western horizon

Like a magician extended his golden wand
o'er the landscape;

Twinkling vapors arose; and sky and water

and forest
Seemed all on fire at the touch, and melted
and mingled together.
Hanging between two skies, a cloud with
edges of silver,
Floated the boat, with its dripping oars, on
the motionless water.
Filled was Evangeline's heart with inexpress-
ible sweetness.
Touched by the magic spell, the sacred
fountains of feeling
Glowed with the light of love, as the skies
and waters around her.
Then from a neighboring thicket the
mocking-bird, wildest of singers,
Swinging aloft on a willow spray that hung
o'er the water,
Shook from his little throat such floods of
delirious music,
That the whole air and the woods and the
waves seemed silent to listen.
Plaintive at first were the tones and sad: then
soaring to madness
Seemed they to follow or guide the revel of
frenzied Bacchantes.
Single notes were then heard, in sorrowful,
low lamentation;
Till, having gathered them all, he flung them
abroad in derision,
As when, after a storm, a gust of wind
through the tree-tops
Shakes down the rattling rain in a crystal

shower on the branches.

With such a prelude as this, and hearts that throbbed with emotion,

Slowly they entered the Têche, where it flows through the green Opelousas,

And, through the amber air, above the crest of the woodland,

Saw the column of smoke that arose from a neighboring dwelling; —

Sounds of a horn they heard, and the distant lowing of cattle.

III.

Near to the bank of the river, o'ershadowed by oaks, from whose branches

Garlands of Spanish moss and of mystic mistletoe flaunted,

Such as the Druids cut down with golden hatchets at Yuletide,

Stood, secluded and still, the house of the herdsman. A garden

Girded it round about with a belt of luxuriant blossoms,

Filling the air with fragrance. The house itself was of timbers

Hewn from the cypress tree, and carefully fitted together.

Large and low was the roof; and on slender columns supported,

Rose-wreathed, vine-encircled, a broad and spacious veranda,

Haunt of the humming-bird and the bee,
    extended around it.
At each end of the house, amid the flowers
    of the garden,
Stationed the dove-cots were, as love's
    perpetual symbol,
Scenes of endless wooing, and endless con-
    tentions of rivals.
Silence reigned o'er the place. The line of
    shadow and sunshine
Ran near the tops of the trees; but the house
    itself was in shadow,
And from its chimney-top, ascending and
    slowly expanding
Into the evening air, a thin blue column of
    smoke rose.
In the rear of the house, from the garden
    gate, ran a pathway
Through the great groves of oak to the skirts
    of the limitless prairie,
Into whose sea of flowers the sun was slowly
    descending.
Full in his track of light, like ships with
    shadowy canvas
Hanging loose from their spars in a motion-
    less calm in the tropics,
Stood a cluster of trees, with tangled cordage
    of grape-vines.

Just where the woodlands met the flowery
    surf of the prairie,
Mounted upon his horse, with Spanish

saddle and stirrups,
Sat a herdsman, arrayed in gaiters and
doublet of deerskin.
Broad and brown was the face that from
under the Spanish sombrero
Gazed on the peaceful scene, with the lordly
look of its master.
Round about him were numberless herds of
kine, that were grazing
Quietly in the meadows, and breathing the
vapory freshness
That uprose from the river, and spread itself
over the landscape.
Slowly lifting the horn that hung at his side,
and expanding
Fully his broad, deep chest, he blew a blast,
that resounded
Wildly and sweet and far, through the still
damp air of the evening.
Suddenly out of the grass the long white
horns of the cattle
Rose like flakes of foam on the adverse cur-
rents of ocean.
Silent a moment they gazed, then bellowing
rushed o'er the prairie,
And the whole mass became a cloud, a shade
in the distance.
Then, as the herdsman turned to the house,
through the gate of the garden
Saw he the forms of the priest and the
maiden advancing to meet him.
Suddenly down from his horse he sprang in

amazement, and forward
Rushed with extended arms and exclama-
tions of wonder;
When they beheld his face, they recognized
Basil the Blacksmith.
Hearty his welcome was, as he led his guests
to the garden.
There in an arbor of roses with endless ques-
tion and answer
Gave they vent to their hearts, and renewed
their friendly embraces,
Laughing and weeping by turns, or sitting
silent and thoughtful.
Thoughtful, for Gabriel came not; and now
dark doubts and misgivings
Stole o'er the maiden's heart; and Basil,
somewhat embarrassed,
Broke the silence and said, "If you came by
the Atchafalaya,
How have you nowhere encountered my Ga-
briel's boat on the bayous?"
Over Evangeline's face at the words of Basil
a shade passed.
Tears came into her eyes, and she said, with
a tremulous accent,
"Gone? is Gabriel gone?" and, concealing
her face on his shoulder,
All her o'erburdened heart gave way, and she
wept and lamented.
Then the good Basil said, — and his voice
grew blithe as he said it, —
"Be of good cheer, my child; it is only to-day

he departed.

Foolish boy! he has left me alone with my herds and my horses.

Moody and restless grown, and tried and troubled, his spirit

Could no longer endure the calm of this quiet existence.

Thinking ever of thee, uncertain and sorrowful ever,

Ever silent, or speaking only of thee and his troubles,

He at length had become so tedious to men and to maidens,

Tedious even to me, that at length I bethought me, and sent him

Unto the town of Adayes to trade for mules with the Spaniards.

Thence he will follow the Indian trails to the Ozark Mountains,

Hunting for furs in the forests, on rivers trapping the beaver.

Therefore be of good cheer; we will follow the fugitive lover;

He is not far on his way, and the Fates and the streams are against him.

Up and away to-morrow, and through the red dew of the morning

We will follow him fast, and bring him back to his prison."

Then glad voices were heard, and up from the banks of the river,

Borne aloft on his comrades' arms, came Michael the fiddler.
Long under Basil's roof had he lived like a god on Olympus,
Having no other care than dispensing music to mortals.
Far renowned was he for his silver locks and his fiddle.
"Long live Michael," they cried, "our brave Acadian minstrel!"
As they bore him aloft in triumphal procession; and straightway
Father Felician advanced with Evangeline, greeting the old man
Kindly and oft, and recalling the past, while Basil, enraptured,
Hailed with hilarious joy his old companions and gossips,
Laughing loud and long, and embracing mothers and daughters.
Much they marvelled to see the wealth of the ci-devant blacksmith,
All his domains and his herds, and his patriarchal demeanor;
Much they marvelled to hear his tales of the soil and the climate,
And of the prairies, whose numberless herds were his who would take them;
Each one thought in his heart, that he, too, would go and do likewise.
Thus they ascended the steps, and crossing the breezy veranda,

Entered the hall of the house, where already
the supper of Basil
Waited his late return; and they rested and
feasted together.

Over the joyous feast the sudden darkness
descended.
All was silent without, and, illuming the
landscape with silver,
Fair rose the dewy moon and the myriad
stars; but within doors,
Brighter than these, shone the faces of
friends in the glimmering lamplight.
Then from his station aloft, at the head of
the table, the herdsman
Poured forth his heart and his wine together
in endless profusion.
Lighting his pipe, that was filled with sweet
Natchitoches tobacco,
Thus he spake to his guests, who listened,
and smiled as they listened: —
"Welcome once more, my friends, who long
have been friendless and homeless,
Welcome once more to a home, that is better
perchance than the old one!
Here no hungry winter congeals our blood
like the rivers;
Here no stony ground provokes the wrath of
the farmer.
Smoothly the ploughshare runs through the
soil, as a keel through the water.
All the year round the orange-groves are in

blossom; and grass grows
More in a single night than a whole Canadian
summer.
Here, too, numberless herds run wild and
unclaimed in the prairies;
Here, too, lands may be had for the asking,
and forests of timber
With a few blows of the axe are hewn and
framed into houses.
After your houses are built, and your fields
are yellow with harvests,
No King George of England shall drive you
away from your homesteads,
Burning your dwellings and barns, and steal-
ing your farms and your cattle."
Speaking these words, he blew a wrathful
cloud from his nostrils,
While his huge, brown hand came thunder-
ing down on the table,
So that the guests all started; and Father Fe-
lician, astounded,
Suddenly paused, with a pinch of snuff half-
way to his nostrils.
But the brave Basil resumed, and his words
were milder and gayer: —
"Only beware of the fever, my friends,
beware of the fever!
For it is not like that of our cold Acadian
climate,
Cured by wearing a spider hung round one's
neck in a nutshell!"
Then there were voices heard at the door,

and footsteps approaching
Sounded upon the stairs and the floor of the
breezy veranda.
It was the neighboring Creoles and small
Acadian planters,
Who had been summoned all to the house of
Basil the Herdsman.
Merry the meeting was of ancient comrades
and neighbors:
Friend clasped friend in his arms; and they
who before were as strangers,
Meeting in exile, became straightway as
friends to each other,
Drawn by the gentle bond of a common
country together.
But in the neighboring hall a strain of music,
proceeding
From the accordant strings of Michael's
melodious fiddle,
Broke up all further speech. Away, like
children delighted,
All things forgotten beside, they gave them-
selves to the maddening
Whirl of the giddy dance, as it swept and
swayed to the music,
Dreamlike, with beaming eyes and the rush
of fluttering garments.

Meanwhile, apart, at the head of the hall,
the priest and the herdsman
Sat, conversing together of past and present
and future;

While Evangeline stood like one entranced, for within her
Olden memories rose, and loud in the midst of the music
Heard she the sound of the sea, and an irrepressible sadness
Came o'er her heart, and unseen she stole forth into the garden.
Beautiful was the night. Behind the black wall of the forest,
Tipping its summit with silver, arose the moon. On the river
Fell here and there through the branches a tremulous gleam of the moonlight,
Like the sweet thoughts of love on a darkened and devious spirit.
Nearer and round about her, the manifold flowers of the garden
Poured out their souls in odors, that were their prayers and confessions
Unto the night, as it went its way, like a silent Carthusian.
Fuller of fragrance than they, and as heavy with shadows and night-dews,
Hung the heart of the maiden. The calm and the magical moonlight
Seemed to inundate her soul with indefinable longings,
As, through the garden-gate, and beneath the shade of the oak-trees,
Passed she along the path to the edge of the measureless prairie.

Silent it lay, with a silvery haze upon it, and
fireflies
Gleamed and floated away in mingled and
infinite numbers.
Over her head the stars, the thoughts of God
in the heavens,
Shone on the eyes of man, who had ceased
to marvel and worship,
Save when a blazing comet was seen on the
walls of that temple,
As if a hand had appeared and written upon
them, "Upharsin."
And the soul of the maiden, between the
stars and the fireflies,
Wandered alone, and she cried, "O Gabriel!
O my beloved!
Art thou so near unto me, and yet I cannot
behold thee?
Art thou so near unto me, and yet thy voice
does not reach me?
Ah! how often thy feet have trod this path to
the prairie!
Ah! how often thine eyes have looked on the
woodlands around me!
Ah! how often beneath this oak, returning
from labor,
Thou hast lain down to rest, and to dream of
me in thy slumbers!
When shall these eyes behold, these arms be
folded about thee?"
Loud and sudden and near the notes of a
whippoorwill sounded

Like a flute in the woods; and anon, through
the neighboring thickets,
Farther and farther away it floated and
dropped into silence.
"Patience!" whispered the oaks from oracular
caverns of darkness:
And, from the moonlit meadow, a sigh
responded, "To-morrow!"

Bright rose the sun next day; and all the
flowers of the garden
Bathed his shining feet with their tears, and
anointed his tresses
With the delicious balm that they bore in
their vases of crystal.
"Farewell!" said the priest, as he stood at the
shadowy threshold;
"See that you bring us the Prodigal Son from
his fasting and famine,
And, too, the Foolish Virgin, who slept when
the bridegroom was coming."
"Farewell!" answered the maiden, and, smil-
ing, with Basil descended
Down to the river's brink, where the boat-
men already were waiting.
Thus beginning their journey with morning,
and sunshine, and gladness,
Swiftly they followed the flight of him who
was speeding before them,
Blown by the blast of fate like a dead leaf
over the desert.
Not that day, nor the next, nor yet the day

that succeeded,
Found they the trace of his course, in lake or
forest or river,
Nor, after many days, had they found him;
but vague and uncertain
Rumors alone were their guides through a
wild and desolate country;
Till, at the little inn of the Spanish town of
Adayes,
Weary and worn, they alighted, and learned
from the garrulous landlord,
That on the day before, with horses and
guides and companions,
Gabriel left the village, and took the road of
the prairies.

IV.

Far in the West there lies a desert land, where
the mountains
Lift, through perpetual snows, their lofty and
luminous summits.
Down from their jagged, deep ravines, where
the gorge, like a gateway,
Opens a passage rude to the wheels of the
emigrant's wagon,
Westward the Oregon flows and the Wall-
esway and Owyhee.
Eastward, with devious course, among the
Wind-river Mountains,
Through the Sweet-water Valley precipitate
leaps the Nebraska;

And to the south, from Fontaine-qui-bout
and the Spanish sierras,
Fretted with sands and rocks, and swept by
the wind of the desert,
Numberless torrents, with ceaseless sound,
descend to the ocean,
Like the great chords of a harp, in loud and
solemn vibrations.
Spreading between these streams are the
wondrous, beautiful prairies;
Billowy bays of grass ever rolling in shadow
and sunshine,
Bright with luxuriant clusters of roses and
purple amorphas.
Over them wandered the buffalo herds, and
the elk and the roebuck;
Over them wandered the wolves, and herds
of riderless horses;
Fires that blast and blight, and winds that
are weary with travel;
Over them wander the scattered tribes of
Ishmael's children,
Staining the desert with blood; and above
their terrible war-trails
Circles and sails aloft, on pinions majestic,
the vulture,
Like the implacable soul of a chieftain
slaughtered in battle,
By invisible stairs ascending and scaling the
heavens.
Here and there rise smokes from the camps
of these savage marauders;

Here and there rise groves from the margins
of swift-running rivers;
And the grim, taciturn bear, the anchorite
monk of the desert,
Climbs down their dark ravines to dig for
roots by the brookside,
And over all is the sky, the clear and crystal-
line heaven,
Like the protecting hand of God inverted
above them.

Into this wonderful land, at the base of the
Ozark Mountains,
Gabriel far had entered, with hunters and
trappers behind him.
Day after day, with their Indian guides, the
maiden and Basil
Followed his flying steps, and thought each
day to o'ertake him.
Sometimes they saw, or thought they saw,
the smoke of his camp-fire
Rise in the morning air from the distant
plain; but at nightfall,
When they had reached the place, they found
only embers and ashes.
And, though their hearts were sad at times
and their bodies were weary,
Hope still guided them on, as the magic Fata
Morgana
Showed them her lakes of light, that retreated
and vanished before them.

Once, as they sat by their evening fire, there
    silently entered
Into their little camp an Indian woman,
    whose features
Wore deep traces of sorrow, and patience as
    great as her sorrow.
She was a Shawnee woman returning home
    to her people,
From the far-off hunting-grounds of the
    cruel Camanches,
Where her Canadian husband, a Coureur-
    des-Bois, had been murdered.
Touched were their hearts at her story, and
    warmest and friendliest welcome
Gave they, with words of cheer, and she sat
    and feasted among them
On the buffalo-meat and the venison cooked
    on the embers.
But when their meal was done, and Basil and
    all his companions,
Worn with the long day's march and the
    chase of the deer and the bison,
Stretched themselves on the ground, and
    slept where the quivering fire-light
Flashed on their swarthy cheeks, and their
    forms wrapped up in their blankets,
Then at the door of Evangeline's tent she sat
    and repeated
Slowly, with soft, low voice, and the charm
    of her Indian accent,
All the tale of her love, with its pleasures,
    and pains, and reverses.

Much Evangeline wept at the tale, and to
know that another
Hapless heart like her own had loved and
had been disappointed.
Moved to the depths of her soul by pity and
woman's compassion,
Yet in her sorrow pleased that one who had
suffered was near her,
She in turn related her love and all its disas-
ters.
Mute with wonder the Shawnee sat, and
when she had ended
Still was mute; but at length, as if a mysteri-
ous horror
Passed through her brain, she spake, and
repeated the tale of the Mowis;
Mowis, the bridegroom of snow, who won
and wedded a maiden,
But, when the morning came, arose and
passed from the wigwam,
Fading and melting away and dissolving into
the sunshine,
Till she beheld him no more, though she fol-
lowed far into the forest.
Then, in those sweet, low tones, that seemed
like a weird incantation,
Told she the tale of the fair Lilinau, who was
wooed by a phantom,
That through the pines o'er her father's
lodge, in the hush of the twilight,
Breathed like the evening wind, and whis-
pered love to the maiden,

Till she followed his green and waving plume
through the forest,
And nevermore returned, nor was seen again
by her people.
Silent with wonder and strange surprise,
Evangeline listened
To the soft flow of her magical words, till the
region around her
Seemed like enchanted ground, and her
swarthy guest the enchantress.
Slowly over the tops of the Ozark Mountains
the moon rose,
Lighting the little tent, and with a mysterious
splendor
Touching the sombre leaves, and embracing
and filling the woodland.
With a delicious sound the brook rushed by,
and the branches
Swayed and sighed overhead in scarcely
audible whispers.
Filled with the thoughts of love was Evange-
line's heart, but a secret,
Subtile sense crept in of pain and indefinite
terror,
As the cold, poisonous snake creeps into the
nest of the swallow.
It was no earthly fear. A breath from the
region of spirits
Seemed to float in the air of night; and she
felt for a moment
That, like the Indian maid, she, too, was
pursuing a phantom.

With this thought she slept, and the fear and
the phantom had vanished.

Early upon the morrow the march was
resumed; and the Shawnee
Said, as they journeyed along, "On the
western slope of these mountains
Dwells in his little village the Black Robe
chief of the Mission.
Much he teaches the people, and tells them
of Mary and Jesus.
Loud laugh their hearts with joy, and weep
with pain, as they hear him."
Then, with a sudden and secret emotion,
Evangeline answered,
"Let us go to the Mission, for there good
tidings await us!"
Thither they turned their steeds; and behind
a spur of the mountains,
Just as the sun went down, they heard a
murmur of voices,
And in a meadow green and broad, by the
bank of a river,
Saw the tents of the Christians, the tents of
the Jesuit Mission.
Under a towering oak, that stood in the midst
of the village,
Knelt the Black Robe chief with his children.
A crucifix fastened
High on the trunk of the tree, and overshad-
owed by grapevines,
Looked with its agonized face on the multi-

tude kneeling beneath it.

This was their rural chapel. Aloft, through the intricate arches
Of its aerial roof, arose the chant of their vespers,
Mingling its notes with the soft susurrus and sighs of the branches.
Silent, with heads uncovered, the travellers, nearer approaching,
Knelt on the swarded floor, and joined in the evening devotions.
But when the service was done, and the benediction had fallen
Forth from the hands of the priest, like seed from the hands of the sower,
Slowly the reverend man advanced to the strangers, and bade them
Welcome; and when they replied, he smiled with benignant expression,
Hearing the homelike sounds of his mother-tongue in the forest,
And, with words of kindness, conducted them into his wigwam.
There upon mats and skins they reposed, and on cakes of the maize-ear
Feasted, and slaked their thirst from the water-gourd of the teacher.
Soon was their story told; and the priest with solemnity answered: —
"Not six suns have risen and set since Gabriel, seated
On this mat by my side, where now the

maiden reposes,
Told me this same sad tale; then arose and
continued his journey!"
Soft was the voice of the priest, and he spake
with an accent of kindness;
But on Evangeline's heart fell his words as in
winter the snow-flakes
Fall into some lone nest from which the birds
have departed.
"Far to the north he has gone," continued
the priest; "but in autumn,
When the chase is done, will return again to
the Mission."
Then Evangeline said, and her voice was
meek and submissive,
"Let me remain with thee, for my soul is sad
and afflicted."
So seemed it wise and well unto all; and be-
times on the morrow,
Mounting his Mexican steed, with his Indian
guides and companions,
Homeward Basil returned, and Evangeline
stayed at the Mission.

Slowly, slowly, slowly the days succeeded
each other, —
Days and weeks and months; and the fields
of maize that were springing
Green from the ground when a stranger she
came, now waving above her,
Lifted their slender shafts, with leaves inter-
lacing, and forming

Cloisters for mendicant crows and granaries
pillaged by squirrels.
Then in the golden weather the maize was
husked, and the maidens
Blushed at each blood-red ear, for that
betokened a lover,
But at the crooked laughed, and called it a
thief in the cornfield.
Even the blood-red ear to Evangeline brought
not her lover.
"Patience!" the priest would say; "have faith,
and thy prayer will be answered!
Look at this vigorous plant that lifts its head
from the meadow,
See how its leaves are turned to the north, as
true as the magnet;
This is the compass-flower, that the finger of
God has planted
Here in the houseless wild, to direct the
traveller's journey
Over the sea-like, pathless, limitless waste of
the desert.
Such in the soul of man is faith. The blos-
soms of passion,
Gay and luxuriant flowers, are brighter and
fuller of fragrance,
But they beguile us, and lead us astray, and
their odor is deadly.
Only this humble plant can guide us here,
and hereafter
Crown us with asphodel flowers, that are wet
with the dews of nepenthe."

So came the autumn, and passed, and the
winter, — yet Gabriel came not;
Blossomed the opening spring, and the notes
of the robin and bluebird
Sounded sweet upon wold and in wood, yet
Gabriel came not.
But on the breath of the summer winds a
rumor was wafted
Sweeter than song of bird, or hue or odor of
blossom.
Far to the north and east, it said, in the
Michigan forests,
Gabriel had his lodge by the banks of the
Saginaw River.
And, with returning guides, that sought the
lakes of St. Lawrence,
Saying a sad farewell, Evangeline went from
the Mission.
When over weary ways, by long and perilous
marches,
She had attained at length the depths of the
Michigan forests,
Found she the hunter's lodge deserted and
fallen to ruin!

Thus did the long sad years glide on, and
in seasons and places
Divers and distant far was seen the wander-
ing maiden; —
Now in the Tents of Grace of the meek
Moravian Missions,
Now in the noisy camps and the battle-fields

of the army,
Now in secluded hamlets, in towns and
populous cities.
Like a phantom she came, and passed away
unremembered.
Fair was she and young, when in hope began
the long journey;
Faded was she and old, when in disappoint-
ment it ended.
Each succeeding year stole something away
from her beauty,
Leaving behind it, broader and deeper, the
gloom and the shadow.
Then there appeared and spread faint streaks
of gray o'er her forehead,
Dawn of another life, that broke o'er her
earthly horizon,
As in the eastern sky the first faint streaks of
the morning.

V.

In that delightful land which is washed by
the Delaware's waters,
Guarding in sylvan shades the name of Penn
the apostle,
Stands on the banks of its beautiful stream
the city he founded.
There all the air is balm, and the peach is
the emblem of beauty,
And the streets still reëcho the names of the
trees of the forest,

As if they fain would appease the Dryads
    whose haunts they molested.
There from the troubled sea had Evangeline
    landed, an exile,
Finding among the children of Penn a home
    and a country.
There old René Leblanc had died; and when
    he departed,
Saw at his side only one of all his hundred
    descendants.
Something at least there was in the friendly
    streets of the city,
Something that spake to her heart, and made
    her no longer a stranger;
And her ear was pleased with the Thee and
    Thou of the Quakers,
For it recalled the past, the old Acadian
    country,
Where all men were equal, and all were
    brothers and sisters.
So, when the fruitless search, the disap-
    pointed endeavor,
Ended, to recommence no more upon earth,
    uncomplaining,
Thither, as leaves to the light, were turned
    her thoughts and her footsteps.
As from the mountain's top the rainy mists
    of the morning
Roll away, and afar we behold the landscape
    below us,
Sun-illumined, with shining rivers and cities
    and hamlets,

So fell the mists from her mind, and she saw
the world far below her,
Dark no longer, but all illumined with love;
and the pathway
Which she had climbed so far, lying smooth
and fair in the distance.
Gabriel was not forgotten. Within her heart
was his image,
Clothed in the beauty of love and youth, as
last she beheld him,
Only more beautiful made by his death-like
silence and absence.
Into her thoughts of him time entered not,
for it was not.
Over him years had no power; he was not
changed, but transfigured;
He had become to her heart as one who is
dead, and not absent;
Patience and abnegation of self, and devo-
tion to others,
This was the lesson a life of trial and sorrow
had taught her.
So was her love diffused, but, like to some
odorous spices,
Suffered no waste nor loss, though filling the
air with aroma.
Other hope had she none, nor wish in life,
but to follow
Meekly, with reverent steps, the sacred feet
of her Saviour.
Thus many years she lived as a Sister of
Mercy; frequenting

Lonely and wretched roofs in the crowded
lanes of the city,
Where distress and want concealed them-
selves from the sunlight,
Where disease and sorrow in garrets lan-
guished neglected.
Night after night, when the world was asleep,
as the watchman repeated
Loud, through the gusty streets, that all was
well in the city,
High at some lonely window he saw the light
of her taper.
Day after day, in the gray of the dawn, as
slow through the suburbs
Plodded the German farmer, with flowers
and fruits for the market,
Met he that meek, pale face, returning home
from its watchings.

Then it came to pass that a pestilence fell
on the city,
Presaged by wondrous signs, and mostly by
flocks of wild pigeons,
Darkening the sun in their flight, with naught
in their craws but an acorn.
And, as the tides of the sea arise in the month
of September,
Flooding some silver stream, till it spreads to
a lake in the meadow,
So death flooded life, and, o'erflowing its
natural margin,
Spread to a brackish lake, the silver stream

of existence.

Wealth had no power to bribe, nor beauty to charm, the oppressor;

But all perished alike beneath the scourge of his anger; —

Only, alas! the poor, who had neither friends nor attendants,

Crept away to die in the almshouse, home of the homeless.

Then in the suburbs it stood, in the midst of meadows and woodlands; —

Now the city surrounds it; but still, with its gateway and wicket

Meek, in the midst of splendor, its humble walls seem to echo

Softly the words of the Lord: "The poor ye always have with you."

Thither, by night and by day, came the Sister of Mercy. The dying

Looked up into her face, and thought, indeed, to behold there

Gleams of celestial light encircle her forehead with splendor,

Such as the artist paints o'er the brows of saints and apostles,

Or such as hangs by night o'er a city seen at a distance.

Unto their eyes it seemed the lamps of the city celestial,

Into whose shining gates erelong their spirits would enter.

Thus, on a Sabbath morn, through the
streets, deserted and silent,
Wending her quiet way, she entered the door
of the almshouse.
Sweet on the summer air was the odor of
flowers in the garden;
And she paused on her way to gather the fair-
est among them,
That the dying once more might rejoice in
their fragrance and beauty.
Then, as she mounted the stairs to the cor-
ridors, cooled by the east-wind,
Distant and soft on her ear fell the chimes
from the belfry of Christ Church,
While, intermingled with these, across the
meadows were wafted
Sounds of psalms, that were sung by the
Swedes in their church at Wicaco.
Soft as descending wings fell the calm of the
hour on her spirit:
Something within her said, "At length thy
trials are ended";
And, with light in her looks, she entered the
chambers of sickness.
Noiselessly moved about the assiduous, care-
ful attendants,
Moistening the feverish lip, and the aching
brow, and in silence
Closing the sightless eyes of the dead, and
concealing their faces,
Where on their pallets they lay, like drifts of
snow by the roadside.

Many a languid head, upraised as Evangeline
    entered,
Turned on its pillow of pain to gaze while
    she passed, for her presence
Fell on their hearts like a ray of the sun on
    the walls of a prison.
And, as she looked around, she saw how
    Death, the consoler,
Laying his hand upon many a heart, had
    healed it forever.
Many familiar forms had disappeared in the
    night time;
Vacant their places were, or filled already by
    strangers.

    Suddenly, as if arrested by fear or a feeling
    of wonder,
Still she stood, with her colorless lips apart,
    while a shudder
Ran through her frame, and, forgotten, the
    flowerets dropped from her fingers,
And from her eyes and cheeks the light and
    bloom of the morning.
Then there escaped from her lips a cry of
    such terrible anguish,
That the dying heard it, and started up from
    their pillows.
On the pallet before her was stretched the
    form of an old man.
Long, and thin, and gray were the locks that
    shaded his temples;
But, as he lay in the morning light, his face

for a moment

Seemed to assume once more the forms of
its earlier manhood;

So are wont to be changed the faces of those
who are dying.

Hot and red on his lips still burned the flush
of the fever,

As if life, like the Hebrew, with blood had
besprinkled its portals,

That the Angel of Death might see the sign,
and pass over.

Motionless, senseless, dying, he lay, and his
spirit exhausted

Seemed to be sinking down through infinite
depths in the darkness,

Darkness of slumber and death, forever sink-
ing and sinking.

Then through those realms of shade, in
multiplied reverberations,

Heard he that cry of pain, and through the
hush that succeeded

Whispered a gentle voice, in accents tender
and saint-like,

"Gabriel! O my beloved!" and died away into
silence.

Then he beheld, in a dream, once more the
home of his childhood;

Green Acadian meadows, with sylvan rivers
among them,

Village, and mountain, and woodlands; and,
walking under their shadow,

As in the days of her youth, Evangeline rose

in his vision.
Tears came into his eyes; and as slowly he
lifted his eyelids,
Vanished the vision away, but Evangeline
knelt by his bedside.
Vainly he strove to whisper her name, for the
accents unuttered
Died on his lips, and their motion revealed
what his tongue would have spoken.
Vainly he strove to rise; and Evangeline,
kneeling beside him,
Kissed his dying lips, and laid his head on
her bosom.
Sweet was the light of his eyes; but it sud-
denly sank into darkness,
As when a lamp is blown out by a gust of
wind at a casement.

All was ended now, the hope, and the fear,
and the sorrow,
All the aching of heart, the restless, unsatis-
fied longing,
All the dull, deep pain, and constant anguish
of patience!
And, as she pressed once more the lifeless
head to her bosom,
Meekly she bowed her own, and murmured,
"Father I thank thee!"

Still stands the forest primeval; but far away
from its shadow,

Side by side, in their nameless graves, the
lovers are sleeping.
Under the humble walls of the little Catholic
churchyard,
In the heart of the city, they lie, unknown
and unnoticed.
Daily the tides of life go ebbing and flowing
beside them,
Thousands of throbbing hearts, where theirs
are at rest and forever,
Thousands of aching brains, where theirs no
longer are busy,
Thousands of toiling hands, where theirs
have ceased from their labors,
Thousands of weary feet, where theirs have
completed their journey!

Still stands the forest primeval; but under
the shade of its branches
Dwells another race, with other customs and
language.
Only along the shore of the mournful and
misty Atlantic
Linger a few Acadian peasants, whose fathers
from exile
Wandered back to their native land to die in
its bosom.
In the fisherman's cot the wheel and the
loom are still busy;
Maidens still wear their Norman caps and
their kirtles of homespun,

And by the evening fire repeat Evangeline's
    story,
While from its rocky caverns the deep-voiced,
    neighboring ocean
Speaks, and in accents disconsolate answers
    the wail of the forest.

The Seaside and the Fireside

The Building of the Ship

"Build me straight, O worthy Master!
  Stanch and strong, a goodly vessel,
That shall laugh at all disaster,
  And with wave and whirlwind wrestle!"

The merchant's word
Delighted the Master heard;
For his heart was in his work, and the heart
Giveth grace unto every Art.
A quiet smile played round his lips,
As the eddies and dimples of the tide
Play round the bows of ships,
That steadily at anchor ride.
And with a voice that was full of glee,
He answered, "Erelong we will launch
A vessel as goodly, and strong, and stanch,
As ever weathered a wintry sea!"
And first with nicest skill and art,
Perfect and finished in every part,
A little model the Master wrought,

Which should be to the larger plan
What the child is to the man,
Its counterpart in miniature;
That with a hand more swift and sure
The greater labor might be brought
To answer to his inward thought.
And as he labored, his mind ran o'er
The various ships that were built of yore,
And above them all, and strangest of all
Towered the Great Harry, crank and tall,
Whose picture was hanging on the wall,
With bows and stern raised high in air,
And balconies hanging here and there,
And signal lanterns and flags afloat,
And eight round towers, like those that frown
From some old castle, looking down
Upon the drawbridge and the moat.
And he said with a smile, "Our ship, I wis,
Shall be of another form than this!"
It was of another form, indeed;
Built for freight, and yet for speed,
A beautiful and gallant craft;
Broad in the beam, that the stress of the blast,
Pressing down upon sail and mast,
Might not the sharp bows overwhelm;
Broad in the beam, but sloping aft
With graceful curve and slow degrees,
That she might be docile to the helm,
And that the currents of parted seas,
Closing behind, with mighty force,
Might aid and not impede her course.

In the ship-yard stood the Master,
With the model of the vessel,
That should laugh at all disaster,
And with wave and whirlwind wrestle!
Covering many a rood of ground,
Lay the timber piled around;
Timber of chestnut, and elm, and oak,
And scattered here and there, with these,
The knarred and crooked cedar knees;
Brought from regions far away,
From Pascagoula's sunny bay,
And the banks of the roaring Roanoke!
Ah! what a wondrous thing it is
To note how many wheels of toil
One thought, one word, can set in motion!
There's not a ship that sails the ocean,
But every climate, every soil,
Must bring its tribute, great or small,
And help to build the wooden wall!
The sun was rising o'er the sea,
And long the level shadows lay,
As if they, too, the beams would be
Of some great, airy argosy,
Framed and launched in a single day.
That silent architect, the sun,
Had hewn and laid them every one,
Ere the work of man was yet begun.
Beside the Master, when he spoke,
A youth, against an anchor leaning,
Listened, to catch his slightest meaning.
Only the long waves, as they broke
In ripples on the pebbly beach,

Interrupted the old man's speech.
Beautiful they were, in sooth,
The old man and the fiery youth!
The old man, in whose busy brain
Many a ship that sailed the main
Was modelled o'er and o'er again; —
The fiery youth, who was to be
The heir of his dexterity,
The heir of his house, and his daughter's
    hand,
When he had built and launched from land
What the elder head had planned.

"Thus," said he, "will we build this ship!
Lay square the blocks upon the slip,
And follow well this plan of mine.
Choose the timbers with greatest care;
Of all that is unsound beware;
For only what is sound and strong
To this vessel shall belong.
Cedar of Maine and Georgia pine
Here together shall combine.
A goodly frame, and a goodly fame,
And the UNION be her name!
For the day that gives her to the sea
Shall give my daughter unto thee!"
The Master's word
Enraptured the young man heard;
And as he turned his face aside,
With a look of joy and a thrill of pride
Standing before
Her father's door,

He saw the form of his promised bride.
The sun shone on her golden hair,
And her cheek was glowing fresh and fair,
With the breath of morn and the soft sea air.
Like a beauteous barge was she,
Still at rest on the sandy beach,
Just beyond the billow's reach;
But he
Was the restless, seething, stormy sea!
Ah, how skilful grows the hand
That obeyeth Love's command!
It is the heart, and not the brain,
That to the highest doth attain,
And he who followeth Love's behest
Far excelleth all the rest!

Thus with the rising of the sun
Was the noble task begun,
And soon throughout the ship-yard's bounds
Were heard the intermingled sounds
Of axes and of mallets, plied
With vigorous arms on every side;
Plied so deftly and so well,
That, ere the shadows of evening fell,
The keel of oak for a noble ship,
Scarfed and bolted, straight and strong,
Was lying ready, and stretched along
The blocks, well placed upon the slip.
Happy, thrice happy, every one
Who sees his labor well begun,
And not perplexed and multiplied,
By idly waiting for time and tide!

And when the hot, long day was o'er,
The young man at the Master's door
Sat with the maiden calm and still,
And within the porch, a little more
Removed beyond the evening chill,
The father sat, and told them tales
Of wrecks in the great September gales,
Of pirates coasting the Spanish Main,
And ships that never came back again,
The chance and change of a sailor's life,
Want and plenty, rest and strife,
His roving fancy, like the wind,
That nothing can stay and nothing can bind,
And the magic charm of foreign lands,
With shadows of palms, and shining sands,
Where the tumbling surf,
O'er the coral reefs of Madagascar,
Washes the feet of the swarthy Lascar,
As he lies alone and asleep on the turf.
And the trembling maiden held her breath
At the tales of that awful, pitiless sea,
With all its terror and mystery,
The dim, dark sea, so like unto Death,
That divides and yet unites mankind!
And whenever the old man paused, a gleam
From the bowl of his pipe would awhile il-
    lume
The silent group in the twilight gloom,
And thoughtful faces, as in a dream;
And for a moment one might mark
What had been hidden by the dark,
That the head of the maiden lay at rest,

Tenderly, on the young man's breast!

Day by day the vessel grew,
With timbers fashioned strong and true,
Stemson and keelson and sternson-knee,
Till, framed with perfect symmetry,
A skeleton ship rose up to view!
And around the bows and along the side
The heavy hammers and mallets plied,
Till after many a week, at length,
Wonderful for form and strength,
Sublime in its enormous bulk,
Loomed aloft the shadowy hulk!
And around it columns of smoke, upwreath-
    ing,
Rose from the boiling, bubbling, seething
Caldron, that glowed,
And overflowed
With the black tar, heated for the sheathing.
And amid the clamors
Of clattering hammers,
He who listened heard now and then
The song of the Master and his men: —

"Build me straight, O worthy Master,
  Staunch and strong, a goodly vessel,
That shall laugh at all disaster,
  And with wave and whirlwind wrestle!"

With oaken brace and copper band,
Lay the rudder on the sand,
That, like a thought, should have control

Over the movement of the whole;
And near it the anchor, whose giant hand
Would reach down and grapple with the land,
And immovable and fast
Hold the great ship against the hallowing
   blast!
And at the bows an image stood,
By a cunning artist carved in wood,
With robes of white, that far behind
Seemed to be fluttering in the wind.
It was not shaped in a classic mould,
Not like a Nymph or Goddess of old,
Or Naiad rising from the water,
But modelled from the Master's daughter!
On many a dreary and misty night,
'T will be seen by the rays of the signal light,
Speeding along through the rain and the
   dark,
Like a ghost in its snow-white sark,
The pilot of some phantom bark,
Guiding the vessel, in its flight,
By a path none other knows aright!

Behold, at last,
Each tall and tapering mast
Is swung into its place;
Shrouds and stays
Holding it firm and fast!

Long ago,
In the deer-haunted forests of Maine,
When upon mountain and plain

Lay the snow,
They fell, — those lordly pines!
Those grand, majestic pines!
'Mid shouts and cheers
The jaded steers,
Panting beneath the goad,
Dragged down the weary, winding road
Those captive kings so straight and tall,
To be shorn of their streaming hair,
And naked and bare,
To feel the stress and the strain
Of the wind and the reeling main,
Whose roar
Would remind them forevermore
Of their native forests they should not see
 again.

And everywhere
The slender, graceful spars
Poise aloft in the air,
And at the mast-head,
White, blue, and red,
A flag unrolls the stripes and stars.
Ah! when the wanderer, lonely, friendless,
In foreign harbors shall behold
That flag unrolled,
'T will be as a friendly hand
Stretched out from his native land,
Filling his heart with memories sweet and
 endless!
All is finished! and at length
Has come the bridal day

Of beauty and of strength.
To-day the vessel shall be launched!
With fleecy clouds the sky is blanched,
And o'er the bay,
Slowly, in all his splendors dight,
The great sun rises to behold the sight.

The ocean old,
Centuries old,
Strong as youth, and as uncontrolled,
Paces restless to and fro,
Up and down the sands of gold.
His beating heart is not at rest;
And far and wide,
With ceaseless flow,
His beard of snow
Heaves with the heaving of his breast.
He waits impatient for his bride.
There she stands,
With her foot upon the sands,
Decked with flags and streamers gay,
In honor of her marriage day,
Her snow-white signals fluttering, blending,
Round her like a veil descending,
Ready to be
The bride of the gray old sea.

On the deck another bride
Is standing by her lover's side.
Shadows from the flags and shrouds,
Like the shadows cast by clouds,
Broken by many a sunny fleck,

Fall around them on the deck.

The prayer is said,
The service read,
The joyous bridegroom bows his head;
And in tears the good old Master
Shakes the brown hand of his son,
Kisses his daughter's glowing cheek
In silence, for he cannot speak,
And ever faster
Down his own the tears begin to run.
The worthy pastor —
The shepherd of that wandering flock,
That has the ocean for its wold,
That has the vessel for its fold,
Leaping ever from rock to rock —
Spake, with accents mild and clear,
Words of warning, words of cheer,
But tedious to the bridegroom's ear.
He knew the chart
Of the sailor's heart,
All its pleasures and its griefs,
All its shallows and rocky reefs,
All those secret currents, that flow
With such resistless undertow,
And lift and drift, with terrible force,
The will from its moorings and its course.
Therefore he spake, and thus said he: —

"Like unto ships far off at sea,
Outward or homeward bound, are we.
Before, behind, and all around,

Floats and swings the horizon's bound,
Seems at its distant rim to rise
And climb the crystal wall of the skies,
And then again to turn and sink,
As if we could slide from its outer brink.
Ah! it is not the sea,
It is not the sea that sinks and shelves,
But ourselves
That rock and rise
With endless and uneasy motion,
Now touching the very skies,
Now sinking into the depths of ocean.
Ah! if our souls but poise and swing
Like the compass in its brazen ring,
Ever level and ever true
To the toil and the task we have to do,
We shall sail securely, and safely reach
The Fortunate Isles, on whose shining beach
The sights we see, and the sounds we hear,
Will be those of joy and not of fear!"

Then the Master,
With a gesture of command,
Waved his hand;
And at the word,
Loud and sudden there was heard,
All around them and below,
The sound of hammers, blow on blow,
Knocking away the shores and spurs.
And see! she stirs!
She starts, — she moves, — she seems to feel
The thrill of life along her keel,

And, spurning with her foot the ground,
With one exulting, joyous bound,
She leaps into the ocean's arms!

And lo! from the assembled crowd
There rose a shout, prolonged and loud,
That to the ocean seemed to say,
"Take her, O bridegroom, old and gray,
Take her to thy protecting arms,
With all her youth and all her charms!"

How beautiful she is! How fair
She lies within those arms, that press
Her form with many a soft caress
Of tenderness and watchful care!
Sail forth into the sea, O ship!
Through wind and wave, right onward steer!
The moistened eye, the trembling lip,
Are not the signs of doubt or fear.

Sail forth into the sea of life,
O gentle, loving, trusting wife,
And safe from all adversity
Upon the bosom of that sea
Thy comings and thy goings be!
For gentleness and love and trust
Prevail o'er angry wave and gust;
And in the wreck of noble lives
Something immortal still survives!

Thou, too, sail on, O Ship of State!
Sail on, O UNION, strong and great!

Humanity with all its fears,
With all the hopes of future years,
Is hanging breathless on thy fate!
We know what Master laid thy keel,
What Workmen wrought thy ribs of steel,
Who made each mast, and sail, and rope,
What anvils rang, what hammers beat,
In what a forge and what a heat
Were shaped the anchors of thy hope!
Fear not each sudden sound and shock,
'T is of the wave and not the rock;
'T is but the flapping of the sail,
And not a rent made by the gale!
In spite of rock and tempest's roar,
In spite of false lights on the shore,
Sail on, nor fear to breast the sea!
Our hearts, our hopes, are all with thee,
Our hearts, our hopes, our prayers, our tears,
Our faith triumphant o'er our fears,
Are all with thee, — are all with thee!

SEAWEED

When descends on the Atlantic
  The gigantic
Storm-wind of the equinox,
Landward in his wrath he scourges
  The toiling surges,
Laden with seaweed from the rocks:

From Bermuda's reefs; from edges

Of sunken ledges,
In some far-off, bright Azore;
From Bahama, and the dashing,
  Silver-flashing
Surges of San Salvador;

From the tumbling surf, that buries
  The Orkneyan skerries,
Answering the hoarse Hebrides;
And from wrecks of ships, and drifting
  Spars, uplifting
On the desolate, rainy seas; —

Ever drifting, drifting, drifting
  On the shifting
Currents of the restless main;
Till in sheltered coves, and reaches
  Of sandy beaches,
All have found repose again.

So when storms of wild emotion
  Strike the ocean
Of the poet's soul, erelong
From each cave and rocky fastness,
  In its vastness,
Floats some fragment of a song:

From the far-off isles enchanted,
  Heaven has planted
With the golden fruit of Truth;
From the flashing surf, whose vision

Gleams Elysian
In the tropic clime of Youth;

From the strong Will, and the Endeavor
  That forever
Wrestle with the tides of Fate;
From the wreck of Hopes far-scattered,
  Tempest-shattered,
Floating waste and desolate; —

Ever drifting, drifting, drifting
  On the shifting
Currents of the restless heart;
Till at length in books recorded,
  They, like hoarded
Household words, no more depart.

CHRYSAOR

Just above yon sandy bar,
  As the day grows fainter and dimmer,
Lonely and lovely, a single star
  Lights the air with a dusky glimmer.

Into the ocean faint and far
  Falls the trail of its golden splendor,
And the gleam of that single star
  Is ever refulgent, soft, and tender.

Chrysaor, rising out of the sea,
  Showed thus glorious and thus emulous,

Leaving the arms of Callirrhoe,
   Forever tender, soft, and tremulous.

Thus o'er the ocean faint and far
   Trailed the gleam of his falchion brightly;
Is it a God, or is it a star
   That, entranced, I gaze on nightly!

TWILIGHT

The twilight is sad and cloudy,
   The wind blows wild and free,
And like the wings of sea-birds
   Flash the white caps of the sea.

But in the fisherman's cottage
   There shines a ruddier light,
And a little face at the window
   Peers out into the night.

Close, close it is pressed to the window,
   As if those childish eyes
Were looking into the darkness
   To see some form arise.

And a woman's waving shadow
   Is passing to and fro,
Now rising to the ceiling,
   Now bowing and bending low.

What tale do the roaring ocean,

And the night-wind, bleak and wild,
  As they beat at the crazy casement,
    Tell to that little child?

And why do the roaring ocean,
    And the night-wind, wild and bleak,
As they beat at the heart of the mother
    Drive the color from her cheek?

SIR HUMPHREY GILBERT

Southward with fleet of ice
  Sailed the corsair Death;
Wild and fast blew the blast,
  And the east-wind was his breath.

His lordly ships of ice
  Glisten in the sun;
On each side, like pennons wide,
  Flashing crystal streamlets run.

His sails of white sea-mist
  Dripped with silver rain;
But where he passed there were cast
  Leaden shadows o'er the main.

Eastward from Campobello
  Sir Humphrey Gilbert sailed;
Three days or more seaward he bore,
  Then, alas! the land-wind failed.

Alas! the land-wind failed,
   And ice-cold grew the night;
And nevermore, on sea or shore,
   Should Sir Humphrey see the light.

He sat upon the deck,
   The Book was in his hand;
"Do not fear! Heaven is as near,"
   He said, "by water as by land!"

In the first watch of the night,
   Without a signal's sound,
Out of the sea, mysteriously,
   The fleet of Death rose all around.

The moon and the evening star
   Were hanging in the shrouds;
Every mast, as it passed,
   Seemed to rake the passing clouds.

They grappled with their prize,
   At midnight black and cold!
As of a rock was the shock;
   Heavily the ground-swell rolled.

Southward through day and dark,
   They drift in close embrace,
With mist and rain, o'er the open main;
   Yet there seems no change of place.

Southward, forever southward,

They drift through dark and day;
And like a dream, in the Gulf-Stream
   Sinking, vanish all away.

THE LIGHTHOUSE

The rocky ledge runs far into the sea,
   And on its outer point, some miles away,
The Lighthouse lifts its massive masonry,
   A pillar of fire by night, of cloud by day.

Even at this distance I can see the tides,
   Upheaving, break unheard along its base,
A speechless wrath, that rises and subsides
   In the white lip and tremor of the face.

And as the evening darkens, lo! how bright,
   Through the deep purple of the twilight
   air,
Beams forth the sudden radiance of its light
   With strange, unearthly splendor in the
   glare!

Not one alone; from each projecting cape
   And perilous reef along the ocean's verge,
Starts into life a dim, gigantic shape,
   Holding its lantern o'er the restless surge.

Like the great giant Christopher it stands
   Upon the brink of the tempestuous wave,
Wading far out among the rocks and sands,

The night-o'ertaken mariner to save.

And the great ships sail outward and return,
  Bending and bowing o'er the billowy swells,
And ever joyful, as they see it burn,
  They wave their silent welcomes and fare-
    wells.

They come forth from the darkness, and their
    sails
  Gleam for a moment only in the blaze,
And eager faces, as the light unveils,
  Gaze at the tower, and vanish while they
    gaze.

The mariner remembers when a child,
  On his first voyage, he saw it fade and sink;
And when, returning from adventures wild,
  He saw it rise again o'er ocean's brink.

Steadfast, serene, immovable, the same
  Year after year, through all the silent night
Burns on forevermore that quenchless flame,
  Shines on that inextinguishable light!

It sees the ocean to its bosom clasp
  The rocks and sea-sand with the kiss of
    peace;
It sees the wild winds lift it in their grasp,
  And hold it up, and shake it like a fleece.

The startled waves leap over it; the storm
  Smites it with all the scourges of the rain,
And steadily against its solid form
  Press the great shoulders of the hurricane.

The sea-bird wheeling round it, with the din
  Of wings and winds and solitary cries,
Blinded and maddened by the light within,
  Dashes himself against the glare, and dies.

A new Prometheus, chained upon the rock,
  Still grasping in his hand the fire of Jove,
It does not hear the cry, nor heed the shock,
  But hails the mariner with words of love.

"Sail on!" it says, "sail on, ye stately ships!
  And with your floating bridge the ocean
    span;
Be mine to guard this light from all eclipse,
  Be yours to bring man nearer unto man!"

THE FIRE OF DRIFT-WOOD

We sat within the farm-house old,
  Whose windows, looking o'er the bay,
Gave to the sea-breeze damp and cold,
  An easy entrance, night and day.

Not far away we saw the port,
  The strange, old-fashioned, silent town,
The lighthouse, the dismantled fort,

The wooden houses, quaint and brown.

We sat and talked until the night,
  Descending, filled the little room;
Our faces faded from the sight,
  Our voices only broke the gloom.

We spake of many a vanished scene,
  Of what we once had thought and said,
Of what had been, and might have been,
  And who was changed, and who was dead;

And all that fills the hearts of friends,
  When first they feel, with secret pain,
Their lives thenceforth have separate ends,
  And never can be one again;

The first slight swerving of the heart,
  That words are powerless to express,
And leave it still unsaid in part,
  Or say it in too great excess.

The very tones in which we spake
  Had something strange, I could but mark;
The leaves of memory seemed to make
  A mournful rustling in the dark.

Oft died the words upon our lips,
  As suddenly, from out the fire
Built of the wreck of stranded ships,
  The flames would leap and then expire.

And, as their splendor flashed and failed,
  We thought of wrecks upon the main,
Of ships dismasted, that were hailed
  And sent no answer back again.

The windows, rattling in their frames,
  The ocean, roaring up the beach,
The gusty blast, the bickering flames,
  All mingled vaguely in our speech;

Until they made themselves a part
  Of fancies floating through the brain,
The long-lost ventures of the heart,
  That send no answers back again.

O flames that glowed! O hearts that yearned!
  They were indeed too much akin,
The drift-wood fire without that burned,
  The thoughts that burned and glowed
  within.

RESIGNATION

There is no flock, however watched and
  tended,
  But one dead lamb is there!
There is no fireside, howsoe'er defended,
  But has one vacant chair!

The air is full of farewells to the dying,
  And mournings for the dead;

The heart of Rachel, for her children crying
  Will not be comforted!

Let us be patient! These severe afflictions
  Not from the ground arise,
But oftentimes celestial benedictions
  Assume this dark disguise.

We see but dimly through the mists and
    vapors;
  Amid these earthly damps
What seem to us but sad, funereal tapers
  May be heaven's distant lamps.

There is no Death! What seems so is transi-
    tion;
  This life of mortal breath
Is but a suburb of the life elysian,
  Whose portal we call Death.

She is not dead, — the child of our affec-
    tion, —
  But gone unto that school
Where she no longer needs our poor protec-
    tion,
  And Christ himself doth rule.

In that great cloister's stillness and seclusion,
  By guardian angels led,
Safe from temptation, safe from sin's pollu-
    tion,

She lives, whom we call dead.

Day after day we think what she is doing
  In those bright realms of air;
Year after year, her tender steps pursuing,
  Behold her grown more fair.

Thus do we walk with her, and keep unbro-
    ken
  The bond which nature gives,
Thinking that our remembrance, though un-
    spoken,
  May reach her where she lives.

Not as a child shall we again behold her;
  For when with raptures wild
In our embraces we again enfold her,
  She will not be a child;

But a fair maiden, in her Father's mansion,
  Clothed with celestial grace;
And beautiful with all the soul's expansion
  Shall we behold her face.

And though at times impetuous with emo-
    tion
  And anguish long suppressed,
The swelling heart heaves moaning like the
    ocean,
  That cannot be at rest, —

We will be patient, and assuage the feeling

We may not wholly stay;
By silence sanctifying, not concealing,
The grief that must have way.

THE BUILDERS

All are architects of Fate,
  Working in these walls of Time;
Some with massive deeds and great,
  Some with ornaments of rhyme.

Nothing useless is, or low;
  Each thing in its place is best;
And what seems but idle show
  Strengthens and supports the rest.

For the structure that we raise,
  Time is with materials filled;
Our to-days and yesterdays
  Are the blocks with which we build.

Truly shape and fashion these;
  Leave no yawning gaps between;
Think not, because no man sees,
  Such things will remain unseen.

In the elder days of Art,
  Builders wrought with greatest care
Each minute and unseen part;
  For the Gods see everywhere.

Let us do our work as well,
  Both the unseen and the seen;
Make the house, where Gods may dwell,
  Beautiful, entire, and clean.

Else our lives are incomplete,
  Standing in these walls of Time,
Broken stairways, where the feet
  Stumble as they seek to climb.

Build to-day, then, strong and sure,
  With a firm and ample base;
And ascending and secure
  Shall to-morrow find its place.

Thus alone can we attain
  To those turrets, where the eye
Sees the world as one vast plain,
  And one boundless reach of sky.

SAND OF THE DESERT IN AN HOUR-GLASS

A handful of red sand, from the hot clime
  Of Arab deserts brought,
Within this glass becomes the spy of Time,
  The minister of Thought.

How many weary centuries has it been
  About those deserts blown!
How many strange vicissitudes has seen,
  How many histories known!

Perhaps the camels of the Ishmaelite
  Trampled and passed it o'er,
When into Egypt from the patriarch's sight
  His favorite son they bore.

Perhaps the feet of Moses, burnt and bare,
  Crushed it beneath their tread,
Or Pharaoh's flashing wheels into the air
  Scattered it as they sped;

Or Mary, with the Christ of Nazareth
  Held close in her caress,
Whose pilgrimage of hope and love and faith
  Illumed the wilderness;

Or anchorites beneath Engaddi's palms
  Pacing the Dead Sea beach,
And singing slow their old Armenian psalms
  In half-articulate speech;

Or caravans, that from Bassora's gate
  With westward steps depart;
Or Mecca's pilgrims, confident of Fate,
  And resolute in heart!

These have passed over it, or may have
    passed!
  Now in this crystal tower
Imprisoned by some curious hand at last,
  It counts the passing hour.

And as I gaze, these narrow walls expand; —
  Before my dreamy eye
Stretches the desert with its shifting sand,
  Its unimpeded sky.

And borne aloft by the sustaining blast,
  This little golden thread
Dilates into a column high and vast,
  A form of fear and dread.

And onward, and across the setting sun,
  Across the boundless plain,
The column and its broader shadow run,
  Till thought pursues in vain.

The vision vanishes! These walls again
  Shut out the lurid sun,
Shut out the hot, immeasurable plain;
  The half-hour's sand is run!

THE OPEN WINDOW

The old house by the lindens
  Stood silent in the shade,
And on the gravelled pathway
  The light and shadow played.

I saw the nursery windows
  Wide open to the air;
But the faces of the children,
  They were no longer there.

The large Newfoundland house-dog
  Was standing by the door;
He looked for his little playmates,
  Who would return no more.

They walked not under the lindens,
  They played not in the hall;
But shadow, and silence, and sadness
  Were hanging over all.

The birds sang in the branches,
  With sweet, familiar tone;
But the voices of the children
  Will be heard in dreams alone!

And the boy that walked beside me,
  He could not understand
Why closer in mine, ah! closer,
  I pressed his warm, soft hand!

THE SONG OF HIAWATHA

Introduction

Should you ask me, whence these stories?
Whence these legends and traditions,
With the odors of the forest,
With the dew and damp of meadows,
With the curling smoke of wigwams,
With the rushing of great rivers,
With their frequent repetitions,
And their wild reverberations,
As of thunder in the mountains?
  I should answer, I should tell you,
"From the forests and the prairies,
From the great lakes of the Northland,
From the land of the Ojibways,
From the land of the Dacotahs,
From the mountains, moors, and fen-lands
Where the heron, the Shuh-shuh-gah,
Feeds among the reeds and rushes.
I repeat them as I heard them
From the lips of Nawadaha,
The musician, the sweet singer."

Should you ask where Nawadaha
Found these songs so wild and wayward,
Found these legends and traditions,
I should answer, I should tell you,
"In the bird's-nests of the forest,
In the lodges of the beaver,
In the hoof-prints of the bison,
In the eyry of the eagle!

"All the wild-fowl sang them to him,
In the moorlands and the fen-lands,
In the melancholy marshes;
Chetowaik, the plover, sang them,
Mahng, the loon, the wild-goose, Wawa,
The blue heron, the Shuh-shuh-gah,
And the grouse, the Mushkodasa!"

If still further you should ask me,
Saying, "Who was Nawadaha?
Tell us of this Nawadaha,"
I should answer your inquiries
Straightway in such words as follow.

"In the vale of Tawasentha,
In the green and silent valley,
By the pleasant water-courses,
Dwelt the singer Nawadaha.
Round about the Indian village
Spread the meadows and the corn-fields,
And beyond them stood the forest,
Stood the groves of singing pine-trees,
Green in Summer, white in Winter,
Ever sighing, ever singing.

"And the pleasant water-courses,
You could trace them through the valley,

By the rushing in the Spring-time,
By the alders in the Summer,
By the white fog in the Autumn,
By the black line in the Winter;
And beside them dwelt the singer,
In the vale of Tawasentha,
In the green and silent valley.
  "There he sang of Hiawatha,
Sang the Song of Hiawatha,
Sang his wondrous birth and being,
How he prayed and how he fasted,
How he lived, and toiled, and suffered,
That the tribes of men might prosper,
That he might advance his people!"
  Ye who love the haunts of Nature,
Love the sunshine of the meadow,
Love the shadow of the forest,
Love the wind among the branches,
And the rain-shower and the snow-storm,
And the rushing of great rivers
Through their palisades of pine-trees,
And the thunder in the mountains,
Whose innumerable echoes
Flap like eagles in their eyries; —
Listen to these wild traditions,
To this Song of Hiawatha!
  Ye who love a nation's legends,
Love the ballads of a people,
That like voices from afar off
Call to us to pause and listen,
Speak in tones so plain and childlike,
Scarcely can the ear distinguish

Whether they are sung or spoken; —
Listen to this Indian Legend,
To this Song of Hiawatha!
  Ye whose hearts are fresh and simple,
Who have faith in God and Nature,
Who believe, that in all ages
Every human heart is human,
That in even savage bosoms
There are longings, yearnings, strivings
For the good they comprehend not,
That the feeble hands and helpless,
Groping blindly in the darkness,
Touch God's right hand in that darkness
And are lifted up and strengthened; —
Listen to this simple story,
To this Song of Hiawatha!
  Ye, who sometimes, in your rambles
Through the green lanes of the country,
Where the tangled barberry-bushes
Hang their tufts of crimson berries
Over stone walls gray with mosses,
Pause by some neglected graveyard,
For a while to muse, and ponder
On a half-effaced inscription,
Written with little skill of song-craft,
Homely phrases, but each letter
Full of hope and yet of heart-break,
Full of all the tender pathos
Of the Here and the Hereafter; —
Stay and read this rude inscription,
Read this Song of Hiawatha!

I

The Peace-Pipe

On the Mountains of the Prairie,
On the great Red Pipe-stone Quarry,
Gitche Manito, the mighty,
He the Master of Life, descending,
On the red crags of the quarry
Stood erect, and called the nations,
Called the tribes of men together.
    From his footprints flowed a river,
Leaped into the light of morning,
O'er the precipice plunging downward
Gleamed like Ishkoodah, the comet.
And the Spirit, stooping earthward,
With his finger on the meadow
Traced a winding pathway for it,
Saying to it, "Run in this way!"
    From the red stone of the quarry
With his hand he broke a fragment,
Moulded it into a pipe-head,
Shaped and fashioned it with figures;
From the margin of the river
Took a long reed for a pipe-stem,
With its dark green leaves upon it;
Filled the pipe with bark of willow,
With the bark of the red willow;
Breathed upon the neighboring forest,
Made its great boughs chafe together,
Till in flame they burst and kindled;
And erect upon the mountains,
Gitche Manito, the mighty,

Smoked the calumet, the Peace-Pipe,
As a signal to the nations.
   And the smoke rose slowly, slowly,
Through the tranquil air of morning,
First a single line of darkness,
Then a denser, bluer vapor,
Then a snow-white cloud unfolding,
Like the tree-tops of the forest,
Ever rising, rising, rising,
Till it touched the top of heaven,
Till it broke against the heaven,
And rolled outward all around it.
   From the Vale of Tawasentha,
From the Valley of Wyoming,
From the groves of Tuscaloosa,
From the far-off Rocky Mountains,
From the Northern lakes and rivers
All the tribes beheld the signal,
Saw the distant smoke ascending,
The Pukwana of the Peace-Pipe.
   And the Prophets of the nations
Said: "Behold it, the Pukwana!
By this signal from afar off,
Bending like a wand of willow,
Waving like a hand that beckons,
Gitche Manito, the mighty,
Calls the tribes of men together,
Calls the warriors to his council!"
   Down the rivers, o'er the prairies,
Came the warriors of the nations,
Came the Delawares and Mohawks,
Came the Choctaws and Camanches,

Came the Shoshonies and Blackfeet,
Came the Pawnees and Omahas,
Came the Mandans and Dacotahs,
Came the Hurons and Ojibways,
All the warriors drawn together
By the signal of the Peace-Pipe,
To the Mountains of the Prairie,
To the great Red Pipe-stone Quarry.
    And they stood there on the meadow,
With their weapons and their war-gear,
Painted like the leaves of Autumn,
Painted like the sky of morning,
Wildly glaring at each other;
In their faces stern defiance,
In their hearts the feuds of ages,
The hereditary hatred,
The ancestral thirst of vengeance.
    Gitche Manito, the mighty,
The creator of the nations,
Looked upon them with compassion,
With paternal love and pity;
Looked upon their wrath and wrangling
But as quarrels among children,
But as feuds and fights of children!
    Over them he stretched his right hand,
To subdue their stubborn natures,
To allay their thirst and fever,
By the shadow of his right hand;
Spake to them with voice majestic
As the sound of far-off waters,
Falling into deep abysses,
Warning, chiding, spake in this wise: —

"O my children! my poor children!
Listen to the words of wisdom,
Listen to the words of warning,
From the lips of the Great Spirit,
From the Master of Life, who made you!
   "I have given you lands to hunt in,
I have given you streams to fish in,
I have given you bear and bison,
I have given you roe and reindeer,
I have given you brant and beaver,
Filled the marshes full of wild-fowl,
Filled the rivers full of fishes;
Why then are you not contented?
Why then will you hunt each other?
   "I am weary of your quarrels,
Weary of your wars and bloodshed,
Weary of your prayers for vengeance,
Of your wranglings and dissensions;
All your strength is in your union,
All your danger is in discord;
Therefore be at peace henceforward,
And as brothers live together.
   "I will send a Prophet to you,
A Deliverer of the nations,
Who shall guide you and shall teach you,
Who shall toil and suffer with you.
If you listen to his counsels,
You will multiply and prosper;
If his warnings pass unheeded,
You will fade away and perish!
   "Bathe now in the stream before you,
Wash the war-paint from your faces,

Wash the blood-stains from your fingers,
Bury your war-clubs and your weapons,
Break the red stone from this quarry,
Mould and make it into Peace-Pipes,
Take the reeds that grow beside you,
Deck them with your brightest feathers,
Smoke the calumet together,
And as brothers live henceforward!"
   Then upon the ground the warriors
Threw their cloaks and shirts of deer-skin,
Threw their weapons and their war-gear,
Leaped into the rushing river,
Washed the war-paint from their faces.
Clear above them flowed the water,
Clear and limpid from the footprints
Of the Master of Life descending;
Dark below them flowed the water,
Soiled and stained with streaks of crimson,
As if blood were mingled with it!
   From the river came the warriors,
Clean and washed from all their war-paint;
On the banks their clubs they buried,
Buried all their warlike weapons.
Gitche Manito, the mighty,
The Great Spirit, the creator,
Smiled upon his helpless children!
   And in silence all the warriors
Broke the red stone of the quarry,
Smoothed and formed it into Peace-Pipes,
Broke the long reeds by the river,
Decked them with their brightest feathers,
And departed each one homeward,

While the Master of Life, ascending,
Through the opening of cloud-curtains,
Through the doorways of the heaven,
Vanished from before their faces,
In the smoke that rolled around him,
The Pukwana of the Peace-Pipe!

II
The Four Winds

"Honor be to Mudjekeewis!"
Cried the warriors, cried the old men,
When he came in triumph homeward
With the sacred Belt of Wampum,
From the regions of the North-Wind,
From the kingdom of Wabasso,
From the land of the White Rabbit.
   He had stolen the Belt of Wampum
From the neck of Mishe-Mokwa,
From the Great Bear of the mountains,
From the terror of the nations,
As he lay asleep and cumbrous
On the summit of the mountains,
Like a rock with mosses on it,
Spotted brown and gray with mosses.
   Silently he stole upon him
Till the red nails of the monster
Almost touched him, almost scared him,
Till the hot breath of his nostrils
Warmed the hands of Mudjekeewis,
As he drew the Belt of Wampum
Over the round ears, that heard not,

Over the small eyes, that saw not,
Over the long nose and nostrils,
The black muffle of the nostrils,
Out of which the heavy breathing
Warmed the hands of Mudjekeewis.

   Then he swung aloft his war-club,
Shouted loud and long his war-cry,
Smote the mighty Mishe-Mokwa
In the middle of the forehead,
Right between the eyes he smote him.

   With the heavy blow bewildered,
Rose the Great Bear of the mountains;
But his knees beneath him trembled,
And he whimpered like a woman,
As he reeled and staggered forward,
As he sat upon his haunches;
And the mighty Mudjekeewis,
Standing fearlessly before him,
Taunted him in loud derision,
Spake disdainfully in this wise: —

   "Hark you, Bear! you are a coward,
And no Brave, as you pretended;
Else you would not cry and whimper
Like a miserable woman!
Bear! you know our tribes are hostile,
Long have been at war together;
Now you find that we are strongest,
You go sneaking in the forest,
You go hiding in the mountains!
Had you conquered me in battle
Not a groan would I have uttered;
But you, Bear! sit here and whimper,

And disgrace your tribe by crying,
Like a wretched Shaugodaya,
Like a cowardly old woman!"
　　Then again he raised his war-club,
Smote again the Mishe-Mokwa
In the middle of his forehead,
Broke his skull, as ice is broken
When one goes to fish in Winter.
Thus was slain the Mishe-Mokwa,
He the Great Bear of the mountains,
He the terror of the nations.
　　"Honor be to Mudjekeewis!"
With a shout exclaimed the people,
"Honor be to Mudjekeewis!
Henceforth he shall be the West-Wind,
And hereafter and forever
Shall he hold supreme dominion
Over all the winds of heaven.
Call him no more Mudjekeewis,
Call him Kabeyun, the West-Wind!"
　　Thus was Mudjekeewis chosen
Father of the Winds of Heaven.
For himself he kept the West-Wind,
Gave the others to his children;
Unto Wabun gave the East-Wind,
Gave the South to Shawondasee,
And the North-Wind, wild and cruel,
To the fierce Kabibonokka.
　　Young and beautiful was Wabun;
He it was who brought the morning,
He it was whose silver arrows
Chased the dark o'er hill and valley;

He it was whose cheeks were painted
With the brightest streaks of crimson,
And whose voice awoke the village,
Called the deer, and called the hunter.

Lonely in the sky was Wabun;
Though the birds sang gayly to him,
Though the wild-flowers of the meadow
Filled the air with odors for him;
Though the forests and the rivers
Sang and shouted at his coming,
Still his heart was sad within him,
For he was alone in heaven.

But one morning, gazing earthward,
While the village still was sleeping,
And the fog lay on the river,
Like a ghost, that goes at sunrise,
He beheld a maiden walking
All alone upon a meadow,
Gathering water-flags and rushes
By a river in the meadow.

Every morning, gazing earthward,
Still the first thing he beheld there
Was her blue eyes looking at him,
Two blue lakes among the rushes.
And he loved the lonely maiden,
Who thus waited for his coming;
For they both were solitary,
She on earth and he in heaven.

And he wooed her with caresses,
Wooed her with his smile of sunshine,
With his flattering words he wooed her,
With his sighing and his singing,

Gentlest whispers in the branches,
Softest music, sweetest odors,
Till he drew her to his bosom,
Folded in his robes of crimson,
Till into a star he changed her,
Trembling still upon his bosom;
And forever in the heavens
They are seen together walking,
Wabun and the Wabun-Annung,
Wabun and the Star of Morning.

But the fierce Kabibonokka
Had his dwelling among icebergs,
In the everlasting snow-drifts,
In the kingdom of Wabasso,
In the land of the White Rabbit.
He it was whose hand in Autumn
Painted all the trees with scarlet,
Stained the leaves with red and yellow;
He it was who sent the snow-flakes,
Sifting, hissing through the forest,
Froze the ponds, the lakes, the rivers,
Drove the loon and sea-gull southward,
Drove the cormorant and curlew
To their nests of sedge and sea-tang
In the realms of Shawondasee.

Once the fierce Kabibonokka
Issued from his lodge of snow-drifts,
From his home among the icebergs,
And his hair, with snow besprinkled,
Streamed behind him like a river,
Like a black and wintry river,
As he howled and hurried southward,

Over frozen lakes and moorlands.
  There among the reeds and rushes
Found he Shingebis, the diver,
Trailing strings of fish behind him,
O'er the frozen fens and moorlands,
Lingering still among the moorlands,
Though his tribe had long departed
To the land of Shawondasee.
  Cried the fierce Kabibonokka,
"Who is this that dares to brave me?
Dares to stay in my dominions,
When the Wawa has departed,
When the wild-goose has gone southward,
And the heron, the Shuh-shuh-gah,
Long ago departed southward?
I will go into his wigwam,
I will put his smouldering fire out!"
  And at night Kabibonokka
To the lodge came wild and wailing,
Heaped the snow in drifts about it,
Shouted down into the smoke-flue,
Shook the lodge-poles in his fury,
Flapped the curtain of the door-way.
Shingebis, the diver, feared not,
Shingebis, the diver, cared not;
Four great logs had he for firewood,
One for each moon of the winter,
And for food the fishes served him.
By his blazing fire he sat there,
Warm and merry, eating, laughing,
Singing, "O Kabibonokka,
You are but my fellow-mortal!"

Then Kabibonokka entered,
And though Shingebis, the diver,
Felt his presence by the coldness,
Felt his icy breath upon him,
Still he did not cease his singing,
Still he did not leave his laughing,
Only turned the log a little,
Only made the fire burn brighter,
Made the sparks fly up the smoke-flue.
   From Kabibonokka's forehead,
From his snow-besprinkled tresses,
Drops of sweat fell fast and heavy,
Making dints upon the ashes,
As along the eaves of lodges,
As from drooping boughs of hemlock,
Drips the melting snow in spring-time,
Making hollows in the snow-drifts.
   Till at last he rose defeated,
Could not bear the heat and laughter,
Could not bear the merry singing,
But rushed headlong through the door way,
Stamped upon the crusted snow-drifts,
Stamped upon the lakes and rivers,
Made the snow upon them harder,
Made the ice upon them thicker,
Challenged Shingebis, the diver,
To come forth and wrestle with him,
To come forth and wrestle naked
On the frozen fens and moorlands.
   Forth went Shingebis, the diver,
Wrestled all night with the North-Wind,
Wrestled naked on the moorlands

With the fierce Kabibonokka,
Till his panting breath grew fainter,
Till his frozen grasp grew feebler,
Till he reeled and staggered backward,
And retreated, baffled, beaten,
To the kingdom of Wabasso,
To the land of the White Rabbit,
Hearing still the gusty laughter,
Hearing Shingebis, the diver,
Singing, "O Kabibonokka,
You are but my fellow-mortal!"
　　Shawondasee, fat and lazy,
Had his dwelling far to southward,
In the drowsy, dreamy sunshine,
In the never-ending Summer.
He it was who sent the wood-birds,
Sent the robin, the Opechee,
Sent the blue-bird, the Owaissa,
Sent the Shawshaw, sent the swallow,
Sent the wild-goose, Wawa, northward,
Sent the melons and tobacco,
And the grapes in purple clusters.
　　From his pipe the smoke ascending
Filled the sky with haze and vapor,
Filled the air with dreamy softness,
Gave a twinkle to the water,
Touched the rugged hills with smoothness,
Brought the tender Indian Summer
To the melancholy north-land,
In the dreary Moon of Snow-shoes.
　　Listless, careless Shawondasee!
In his life he had one shadow,

In his heart one sorrow had he.
Once, as he was gazing northward,
Far away upon a prairie
He beheld a maiden standing,
Saw a tall and slender maiden
All alone upon a prairie;
Brightest green were all her garments,
And her hair was like the sunshine.
  Day by day he gazed upon her,
Day by day he sighed with passion,
Day by day his heart within him
Grew more hot with love and longing
For the maid with yellow tresses.
But he was too fat and lazy
To bestir himself and woo her.
Yes, too indolent and easy
To pursue her and persuade her;
So he only gazed upon her,
Only sat and sighed with passion
For the maiden of the prairie.
  Till one morning, looking northward,
He beheld her yellow tresses
Changed and covered o'er with whiteness,
Covered as with whitest snow-flakes.
"Ah! my brother from the North-land,
From the kingdom of Wabasso,
From the land of the White Rabbit!
You have stolen the maiden from me,
You have laid your hand upon her,
You have wooed and won my maiden,
With your stories of the North-land!"
  Thus the wretched Shawondasee

Breathed into the air his sorrow;
And the South-Wind o'er the prairie
Wandered warm with sighs of passion,
With the sighs of Shawondasee,
Till the air seemed full of snow-flakes,
Full of thistle-down the prairie,
And the maid with hair like sunshine
Vanished from his sight forever;
Never more did Shawondasee
See the maid with yellow tresses!
   Poor, deluded Shawondasee!
'T was no woman that you gazed at,
'T was no maiden that you sighed for,
'T was the prairie dandelion
That through all the dreamy Summer
You had gazed at with such longing,
You had sighed for with such passion,
And had puffed away forever,
Blown into the air with sighing.
Ah! deluded Shawondasee!
   Thus the Four Winds were divided;
Thus the sons of Mudjekeewis
Had their stations in the heavens,
At the corners of the heavens;
For himself the West-Wind only
Kept the mighty Mudjekeewis.

III
Hiawatha's Childhood

Downward through the evening twilight,
In the days that are forgotten,

In the unremembered ages,
From the full moon fell Nokomis,
Fell the beautiful Nokomis,
She a wife, but not a mother.
   She was sporting with her women,
Swinging in a swing of grape-vines,
When her rival the rejected,
Full of jealousy and hatred,
Cut the leafy swing asunder,
Cut in twain the twisted grape-vines,
And Nokomis fell affrighted
Downward through the evening twilight,
On the Muskoday, the meadow,
On the prairie fall of blossoms.
"See! a star falls!" said the people;
"From the sky a star is falling!"
   There among the ferns and mosses,
There among the prairie lilies,
On the Muskoday, the meadow,
In the moonlight and the starlight,
Fair Nokomis bore a daughter.
And she called her name Wenonah,
As the first-born of her daughters.
And the daughter of Nokomis
Grew up like the prairie lilies,
Grew a tall and slender maiden,
With the beauty of the moonlight,
With the beauty of the starlight.
   And Nokomis warned her often,
Saying oft, and oft repeating,
"Oh, beware of Mudjekeewis,
Of the West-Wind, Mudjekeewis;

Listen not to what he tells you;
Lie not down upon the meadow,
Stoop not down among the lilies,
Lest the West-Wind come and harm you!"
    But she heeded not the warning,
Heeded not those words of wisdom,
And the West-Wind came at evening,
Walking lightly o'er the prairie,
Whispering to the leaves and blossoms,
Bending low the flowers and grasses,
Found the beautiful Wenonah,
Lying there among the lilies,
Wooed her with his words of sweetness,
Wooed her with his soft caresses,
Till she bore a son in sorrow,
Bore a son of love and sorrow.
    Thus was born my Hiawatha,
Thus was born the child of wonder;
But the daughter of Nokomis,
Hiawatha's gentle mother,
In her anguish died deserted
By the West-Wind, false and faithless,
By the heartless Mudjekeewis.
    For her daughter long and loudly
Wailed and wept the sad Nokomis;
"Oh that I were dead!" she murmured,
"Oh that I were dead, as thou art!
No more work, and no more weeping,
Wahonowin! Wahonowin!"
    By the shores of Gitche Gumee,
By the shining Big-Sea-Water,
Stood the wigwam of Nokomis,

Daughter of the Moon, Nokomis.
Dark behind it rose the forest,
Rose the black and gloomy pine-trees,
Rose the firs with cones upon them;
Bright before it beat the water,
Beat the clear and sunny water,
Beat the shining Big-Sea-Water.
    There the wrinkled old Nokomis
Nursed the little Hiawatha,
Rocked him in his linden cradle,
Bedded soft in moss and rushes,
Safely bound with reindeer sinews;
Stilled his fretful wail by saying,
"Hush! the Naked Bear will hear thee!"
Lulled him into slumber, singing,
"Ewa-yea! my little owlet!
Who is this, that lights the wigwam?
With his great eyes lights the wigwam?
Ewa-yea! my little owlet!"
    Many things Nokomis taught him
Of the stars that shine in heaven;
Showed him Ishkoodah, the comet,
Ishkoodah, with fiery tresses;
Showed the Death-Dance of the spirits,
Warriors with their plumes and war-clubs,
Flaring far away to northward
In the frosty nights of Winter;
Showed the broad white road in heaven,
Pathway of the ghosts, the shadows,
Running straight across the heavens,
Crowded with the ghosts, the shadows.
    At the door on summer evenings

Sat the little Hiawatha;
Heard the whispering of the pine-trees,
Heard the lapping of the waters,
Sounds of music, words of wonder;
"Minne-wawa!" said the pine-trees,
"Mudway-aushka!" said the water.
  Saw the fire-fly, Wah-wah-taysee,
Flitting through the dusk of evening,
With the twinkle of its candle
Lighting up the brakes and bushes,
And he sang the song of children,
Sang the song Nokomis taught him:
"Wah-wah-taysee, little fire-fly,
Little, flitting, white-fire insect,
Little, dancing, white-fire creature,
Light me with your little candle,
Ere upon my bed I lay me,
Ere in sleep I close my eyelids!"
  Saw the moon rise from the water
Rippling, rounding from the water,
Saw the flecks and shadows on it,
Whispered, "What is that, Nokomis?"
And the good Nokomis answered:
"Once a warrior, very angry,
Seized his grandmother, and threw her
Up into the sky at midnight;
Right against the moon he threw her;
'T is her body that you see there."
  Saw the rainbow in the heaven,
In the eastern sky, the rainbow,
Whispered, "What is that, Nokomis?"
And the good Nokomis answered:

" 'T is the heaven of flowers you see there;
All the wild-flowers of the forest,
All the lilies of the prairie,
When on earth they fade and perish,
Blossom in that heaven above us."
    When he heard the owls at midnight,
Hooting, laughing in the forest,
"What is that?" he cried in terror,
"What is that," he said, "Nokomis?"
And the good Nokomis answered:
"That is but the owl and owlet,
Talking in their native language,
Talking, scolding at each other."
    Then the little Hiawatha
Learned of every bird its language,
Learned their names and all their secrets,
How they built their nests in Summer,
Where they hid themselves in Winter,
Talked with them whene'er he met them,
Called them "Hiawatha's Chickens."
    Of all beasts he learned the language,
Learned their names and all their secrets,
How the beavers built their lodges,
Where the squirrels hid their acorns,
How the reindeer ran so swiftly,
Why the rabbit was so timid,
Talked with them whene'er he met them,
Called them "Hiawatha's Brothers."
    Then Iagoo, the great boaster,
He the marvellous story-teller,
He the traveller and the talker,
He the friend of old Nokomis,

Made a bow for Hiawatha;
From a branch of ash he made it,
From an oak-bough made the arrows,
Tipped with flint, and winged with feathers,
And the cord he made of deer-skin.
　　Then he said to Hiawatha:
"Go, my son, into the forest,
Where the red deer herd together,
Kill for us a famous roebuck,
Kill for us a deer with antlers!"
　　Forth into the forest straightway
All alone walked Hiawatha
Proudly, with his bow and arrows;
And the birds sang round him, o'er him,
"Do not shoot us, Hiawatha!"
Sang the robin, the Opechee,
Sang the bluebird, the Owaissa,
"Do not shoot us, Hiawatha!"
　　Up the oak-tree, close beside him,
Sprang the squirrel, Adjidaumo,
In and our among the branches,
Coughed and chartered from the oak-tree,
Laughed, and said between his laughing,
"Do not shoot me, Hiawatha!"
　　And the rabbit from his pathway
Leaped aside, and at a distance
Sat erect upon his haunches,
Half in fear and half in frolic,
Saying to the little hunter,
"Do not shoot me, Hiawatha!"
　　But he heeded not, nor heard them,
For his thoughts were with the red deer;

On their tracks his eyes were fastened,
Leading downward to the river,
To the ford across the river,
And as one in slumber walked he.
  Hidden in the alder-bushes,
There he waited till the deer came,
Till he saw two antlers lifted,
Saw two eyes look from the thicket,
Saw two nostrils point to windward,
And a deer came down the pathway,
Flecked with leafy light and shadow.
And his heart within him fluttered,
Trembled like the leaves above him,
Like the birch-leaf palpitated,
As the deer came down the pathway.
  Then, upon one knee uprising,
Hiawatha aimed an arrow;
Scarce a twig moved with his motion,
Scarce a leaf was stirred or rustled,
But the wary roebuck started,
Stamped with all his hoofs together,
Listened with one foot uplifted,
Leaped as if to meet the arrow;
Ah! the singing, fatal arrow,
Like a wasp it buzzed and stung him!
  Dead he lay there in the forest,
By the ford across the river;
Beat his timid heart no longer,
But the heart of Hiawatha
Throbbed and shouted and exulted,
As he bore the red deer homeward,
And Iagoo and Nokomis

Hailed his coming with applauses.
   From the red deer's hide Nokomis
Made a cloak for Hiawatha,
From the red deer's flesh Nokomis
Made a banquet to his honor.
All the village came and feasted,
All the guests praised Hiawatha,
Called him Strong-Heart, Soan-ge-taha!
Called him Loon-Heart, Mahn-go-taysee!

IV
Hiawatha and Mudjekeewis

Out of childhood into manhood
Now had grown my Hiawatha,
Skilled in all the craft of hunters,
Learned in all the lore of old men,
In all youthful sports and pastimes,
In all manly arts and labors.
   Swift of foot was Hiawatha;
He could shoot an arrow from him,
And run forward with such fleetness,
That the arrow fell behind him!
Strong of arm was Hiawatha;
He could shoot ten arrows upward,
Shoot them with such strength and swiftness,
That the tenth had left the bow-string
Ere the first to earth had fallen!
   He had mittens, Minjekahwun,
Magic mittens made of deer-skin;
When upon his hands he wore them,
He could smite the rocks asunder,

He could grind them into powder.
He had moccasins enchanted,
Magic moccasins of deer-skin;
When he bound them round his ankles,
When upon his feet he tied them,
At each stride a mile he measured!
　Much he questioned old Nokomis
Of his father Mudjekeewis;
Learned from her the fatal secret
Of the beauty of his mother,
Of the falsehood of his father;
And his heart was hot within him,
Like a living coal his heart was.
　Then he said to old Nokomis,
"I will go to Mudjekeewis,
See how fares it with my father,
At the doorways of the West-Wind,
At the portals of the Sunset!"
　From his lodge went Hiawatha,
Dressed for travel, armed for hunting;
Dressed in deer-skin shirt and leggings,
Richly wrought with quills and wampum;
On his head his eagle-feathers,
Round his waist his belt of wampum,
In his hand his bow of ash-wood,
Strung with sinews of the reindeer;
In his quiver oaken arrows,
Tipped with jasper, winged with feathers;
With his mittens, Minjekahwun,
With his moccasins enchanted.
　Warning said the old Nokomis,
"Go not forth, O Hiawatha!

To the kingdom of the West-Wind,
To the realms of Mudjekeewis,
Lest he harm you with his magic,
Lest he kill you with his cunning!"
  But the fearless Hiawatha
Heeded not her woman's warning;
Forth he strode into the forest,
At each stride a mile he measured;
Lurid seemed the sky above him,
Lurid seemed the earth beneath him,
Hot and close the air around him,
Filled with smoke and fiery vapors,
As of burning woods and prairies,
For his heart was hot within him,
Like a living coal his heart was.
  So he journeyed westward, westward,
Left the fleetest deer behind him,
Left the antelope and bison;
Crossed the rushing Esconaba,
Crossed the mighty Mississippi,
Passed the Mountains of the Prairie,
Passed the land of Crows and Foxes,
Passed the dwellings of the Blackfeet,
Came unto the Rocky Mountains,
To the kingdom of the West-Wind,
Where upon the gusty summits
Sat the ancient Mudjekeewis,
Ruler of the winds of heaven.
  Filled with awe was Hiawatha
At the aspect of his father.
On the air about him wildly
Tossed and streamed his cloudy tresses,

Gleamed like drifting snow his tresses,
Glared like Ishkoodah, the comet,
Like the star with fiery tresses.

   Filled with joy was Mudjekeewis
When he looked on Hiawatha,
Saw his youth rise up before him
In the face of Hiawatha,
Saw the beauty of Wenonah
From the grave rise up before him.

   "Welcome!" said he, "Hiawatha,
To the kingdom of the West-Wind!
Long have I been waiting for you!
Youth is lovely, age is lonely,
Youth is fiery, age is frosty;
You bring back the days departed,
You bring back my youth of passion,
And the beautiful Wenonah!"

   Many days they talked together,
Questioned, listened, waited, answered;
Much the mighty Mudjekeewis
Boasted of his ancient prowess,
Of his perilous adventures,
His indomitable courage,
His invulnerable body.

   Patiently sat Hiawatha,
Listening to his father's boasting;
With a smile he sat and listened,
Uttered neither threat nor menace,
Neither word nor look betrayed him,
But his heart was hot within him,
Like a living coal his heart was.

   Then he said, "O Mudjekeewis,

Is there nothing that can harm you?
Nothing that you are afraid of?"
And the mighty Mudjekeewis,
Grand and gracious in his boasting,
Answered, saying, "There is nothing,
Nothing but the black rock yonder,
Nothing but the fatal Wawbeek!"
   And he looked at Hiawatha
With a wise look and benignant,
With a countenance paternal,
Looked with pride upon the beauty
Of his tall and graceful figure,
Saying, "O my Hiawatha!
Is there anything can harm you?
Anything you are afraid of?"
   But the wary Hiawatha
Paused awhile, as if uncertain,
Held his peace, as if resolving,
And then answered, "There is nothing,
Nothing but the bulrush yonder,
Nothing but the great Apukwa!"
   And as Mudjekeewis, rising,
Stretched his hand to pluck the bulrush,
Hiawatha cried in terror,
Cried in well-dissembled terror,
"Kago! kago! do not touch it!"
"Ah, kaween!" said Mudjekeewis,
"No indeed, I will not touch it!"
   Then they talked of other matters;
First of Hiawatha's brothers,
First of Wabun, of the East-Wind,
Of the South-Wind, Shawondasee,

Of the North, Kabibonokka;
Then of Hiawatha's mother,
Of the beautiful Wenonah,
Of her birth upon the meadow,
Of her death, as old Nokomis
Had remembered and related.

And he cried, "O Mudjekeewis,
It was you who killed Wenonah,
Took her young life and her beauty,
Broke the Lily of the Prairie,
Trampled it beneath your footsteps;
You confess it! you confess it!"
And the mighty Mudjekeewis
Tossed upon the wind his tresses,
Bowed his hoary, head in anguish,
With a silent nod assented.

Then up started Hiawatha,
And with threatening look and gesture
Laid his hand upon the black rock,
On the fatal Wawbeek laid it,
With his mittens, Minjekahwun,
Rent the jutting crag asunder,
Smote and crushed it into fragments,
Hurled them madly at his father,
The remorseful Mudjekeewis,
For his heart was hot within him,
Like a living coal his heart was.

But the ruler of the West-Wind
Blew the fragments backward from him,
With the breathing of his nostrils,
With the tempest of his anger,
Blew them back at his assailant;

Seized the bulrush, the Apukwa,
Dragged it with its roots and fibres
From the margin of the meadow,
From its ooze the giant bulrush;
Long and loud laughed Hiawatha!
   Then began the deadly conflict,
Hand to hand among the mountains;
From his eyry screamed the eagle,
The Keneu, the great war-eagle,
Sat upon the crags around them,
Wheeling flapped his wings above them.
   Like a tall tree in the tempest
Bent and lashed the giant bulrush;
And in masses huge and heavy
Crashing fell the fatal Wawbeek;
Till the earth shook with the tumult
And confusion of the battle,
And the air was full of shoutings,
And the thunder of the mountains,
Starting, answered, "Baim-wawa!"
   Back retreated Mudjekeewis,
Rushing westward o'er the mountains,
Stumbling westward down the mountains,
Three whole days retreated fighting,
Still pursued by Hiawatha
To the doorways of the West-Wind,
To the portals of the Sunset,
To the earth's remotest border,
Where into the empty spaces
Sinks the sun, as a flamingo
Drops into her nest at nightfall
In the melancholy marshes.

"Hold!" at length cried Mudjekeewis,
"Hold, my son, my Hiawatha!
'T is impossible to kill me,
For you cannot kill the immortal.
I have put you to this trial,
But to know and prove your courage;
Now receive the prize of valor!

"Go back to your home and people,
Live among them, toil among them,
Cleanse the earth from all that harms it,
Clear the fishing-grounds and rivers,
Slay all monsters and magicians,
All the Wendigoes, the giants,
All the serpents, the Kenabeeks,
As I slew the Mishe-Mokwa,
Slew the Great Bear of the mountains.

"And at last when Death draws near you,
When the awful eyes of Pauguk
Glare upon you in the darkness,
I will share my kingdom with you,
Ruler shall you be thenceforward
Of the Northwest-Wind, Keewaydin,
Of the home-wind, the Keewaydin."

Thus was fought that famous battle
In the dreadful days of Shah-shah,
In the days long since departed,
In the kingdom of the West-Wind.
Still the hunter sees its traces
Scattered far o'er hill and valley;
Sees the giant bulrush growing
By the ponds and water-courses,
Sees the masses of the Wawbeek

Lying still in every valley.
  Homeward now went Hiawatha;
Pleasant was the landscape round him,
Pleasant was the air above him,
For the bitterness of anger
Had departed wholly from him,
From his brain the thought of vengeance,
From his heart the burning fever.
  Only once his pace he slackened,
Only once he paused or halted,
Paused to purchase heads of arrows
Of the ancient Arrow-maker,
In the land of the Dacotahs,
Where the Falls of Minnehaha
Flash and gleam among the oak-trees,
Laugh and leap into the valley.
  There the ancient Arrow-maker
Made his arrow-heads of sandstone,
Arrow-heads of chalcedony,
Arrow-heads of flint and jasper,
Smoothed and sharpened at the edges,
Hard and polished, keen and costly.
  With him dwelt his dark-eyed daughter,
Wayward as the Minnehaha,
With her moods of shade and sunshine,
Eyes that smiled and frowned alternate,
Feet as rapid as the river,
Tresses flowing like the water,
And as musical a laughter:
And he named her from the river,
From the water-fall he named her,
Minnehaha, Laughing Water.

Was it then for heads of arrows,
Arrow-heads of chalcedony,
Arrow-heads of flint and jasper,
That my Hiawatha halted
In the land of the Dacotahs?
Was it not to see the maiden,
See the face of Laughing Water
Peeping from behind the curtain,
Hear the rustling of her garments
From behind the waving curtain,
As one sees the Minnehaha
Gleaming, glancing through the branches,
As one hears the Laughing Water
From behind its screen of branches?
Who shall say what thoughts and visions
Fill the fiery brains of young men?
Who shall say what dreams of beauty
Filled the heart of Hiawatha?
All he told to old Nokomis,
When he reached the lodge at sunset,
Was the meeting with his father,
Was his fight with Mudjekeewis;
Not a word he said of arrows,
Not a word of Laughing Water.

V

Hiawatha's Fasting

You shall hear how Hiawatha
Prayed and fasted in the forest,
Not for greater skill in hunting,
Not for greater craft in fishing,

Not for triumphs in the battle,
And renown among the warriors,
But for profit of the people,
For advantage of the nations.

  First he built a lodge for fasting,
Built a wigwam in the forest,
By the shining Big-Sea-Water,
In the blithe and pleasant Spring-time,
In the Moon of Leaves he built it,
And, with dreams and visions many,
Seven whole days and nights he fasted.

  On the first day of his fasting
Through the leafy woods he wandered;
Saw the deer start from the thicket,
Saw the rabbit in his burrow,
Heard the pheasant, Bena, drumming,
Heard the squirrel, Adjidaumo,
Rattling in his hoard of acorns,
Saw the pigeon, the Omeme,
Building nests among the pine-trees,
And in flocks the wild-goose, Wawa,
Flying to the fen-lands northward,
Whirring, wailing far above him.
"Master of Life!" he cried, desponding,
"Must our lives depend on these things?"

  On the next day of his fasting
By the river's brink he wandered,
Through the Muskoday, the meadow,
Saw the wild rice, Mahnomonee,
Saw the blueberry, Meenahga,
And the strawberry, Odahmin,
And the gooseberry, Shahbomin,

And the grape-vine, the Bemahgut,
Trailing o'er the alder-branches,
Filling all the air with fragrance!
"Master of Life!" he cried, desponding,
"Must our lives depend on these things?"
  On the third day of his fasting
By the lake he sat and pondered,
By the still, transparent water;
Saw the sturgeon, Nahma, leaping,
Scattering drops like beads of wampum,
Saw the yellow perch, the Sahwa,
Like a sunbeam in the water,
Saw the pike, the Maskenozha,
And the herring, Okahahwis,
And the Shawgashee, the craw-fish!
"Master of Life!" he cried, desponding,
"Must our lives depend on these things?"
  On the fourth day of his fasting
In his lodge he lay exhausted;
From his couch of leaves and branches
Gazing with half-open eyelids,
Full of shadowy dreams and visions,
On the dizzy, swimming landscape,
On the gleaming of the water,
On the splendor of the sunset.
  And he saw a youth approaching,
Dressed in garments green and yellow,
Coming through the purple twilight,
Through the splendor of the sunset;
Plumes of green bent o'er his forehead,
And his hair was soft and golden.
  Standing at the open doorway,

Long he looked at Hiawatha,
Looked with pity and compassion
On his wasted form and features,
And, in accents like the sighing
Of the South-Wind in the tree-tops,
Said he, "O my Hiawatha!
All your prayers are heard in heaven,
For you pray not like the others;
Not for greater skill in hunting,
Not for greater craft in fishing,
Not for triumph in the battle,
Nor renown among the warriors,
But for profit of the people,
For advantage of the nations.
    "From the Master of Life descending,
I, the friend of man, Mondamin,
Come to warn you and instruct you,
How by struggle and by labor
You shall gain what you have prayed for.
Rise up from your bed of branches,
Rise, O youth, and wrestle with me!"
    Faint with famine, Hiawatha
Started from his bed of branches,
From the twilight of his wigwam
Forth into the flush of sunset
Came, and wrestled with Mondamin;
At his touch he felt new courage
Throbbing in his brain and bosom,
Felt new life and hope and vigor
Run through every nerve and fibre.
    So they wrestled there together
In the glory of the sunset,

And the more they strove and struggled,
Stronger still grew Hiawatha;
Till the darkness fell around them,
And the heron, the Shuh-shuh-gah,
From her nest among the pine-trees,
Gave a cry of lamentation,
Gave a scream of pain and famine.
  " 'T is enough!" then said Mondamin,
Smiling upon Hiawatha,
"But to-morrow, when the sun sets,
I will come again to try you."
And he vanished, and was seen not;
Whether sinking as the rain sinks,
Whether rising as the mists rise,
Hiawatha saw not, knew not,
Only saw that he had vanished,
Leaving him alone and fainting,
With the misty lake below him,
And the reeling stars above him.
  On the morrow and the next day,
When the sun through heaven descending,
Like a red and burning cinder
From the hearth of the Great Spirit,
Fell into the western waters,
Came Mondamin for the trial,
For the strife with Hiawatha;
Came as silent as the dew comes,
From the empty air appearing,
Into empty air returning,
Taking shape when earth it touches,
But invisible to all men
In its coming and its going.

Thrice they wrestled there together
In the glory of the sunset,
Till the darkness fell around them,
Till the heron, the Shuh-shuh-gah,
From her nest among the pine-trees,
Uttered her loud cry of famine,
And Mondamin paused to listen.

Tall and beautiful he stood there,
In his garments green and yellow;
To and fro his plumes above him
Waved and nodded with his breathing,
And the sweat of the encounter
Stood like drops of dew upon him.

And he cried, "O Hiawatha!
Bravely have you wrestled with me,
Thrice have wrestled stoutly with me,
And the Master of Life, who sees us,
He will give to you the triumph!"

Then he smiled, and said: "To-morrow
Is the last day of your conflict,
Is the last day of your fasting.
You will conquer and o'ercome me;
Make a bed for me to lie in,
Where the rain may fall upon me,
Where the sun may come and warm me;
Strip these garments, green and yellow,
Strip this nodding plumage from me,
Lay me in the earth, and make it
Soft and loose and light above me.

"Let no hand disturb my slumber,
Let no weed nor worm molest me,
Let not Kahgahgee, the raven,

Come to haunt me and molest me,
Only come yourself to watch me,
Till I wake, and start, and quicken,
Till I leap into the sunshine."
  And thus saying, he departed;
Peacefully slept Hiawatha,
But he heard the Wawonaissa,
Heard the whippoorwill complaining,
Perched upon his lonely wigwam;
Heard the rushing Sebowisha,
Heard the rivulet rippling near him,
Talking to the darksome forest;
Heard the sighing of the branches,
As they lifted and subsided
At the passing of the night-wind,
Heard them, as one hears in slumber
Far-off murmurs, dreamy whispers:
Peacefully slept Hiawatha.
  On the morrow came Nokomis,
On the seventh day of his fasting,
Came with food for Hiawatha,
Came imploring and bewailing,
Lest his hunger should o'ercome him,
Lest his fasting should be fatal.
  But he tasted not, and touched not,
Only said to her, "Nokomis,
Wait until the sun is setting,
Till the darkness falls around us,
Till the heron, the Shuh-shuh-gah,
Crying from the desolate marshes,
Tells us that the day is ended."
  Homeward weeping went Nokomis,

Sorrowing for her Hiawatha,
Fearing lest his strength should fail him,
Lest his fasting should be fatal.
He meanwhile sat weary waiting
For the coming of Mondamin,
Till the shadows, pointing eastward,
Lengthened over field and forest,
Till the sun dropped from the heaven,
Floating on the waters westward,
As a red leaf in the Autumn
Falls and floats upon the water,
Falls and sinks into its bosom.
    And behold! the young Mondamin,
With his soft and shining tresses,
With his garments green and yellow,
With his long and glossy plumage,
Stood and beckoned at the doorway.
And as one in slumber walking,
Pale and haggard, but undaunted,
From the wigwam Hiawatha
Came and wrestled with Mondamin.
    Round about him spun the landscape,
Sky and forest reeled together,
And his strong heart leaped within him,
As the sturgeon leaps and struggles
In a net to break its meshes.
Like a ring of fire around him
Blazed and flared the red horizon,
And a hundred suns seemed looking
At the combat of the wrestlers.
    Suddenly upon the greensward
All alone stood Hiawatha,

Panting with his wild exertion,
Palpitating with the struggle;
And before him breathless, lifeless,
Lay the youth, with hair dishevelled,
Plumage torn, and garments tattered,
Dead he lay there in the sunset.
　　And victorious Hiawatha
Made the grave as he commanded,
Stripped the garments from Mondamin,
Stripped his tattered plumage from him,
Laid him in the earth, and made it
Soft and loose and light above him;
And the heron, the Shuh-shuh-gah,
From the melancholy moorlands,
Gave a cry of lamentation,
Gave a cry of pain and anguish!
　　Homeward then went Hiawatha
To the lodge of old Nokomis,
And the seven days of his fasting
Were accomplished and completed.
But the place was not forgotten
Where he wrestled with Mondamin;
Nor forgotten nor neglected
Was the grave where lay Mondamin,
Sleeping in the rain and sunshine,
Where his scattered plumes and garments
Faded in the rain and sunshine.
　　Day by day did Hiawatha
Go to wait and watch beside it;
Kept the dark mould soft above it,
Kept it clean from weeds and insects,
Drove away, with scoffs and shoutings,

Kahgahgee, the king of ravens.
  Till at length a small green feather
From the earth shot slowly upward,
Then another and another,
And before the Summer ended
Stood the maize in all its beauty,
With its shining robes about it,
And its long, soft, yellow tresses;
And in rapture Hiawatha
Cried aloud, "It is Mondamin!
Yes, the friend of man, Mondamin!"
  Then he called to old Nokomis
And Iagoo, the great boaster,
Showed them where the maize was growing,
Told them of his wondrous vision,
Of his wrestling and his triumph,
Of this new gift to the nations,
Which should be their food forever.
  And still later, when the Autumn
Changed the long, green leaves to yellow,
And the soft and juicy kernels
Grew like wampum hard and yellow,
Then the ripened ears he gathered,
Stripped the withered husks from off them,
As he once had stripped the wrestler,
Gave the first Feast of Mondamin,
And made known unto the people
This new gift of the Great Spirit.

VI
Hiawatha's Friends

Two good friends had Hiawatha,
Singled out from all the others,
Bound to him in closest union,
And to whom he gave the right hand
Of his heart, in joy and sorrow;
Chibiabos, the musician,
And the very strong man, Kwasind.
   Straight between them ran the pathway,
Never grew the grass upon it;
Singing birds, that utter falsehoods,
Story-tellers, mischief-makers,
Found no eager ear to listen,
Could not breed ill-will between them,
For they kept each other's counsel,
Spake with naked hearts together,
Pondering much and much contriving
How the tribes of men might prosper.
   Most beloved by Hiawatha
Was the gentle Chibiabos,
He the best of all musicians,
He the sweetest of all singers.
Beautiful and childlike was he,
Brave as man is, soft as woman,
Pliant as a wand of willow,
Stately as a deer with antlers.
   When he sang, the village listened;
All the warriors gathered round him,
All the women came to hear him;
Now he stirred their souls to passion,

Now he melted them to pity.
From the hollow reeds he fashioned
Flutes so musical and mellow,
That the brook, the Sebowisha,
Ceased to murmur in the woodland,
That the wood-birds ceased from singing,
And the squirrel, Adjidaumo,
Ceased his chatter in the oak-tree,
And the rabbit, the Wabasso,
Sat upright to look and listen.
Yes, the brook, the Sebowisha,
Pausing, said, "O Chibiabos,
Teach my waves to flow in music,
Softly as your words in singing!"
Yes, the bluebird, the Owaissa,
Envious, said, "O Chibiabos,
Teach me tones as wild and wayward,
Teach me songs as full of frenzy!"
Yes, the robin, the Opechee,
Joyous, said, "O Chibiabos,
Teach me tones as sweet and tender,
Teach me songs as full of gladness!"
And the whippoorwill, Wawonaissa,
Sobbing, said, "O Chibiabos,
Teach me tones as melancholy,
Teach me songs as full of sadness!"
All the many sounds of nature
Borrowed sweetness from his singing;
All the hearts of men were softened
By the pathos of his music;
For he sang of peace and freedom,
Sang of beauty, love, and longing;

Sang of death, and life undying
In the Islands of the Blessed,
In the kingdom of Ponemah,
In the land of the Hereafter.
    Very dear to Hiawatha
Was the gentle Chibiabos,
He the best of all musicians,
He the sweetest of all singers;
For his gentleness he loved him,
And the magic of his singing.
    Dear, too, unto Hiawatha
Was the very strong man, Kwasind,
He the strongest of all mortals,
He the mightiest among many;
For his very strength he loved him,
For his strength allied to goodness.
    Idle in his youth was Kwasind,
Very listless, dull, and dreamy,
Never played with other children,
Never fished and never hunted,
Not like other children was he;
But they saw that much he fasted,
Much his Manito entreated,
Much besought his Guardian Spirit.
    "Lazy Kwasind!" said his mother,
"In my work you never help me!
In the Summer you are roaming
Idly in the fields and forests;
In the Winter you are cowering
O'er the firebrands in the wigwam!
In the coldest days of Winter
I must break the ice for fishing;

With my nets you never help me!
At the door my nets are hanging,
Dripping, freezing with the water;
Go and wring them, Yenadizze!
Go and dry them in the sunshine!"
   Slowly, from the ashes, Kwasind
Rose, but made no angry answer;
From the lodge went forth in silence,
Took the nets, that hung together,
Dripping, freezing at the doorway;
Like a wisp of straw he wrung them,
Like a wisp of straw he broke them,
Could not wring them without breaking,
Such the strength was in his fingers.
   "Lazy Kwasind!" said his father,
"In the hunt you never help me;
Every bow you touch is broken,
Snapped asunder every arrow;
Yet come with me to the forest,
You shall bring the hunting homeward."
   Down a narrow pass they wandered,
Where a brooklet led them onward,
Where the trail of deer and bison
Marked the soft mud on the margin,
Till they found all further passage
Shut against them, barred securely
By the trunks of trees uprooted,
Lying lengthwise, lying crosswise,
And forbidding further passage.
   "We must go back," said the old man,
"O'er these logs we cannot clamber;
Not a woodchuck could get through them,

Not a squirrel clamber o'er them!"
And straightway his pipe he lighted,
And sat down to smoke and ponder.
But before his pipe was finished,
Lo! the path was cleared before him;
All the trunks had Kwasind lifted,
To the right hand, to the left hand,
Shot the pine-trees swift as arrows,
Hurled the cedars light as lances.
    "Lazy Kwasind!" said the young men,
As they sported in the meadow:
"Why stand idly looking at us,
Leaning on the rock behind you?
Come and wrestle with the others,
Let us pitch the quoit together!"
    Lazy Kwasind made no answer,
To their challenge made no answer,
Only rose, and slowly turning,
Seized the huge rock in his fingers,
Tore it from its deep foundation,
Poised it in the air a moment,
Pitched it sheer into the river,
Sheer into the swift Pauwating,
Where it still is seen in Summer.
    Once as down that foaming river,
Down the rapids of Pauwating,
Kwasind sailed with his companions,
In the stream he saw a beaver,
Saw Ahmeek, the King of Beavers,
Struggling with the rushing currents,
Rising, sinking in the water.
    Without speaking, without pausing,

Kwasind leaped into the river,
Plunged beneath the bubbling surface,
Through the whirlpools chased the beaver,
Followed him among the islands,
Stayed so long beneath the water,
That his terrified companions
Cried, "Alas! good-by to Kwasind!
We shall never more see Kwasind!"
But he reappeared triumphant,
And upon his shining shoulders
Brought the beaver, dead and dripping,
Brought the King of all the Beavers.
   And these two, as I have told you,
Were the friends of Hiawatha,
Chibiabos, the musician,
And the very strong man, Kwasind.
Long they lived in peace together,
Spake with naked hearts together,
Pondering much and much contriving
How the tribes of men might prosper.

VII
Hiawatha's Sailing

"Give me of your bark, O Birch-tree!
Of your yellow bark, O Birch-tree!
Growing by the rushing river,
Tall and stately in the valley!
I a light canoe will build me,
Build a swift Cheemaun for sailing,
That shall float upon the river,
Like a yellow leaf in Autumn,

Like a yellow water-lily!
    "Lay aside your cloak, O Birch-tree!
Lay aside your white-skin wrapper,
For the Summer-time is coming,
And the sun is warm in heaven,
And you need no white-skin wrapper!"
    Thus aloud cried Hiawatha
In the solitary forest,
By the rushing Taquamenaw,
When the birds were singing gayly,
In the Moon of Leaves were singing,
And the sun, from sleep awaking,
Started up and said, "Behold me!
Gheezis, the great Sun, behold me!"
    And the tree with all its branches
Rustled in the breeze of morning,
Saying, with a sigh of patience,
"Take my cloak, O Hiawatha!"
    With his knife the tree he girdled;
Just beneath its lowest branches,
Just above the roots, he cut it,
Till the sap came oozing outward;
Down the trunk, from top to bottom,
Sheer he cleft the bark asunder,
With a wooden wedge he raised it,
Stripped it from the trunk unbroken.
    "Give me of your boughs, O Cedar!
Of your strong and pliant branches,
My canoe to make more steady,
Make more strong and firm beneath me!"
    Through the summit of the Cedar
Went a sound, a cry of horror,

Went a murmur of resistance;
But it whispered, bending downward,
"Take my boughs, O Hiawatha!"
    Down he hewed the boughs of cedar,
Shaped them straightway to a frame-work,
Like two bows he formed and shaped them,
Like two bended bows together.
    "Give me of your roots, O Tamarack!
Of your fibrous roots, O Larch-tree!
My canoe to bind together,
So to bind the ends together
That the water may not enter,
That the river may not wet me!"
    And the Larch, with all its fibres,
Shivered in the air of morning,
Touched his forehead with its tassels,
Said, with one long sigh of sorrow,
"Take them all, O Hiawatha!"
    From the earth he tore the fibres,
Tore the tough roots of the Larch-tree,
Closely sewed the bark together,
Bound it closely to the frame-work.
    "Give me of your balm, O Fir-tree!
Of your balsam and your resin,
So to close the seams together
That the water may not enter,
That the river may not wet me!"
    And the Fir-tree, tall and sombre,
Sobbed through all its robes of darkness,
Rattled like a shore with pebbles,
Answered wailing, answered weeping,
"Take my balm, O Hiawatha!"

And he took the tears of balsam,
Took the resin of the Fir-tree,
Smeared therewith each seam and fissure,
Made each crevice safe from water.
   "Give me of your quills, O Hedgehog!
All your quills, O Kagh, the Hedgehog!
I will make a necklace of them,
Make a girdle for my beauty,
And two stars to deck her bosom!"
   From a hollow tree the Hedgehog
With his sleepy eyes looked at him,
Shot his shining quills, like arrows,
Saying with a drowsy murmur,
Through the tangle of his whiskers,
"Take my quills, O Hiawatha!"
   From the ground the quills he gathered,
All the little shining arrows,
Stained them red and blue and yellow,
With the juice of roots and berries;
Into his canoe he wrought them,
Round its waist a shining girdle,
Round its bows a gleaming necklace,
On its breast two stars resplendent.
   Thus the Birch Canoe was builded
In the valley, by the river,
In the bosom of the forest;
And the forest's life was in it,
All its mystery and its magic,
All the lightness of the birch-tree,
All the toughness of the cedar,
All the larch's supple sinews;
And it floated on the river

Like a yellow leaf in Autumn,
Like a yellow water-lily.
　　Paddles none had Hiawatha,
Paddles none he had or needed,
For his thoughts as paddles served him,
And his wishes served to guide him;
Swift or slow at will he glided,
Veered to right or left at pleasure.
　　Then he called aloud to Kwasind,
To his friend, the strong man, Kwasind,
Saying, "Help me clear this river
Of its sunken logs and sand-bars."
　　Straight into the river Kwasind
Plunged as if he were an otter,
Dived as if he were a beaver,
Stood up to his waist in water,
To his arm-pits in the river,
Swam and shouted in the river,
Tugged at sunken logs and branches,
With his hands he scooped the sand-bars,
With his feet the ooze and tangle.
　　And thus sailed my Hiawatha
Down the rushing Taquamenaw,
Sailed through all its bends and windings,
Sailed through all its deeps and shallows,
While his friend, the strong man, Kwasind,
Swam the deeps, the shallows waded.
　　Up and down the river went they,
In and out among its islands,
Cleared its bed of root and sand-bar,
Dragged the dead trees from its channel,
Made its passage safe and certain,

Made a pathway for the people,
From its springs among the mountains,
To the waters of Pauwating,
To the bay of Taquamenaw.

VIII
Hiawatha's Fishing

Forth upon the Gitche Gumee,
On the shining Big-Sea-Water,
With his fishing-line of cedar,
Of the twisted bark of cedar,
Forth to catch the sturgeon Nahma,
Mishe-Nahma, King of Fishes,
In his birch canoe exulting
All alone went Hiawatha.
   Through the clear, transparent water
He could see the fishes swimming
Far down in the depths below him;
See the yellow perch, the Sahwa,
Like a sunbeam in the water,
See the Shawgashee, the craw-fish,
Like a spider on the bottom,
On the white and sandy bottom.
   At the stern sat Hiawatha,
With his fishing-line of cedar;
In his plumes the breeze of morning
Played as in the hemlock branches;
On the bows, with tail erected,
Sat the squirrel, Adjidaumo;
In his fur the breeze of morning
Played as in the prairie grasses.

On the white sand of the bottom
Lay the monster Mishe-Nahma,
Lay the sturgeon, King of Fishes;
Through his gills he breathed the water,
With his fins he fanned and winnowed,
With his tail he swept the sand-floor.
    There he lay in all his armor;
On each side a shield to guard him,
Plates of bone upon his forehead,
Down his sides and back and shoulders
Plates of bone with spines projecting!
Painted was he with his war-paints,
Stripes of yellow, red, and azure,
Spots of brown and spots of sable;
And he lay there on the bottom,
Fanning with his fins of purple,
As above him Hiawatha
In his birch canoe came sailing,
With his fishing-line of cedar.
    "Take my bait," cried Hiawatha,
Down into the depths beneath him,
"Take my bait, O Sturgeon, Nahma!
Come up from below the water,
Let us see which is the stronger!"
And he dropped his line of cedar
Through the clear, transparent water,
Waited vainly for an answer,
Long sat waiting for an answer,
And repeating loud and louder,
"Take my bait, O King of Fishes!"
    Quiet lay the sturgeon, Nahma,
Fanning slowly in the water,

Looking up at Hiawatha,
Listening to his call and clamor,
His unnecessary tumult,
Till he wearied of the shouting;
And he said to the Kenozha,
To the pike, the Maskenozha,
"Take the bait of this rude fellow,
Break the line of Hiawatha!"
    In his fingers Hiawatha
Felt the loose line jerk and tighten;
As he drew it in, it tugged so
That the birch canoe stood endwise,
Like a birch log in the water,
With the squirrel, Adjidaumo,
Perched and frisking on the summit.
    Full of scorn was Hiawatha
When he saw the fish rise upward,
Saw the pike, the Maskenozha,
Coming nearer, nearer to him,
And he shouted through the water,
"Esa! esa! shame upon you!
You are but the pike, Kenozha,
You are not the fish I wanted,
You are not the King of Fishes!"
    Reeling downward to the bottom
Sank the pike in great confusion,
And the mighty sturgeon, Nahma,
Said to Ugudwash, the sun-fish,
To the bream, with scales of crimson,
"Take the bait of this great boaster,
Break the line of Hiawatha!"
    Slowly upward, wavering, gleaming,

Rose the Ugudwash, the sun-fish,
Seized the line of Hiawatha,
Swung with all his weight upon it,
Made a whirlpool in the water,
Whirled the birch canoe in circles,
Round and round in gurgling eddies,
Till the circles in the water
Reached the far-off sandy beaches,
Till the water-flags and rushes
Nodded on the distant margins.
  But when Hiawatha saw him
Slowly rising through the water,
Lifting up his disk refulgent,
Loud he shouted in derision,
"Esa! esa! shame upon you!
You are Ugudwash, the sun-fish,
You are not the fish I wanted,
You are not the King of Fishes!"
  Slowly downward, wavering, gleaming,
Sank the Ugudwash, the sun-fish,
And again the sturgeon, Nahma,
Heard the shout of Hiawatha,
Heard his challenge of defiance,
The unnecessary tumult,
Ringing far across the water.
  From the white sand of the bottom
Up he rose with angry gesture,
Quivering in each nerve and fibre,
Clashing all his plates of armor,
Gleaming bright with all his war-paint;
In his wrath he darted upward,
Flashing leaped into the sunshine,

Opened his great jaws, and swallowed
Both canoe and Hiawatha.
　Down into that darksome cavern
Plunged the headlong Hiawatha,
As a log on some black river
Shoots and plunges down the rapids,
Found himself in utter darkness,
Groped about in helpless wonder,
Till he felt a great heart beating,
Throbbing in that utter darkness.
　And he smote it in his anger,
With his fist, the heart of Nahma,
Felt the mighty King of Fishes
Shudder through each nerve and fibre,
Heard the water gurgle round him
As he leaped and staggered through it,
Sick at heart, and faint and weary.
　Crosswise then did Hiawatha
Drag his birch-canoe for safety,
Lest from out the jaws of Nahma,
In the turmoil and confusion,
Forth he might be hurled and perish.
And the squirrel, Adjidaumo,
Frisked and chatted very gayly,
Toiled and tugged with Hiawatha
Till the labor was completed.
　Then said Hiawatha to him,
"O my little friend, the squirrel,
Bravely have you toiled to help me;
Take the thanks of Hiawatha,
And the name which now he gives you;
For hereafter and forever

Boys shall call you Adjidaumo,
Tail-in-air the boys shall call you!"
  And again the sturgeon, Nahma,
Gasped and quivered in the water,
Then was still, and drifted landward
Till he grated on the pebbles,
Till the listening Hiawatha
Heard him grate upon the margin,
Felt him strand upon the pebbles,
Knew that Nahma, King of Fishes,
Lay there dead upon the margin.
  Then he heard a clang and flapping,
As of many wings assembling,
Heard a screaming and confusion,
As of birds of prey contending,
Saw a gleam of light above him,
Shining through the ribs of Nahma,
Saw the glittering eyes of sea-gulls,
Of Kayoshk, the sea-gulls, peering,
Gazing at him through the opening,
Heard them saying to each other,
" 'T is our brother, Hiawatha!"
  And he shouted from below them,
Cried exulting from the caverns:
"O ye sea-gulls! O my brothers!
I have slain the sturgeon, Nahma;
Make the rifts a little larger,
With your claws the openings widen,
Set me free from this dark prison,
And henceforward and forever
Men shall speak of your achievements,
Calling you Kayoshk, the sea-gulls,

Yes, Kayoshk, the Noble Scratchers!"
And the wild and clamorous sea-gulls
Toiled with beak and claws together,
Made the rifts and openings wider
In the mighty ribs of Nahma,
And from peril and from prison,
From the body of the sturgeon,
From the peril of the water,
They released my Hiawatha.

He was standing near his wigwam,
On the margin of the water,
And he called to old Nokomis,
Called and beckoned to Nokomis,
Pointed to the sturgeon, Nahma,
Lying lifeless on the pebbles,
With the sea-gulls feeding on him.

"I have slain the Mishe-Nahma,
Slain the King of Fishes!" said he;
"Look! the sea-gulls feed upon him,
Yes, my friends Kayoshk, the sea-gulls;
Drive them not away, Nokomis,
They have saved me from great peril
In the body of the sturgeon,
Wait until their meal is ended,
Till their craws are full with feasting,
Till they homeward fly, at sunset,
To their nests among the marshes;
Then bring all your pots and kettles,
And make oil for us in Winter."

And she waited till the sun set,
Till the pallid moon, the Night-sun,
Rose above the tranquil water,

Till Kayoshk, the sated sea-gulls,
From their banquet rose with clamor,
And across the fiery sunset
Winged their way to far-off islands,
To their nests among the rushes.
　To his sleep went Hiawatha,
And Nokomis to her labor,
Toiling patient in the moonlight,
Till the sun and moon changed places,
Till the sky was red with sunrise,
And Kayoshk, the hungry sea-gulls,
Came back from the reedy islands,
Clamorous for their morning banquet.
　Three whole days and nights alternate
Old Nokomis and the sea-gulls
Stripped the oily flesh of Nahma,
Till the waves washed through the rib-bones,
Till the sea-gulls came no longer,
And upon the sands lay nothing
But the skeleton of Nahma.

IX
Hiawatha and the Pearl-Feather

On the shores of Gitche Gumee,
Of the shining Big-Sea-Water,
Stood Nokomis, the old woman,
Pointing with her finger westward,
O'er the water pointing westward,
To the purple clouds of sunset.
　Fiercely the red sun descending
Burned his way along the heavens,

Set the sky on fire behind him,
As war-parties, when retreating,
Burn the prairies on their war-trail;
And the moon, the Night-sun, eastward,
Suddenly starting from his ambush,
Followed fast those bloody footprints,
Followed in that fiery war-trail,
With its glare upon his features.
  And Nokomis, the old woman,
Pointing with her finger westward,
Spake these words to Hiawatha:
"Yonder dwells the great Pearl-Feather,
Megissogwon, the Magician,
Manito of Wealth and Wampum,
Guarded by his fiery serpents,
Guarded by the black pitch-water.
You can see his fiery serpents,
The Kenabeek, the great serpents,
Coiling, playing in the water;
You can see the black pitch-water
Stretching far away beyond them,
To the purple clouds of sunset!
  "He it was who slew my father,
By his wicked wiles and cunning,
When he from the moon descended,
When he came on earth to seek me.
He, the mightiest of Magicians,
Sends the fever from the marshes,
Sends the pestilential vapors,
Sends the poisonous exhalations,
Sends the white fog from the fen-lands,
Sends disease and death among us!

"Take your bow, O Hiawatha,
Take your arrows, jasper-headed,
Take your war-club, Puggawaugun,
And your mittens, Minjekahwun,
And your birch-canoe for sailing,
And the oil of Mishe-Nahma,
So to smear its sides, that swiftly
You may pass the black pitch-water;
Slay this merciless magician,
Save the people from the fever
That he breathes across the fen-lands,
And avenge my father's murder!"
    Straightway then my Hiawatha
Armed himself with all his war-gear,
Launched his birch-canoe for sailing;
With his palm its sides he patted,
Said with glee, "Cheemaun, my darling,
O my Birch-canoe! leap forward,
Where you see the fiery serpents,
Where you see the black pitch-water!"
    Forward leaped Cheemaun exulting,
And the noble Hiawatha
Sang his war-song wild and woful,
And above him the war-eagle,
The Keneu, the great war-eagle,
Master of all fowls with feathers,
Screamed and hurtled through the heavens.
    Soon he reached the fiery serpents,
The Kenabeek, the great serpents,
Lying huge upon the water,
Sparkling, rippling in the water,
Lying coiled across the passage,

With their blazing crests uplifted,
Breathing fiery fogs and vapors,
So that none could pass beyond them.
  But the fearless Hiawatha
Cried aloud, and spake in this wise:
"Let me pass my way, Kenabeek,
Let me go upon my journey!"
And they answered, hissing fiercely,
With their fiery breath made answer:
"Back, go back! O Shaugodaya!
Back to old Nokomis, Faint-heart!"
  Then the angry Hiawatha
Raised his mighty bow of ash-tree,
Seized his arrows, jasper-headed,
Shot them fast among the serpents;
Every twanging of the bow-string
Was a war-cry and a death-cry,
Every whizzing of an arrow
Was a death-song of Kenabeek.
  Weltering in the bloody water,
Dead lay all the fiery serpents,
And among them Hiawatha
Harmless sailed, and cried exulting:
"Onward, O Cheemaun, my darling!
Onward to the black pitch-water!"
  Then he took the oil of Nahma,
And the bows and sides anointed,
Smeared them well with oil, that swiftly
He might pass the black pitch-water.
  All night long he sailed upon it,
Sailed upon that sluggish water,
Covered with its mould of ages,

Black with rotting water-rushes,
Rank with flags and leaves of lilies,
Stagnant, lifeless, dreary, dismal,
Lighted by the shimmering moonlight,
And by will-o'-the-wisps illumined,
Fires by ghosts of dead men kindled,
In their weary night-encampments.
   All the air was white with moonlight,
All the water black with shadow,
And around him the Suggema,
The mosquito, sang his war-song,
And the fire-flies, Wah-wah-taysee,
Waved their torches to mislead him;
And the bull-frog, the Dahinda,
Thrust his head into the moonlight,
Fixed his yellow eyes upon him,
Sobbed and sank beneath the surface;
And anon a thousand whistles,
Answered over all the fen-lands,
And the heron, the Shuh-shuh-gah,
Far off on the reedy margin,
Heralded the hero's coming.
   Westward thus fared Hiawatha,
Toward the realm of Megissogwon,
Toward the land of the Pearl-Feather,
Till the level moon stared at him,
In his face stared pale and haggard,
Till the sun was hot behind him,
Till it burned upon his shoulders,
And before him on the upland
He could see the Shining Wigwam
Of the Manito of Wampum,

Of the mightiest of Magicians.
  Then once more Cheemaun he patted,
To his birch-canoe said, "Onward!"
And it stirred in all its fibres,
And with one great bound of triumph
Leaped across the water-lilies,
Leaped through tangled flags and rushes,
And upon the beach beyond them
Dry-shod landed Hiawatha.
  Straight he took his bow of ash-tree,
On the sand one end he rested,
With his knee he pressed the middle,
Stretched the faithful bow-string tighter,
Took an arrow, jasper-headed,
Shot it at the Shining Wigwam,
Sent it singing as a herald,
As a bearer of his message,
Of his challenge loud and lofty:
"Come forth from your lodge, Pearl-Feather!
Hiawatha waits your coming!"
  Straightway from the Shining Wigwam
Came the mighty Megissogwon,
Tall of stature, broad of shoulder,
Dark and terrible in aspect,
Clad from head to foot in wampum,
Armed with all his warlike weapons,
Painted like the sky of morning,
Streaked with crimson, blue, and yellow,
Crested with great eagle-feathers,
Streaming upward, streaming outward.
  "Well I know you, Hiawatha!"
Cried he in a voice of thunder,

In a tone of loud derision.
"Hasten back, O Shaugodaya!
Hasten back among the women,
Back to old Nokomis, Faint-heart!
I will slay you as you stand there,
As of old I slew her father!"

But my Hiawatha answered,
Nothing daunted, fearing nothing:
"Big words do not smite like war-clubs,
Boastful breath is not a bow-string,
Taunts are not so sharp as arrows,
Deeds are better things than words are,
Actions mightier than boastings!"

Then began the greatest battle
That the sun had ever looked on,
That the war-birds ever witnessed.
All a Summer's day it lasted,
From the sunrise to the sunset;
For the shafts of Hiawatha
Harmless hit the shirt of wampum,
Harmless fell the blows he dealt it
With his mittens, Minjekahwun,
Harmless fell the heavy war-club;
It could dash the rocks asunder,
But it could not break the meshes
Of that magic shirt of wampum.

Till at sunset Hiawatha,
Leaning on his bow of ash-tree,
Wounded, weary, and desponding,
With his mighty war-club broken,
With his mittens torn and tattered,
And three useless arrows only,

Paused to rest beneath a pine-tree,
From whose branches trailed the mosses,
And whose trunk was coated over
With the Dead-man's Moccasin-leather,
With the fungus white and yellow.
   Suddenly from the boughs above him
Sang the Mama, the woodpecker:
"Aim your arrows, Hiawatha,
At the head of Megissogwon,
Strike the tuft of hair upon it,
At their roots the long black tresses;
There alone can he be wounded!"
   Winged with feathers, tipped with jasper,
Swift flew Hiawatha's arrow,
Just as Megissogwon, stooping,
Raised a heavy stone to throw it.
Full upon the crown it struck him,
At the roots of his long tresses,
And he reeled and staggered forward,
Plunging like a wounded bison,
Yes, like Pezhekee, the bison,
When the snow is on the prairie.
   Swifter flew the second arrow,
In the pathway of the other,
Piercing deeper than the other,
Wounding sorer than the other;
And the knees of Megissogwon
Shook like windy reeds beneath him,
Bent and trembled like the rushes.
   But the third and latest arrow
Swiftest flew, and wounded sorest,
And the mighty Megissogwon

Saw the fiery eyes of Pauguk,
Saw the eyes of Death glare at him,
Heard his voice call in the darkness;
At the feet of Hiawatha
Lifeless lay the great Pearl-Feather,
Lay the mightiest of Magicians.
  Then the grateful Hiawatha
Called the Mama, the woodpecker,
From his perch among the branches
Of the melancholy pine-tree,
And, in honor of his service,
Stained with blood the tuft of feathers
On the little head of Mama;
Even to this day he wears it,
Wears the tuft of crimson feathers,
As a symbol of his service.
  Then he stripped the shirt of wampum
From the back of Megissogwon,
As a trophy of the battle,
As a signal of his conquest.
On the shore he left the body,
Half on land and half in water,
In the sand his feet were buried,
And his face was in the water.
And above him, wheeled and clamored
The Keneu, the great war-eagle,
Sailing round in narrower circles,
Hovering nearer, nearer, nearer.
  From the wigwam Hiawatha
Bore the wealth of Megissogwon,
All his wealth of skins and wampum,
Furs of bison and of beaver,

Furs of sable and of ermine,
Wampum belts and strings and pouches,
Quivers wrought with beads of wampum,
Filled with arrows, silver-headed.
    Homeward then he sailed exulting,
Homeward through the black pitch-water,
Homeward through the weltering serpents,
With the trophies of the battle,
With a shout and song of triumph.
    On the shore stood old Nokomis,
On the shore stood Chibiabos,
And the very strong man, Kwasind,
Waiting for the hero's coming,
Listening to his songs of triumph.
And the people of the village
Welcomed him with songs and dances,
Made a joyous feast, and shouted:
"Honor be to Hiawatha!
He has slain the great Pearl-Feather,
Slain the mightiest of magicians,
Him, who sent the fiery fever,
Sent the white fog from the fen-lands,
Sent disease and death among us!"
    Ever dear to Hiawatha
Was the memory of Mama!
And in token of his friendship,
As a mark of his remembrance,
He adorned and decked his pipe-stem
With the crimson tuft of feathers,
With the blood-red crest of Mama.
But the wealth of Megissogwon,
All the trophies of the battle,

He divided with his people,
Shared it equally among them.

X
Hiawatha's Wooing

"As unto the bow the cord is,
So unto the man is woman,
Though she bends him, she obeys him,
Though she draws him, yet she follows,
Useless each without the other!"
    Thus the youthful Hiawatha
Said within himself and pondered,
Much perplexed by various feelings,
Listless, longing, hoping, fearing,
Dreaming still of Minnehaha,
Of the lovely Laughing Water,
In the land of the Dacotahs.
    "Wed a maiden of your people,"
Warning said the old Nokomis;
"Go not eastward, go not westward,
For a stranger, whom we know not!
Like a fire upon the hearth-stone
Is a neighbor's homely daughter,
Like the starlight or the moonlight
Is the handsomest of strangers!"
    Thus dissuading spake Nokomis,
And my Hiawatha answered
Only this: "Dear old Nokomis,
Very pleasant is the firelight,
But I like the starlight better,
Better do I like the moonlight!"

Gravely then said old Nokomis:
"Bring not here an idle maiden,
Bring not here a useless woman,
Hands unskilful, feet unwilling;
Bring a wife with nimble fingers,
Heart and hand that move together,
Feet that run on willing errands!"
    Smiling answered Hiawatha:
"In the land of the Dacotahs
Lives the Arrow-maker's daughter,
Minnehaha, Laughing Water,
Handsomest of all the women.
I will bring her to your wigwam,
She shall run upon your errands,
Be your starlight, moonlight, firelight,
Be the sunlight of my people!"
    Still dissuading said Nokomis:
"Bring not to my lodge a stranger
From the land of the Dacotahs!
Very fierce are the Dacotahs,
Often is there war between us,
There are feuds yet unforgotten,
Wounds that ache and still may open!"
    Laughing answered Hiawatha:
"For that reason, if no other,
Would I wed the fair Dacotah,
That our tribes might be united,
That old feuds might be forgotten,
And old wounds be healed forever!"
    Thus departed Hiawatha
To the land of the Dacotahs,
To the land of handsome women;

Striding over moor and meadow,
Through interminable forests,
Through uninterrupted silence.
  With his moccasins of magic,
At each stride a mile he measured;
Yet the way seemed long before him,
And his heart outran his footsteps;
And he journeyed without resting,
Till he heard the cataract's laughter,
Heard the Falls of Minnehaha
Calling to him through the silence.
"Pleasant is the sound!" he murmured,
"Pleasant is the voice that calls me!"
  On the outskirts of the forests,
'Twixt the shadow and the sunshine,
Herds of fallow deer were feeding,
But they saw not Hiawatha;
To his bow he whispered, "Fail not!"
To his arrow whispered, "Swerve not!"
Sent it singing on its errand,
To the red heart of the roebuck;
Threw the deer across his shoulder,
And sped forward without pausing.
  At the doorway of his wigwam
Sat the ancient Arrow-maker,
In the land of the Dacotahs,
Making arrow-heads of jasper,
Arrow-heads of chalcedony.
At his side, in all her beauty,
Sat the lovely Minnehaha,
Sat his daughter, Laughing Water,
Plaiting mats of flags and rushes;

Of the past the old man's thoughts were,
And the maiden's of the future.
　He was thinking, as he sat there,
Of the days when with such arrows
He had struck the deer and bison,
On the Muskoday, the meadow;
Shot the wild goose, flying southward,
On the wing, the clamorous Wawa;
Thinking of the great war-parties,
How they came to buy his arrows,
Could not fight without his arrows.
Ah, no more such noble warriors
Could be found on earth as they were!
Now the men were all like women,
Only used their tongues for weapons!
　She was thinking of a hunter,
From another tribe and country,
Young and tall and very handsome,
Who one morning, in the Spring-time,
Came to buy her father's arrows,
Sat and rested in the wigwam,
Lingered long about the doorway,
Looking back as he departed.
She had heard her father praise him,
Praise his courage and his wisdom;
Would he come again for arrows
To the Falls of Minnehaha?
On the mat her hands lay idle,
And her eyes were very dreamy.
　Through their thoughts they heard a foot-
　　step,
Heard a rustling in the branches,

And with glowing cheek and forehead,
With the deer upon his shoulders,
Suddenly from out the woodlands
Hiawatha stood before them.
    Straight the ancient Arrow-maker
Looked up gravely from his labor,
Laid aside the unfinished arrow,
Bade him enter at the doorway,
Saying, as he rose to meet him,
"Hiawatha, you are welcome!"
    At the feet of Laughing Water
Hiawatha laid his burden,
Threw the red deer from his shoulders;
And the maiden looked up at him,
Looked up from her mat of rushes,
Said with gentle look and accent,
"You are welcome, Hiawatha!"
    Very spacious was the wigwam,
Made of deer-skins dressed and whitened,
With the Gods of the Dacotahs
Drawn and painted on its curtains,
And so tall the doorway, hardly
Hiawatha stooped to enter,
Hardly touched his eagle-feathers
As he entered at the doorway.
    Then uprose the Laughing Water,
From the ground fair Minnehaha,
Laid aside her mat unfinished,
Brought forth food and set before them,
Water brought them from the brooklet,
Gave them food in earthen vessels,
Gave them drink in bowls of bass-wood,

Listened while the guest was speaking,
Listened while her father answered,
But not once her lips she opened,
Not a single word she uttered.
  Yes, as in a dream she listened
To the words of Hiawatha,
As he talked of old Nokomis,
Who had nursed him in his childhood,
As he told of his companions,
Chibiabos, the musician,
And the very strong man, Kwasind,
And of happiness and plenty
In the land of the Ojibways,
In the pleasant land and peaceful.
  "After many years of warfare,
Many years of strife and bloodshed,
There is peace between the Ojibways
And the tribe of the Dacotahs."
Thus continued Hiawatha,
And then added, speaking slowly,
"That this peace may last forever,
And our hands be clasped more closely,
And our hearts be more united,
Give me as my wife this maiden,
Minnehaha, Laughing Water,
Loveliest of Dacotah women!"
  And the ancient Arrow-maker
Paused a moment ere he answered,
Smoked a little while in silence,
Looked at Hiawatha proudly,
Fondly looked at Laughing Water,
And made answer very gravely:

"Yes, if Minnehaha wishes;
Let your heart speak, Minnehaha!"
   And the lovely Laughing Water
Seemed more lovely as she stood there,
Neither willing nor reluctant,
As she went to Hiawatha,
Softly took the seat beside him,
While she said, and blushed to say it,
"I will follow you, my husband!"
   This was Hiawatha's wooing!
Thus it was he won the daughter
Of the ancient Arrow-maker,
In the land of the Dacotahs!
   From the wigwam he departed,
Leading with him Laughing Water;
Hand in hand they went together,
Through the woodland and the meadow,
Left the old man standing lonely
At the doorway of his wigwam,
Heard the Falls of Minnehaha
Calling to them from the distance,
Crying to them from afar off,
"Fare thee well, O Minnehaha!"
   And the ancient Arrow-maker
Turned again unto his labor,
Sat down by his sunny doorway,
Murmuring to himself, and saying:
"Thus it is our daughters leave us,
Those we love, and those who love us!
Just when they have learned to help us,
When we are old and lean upon them,
Comes a youth with flaunting feathers,

With his flute of reeds, a stranger
Wanders piping through the village,
Beckons to the fairest maiden,
And she follows where he leads her,
Leaving all things for the stranger!"
    Pleasant was the journey homeward,
Through interminable forests,
Over meadow, over mountain,
Over river, hill, and hollow.
Short it seemed to Hiawatha,
Though they journeyed very slowly,
Though his pace he checked and slackened
To the steps of Laughing Water.
    Over wide and rushing rivers
In his arms he bore the maiden;
Light he thought her as a feather,
As the plume upon his head-gear;
Cleared the tangled pathway for her,
Bent aside the swaying branches,
Made at night a lodge of branches,
And a bed with boughs of hemlock,
And a fire before the doorway
With the dry cones of the pine-tree.
    All the travelling winds went with them,
O'er the meadows, through the forest;
All the stars of night looked at them,
Watched with sleepless eyes their slumber;
From his ambush in the oak-tree
Peeped the squirrel, Adjidaumo,
Watched with eager eyes the lovers;
And the rabbit, the Wabasso,
Scampered from the path before them,

Peering, peeping from his burrow,
Sat erect upon his haunches,
Watched with curious eyes the lovers.
　　Pleasant was the journey homeward!
All the birds sang loud and sweetly
Songs of happiness and heart's-ease;
Sang the bluebird, the Owaissa,
"Happy are you, Hiawatha,
Having such a wife to love you!"
Sang the robin, the Opechee,
"Happy are you, Laughing Water,
Having such a noble husband!"
　　From the sky the sun benignant
Looked upon them through the branches,
Saying to them, "O my children,
Love is sunshine, hate is shadow,
Life is checkered shade and sunshine,
Rule by love, O Hiawatha!"
　　From the sky the moon looked at them,
Filled the lodge with mystic splendors,
Whispered to them, "O my children,
Day is restless; night is quiet,
Man imperious, woman feeble;
Half is mine, although I follow;
Rule by patience, Laughing Water!"
　　Thus it was they journeyed homeward;
Thus it was that Hiawatha
To the lodge of old Nokomis
Brought the moonlight, starlight, firelight,
Brought the sunshine of his people,
Minnehaha, Laughing Water,
Handsomest of all the women

In the land of the Dacotahs,
In the land of handsome women.

XI
Hiawatha's Wedding-Feast

You shall hear how Pau-Puk-Keewis,
How the handsome Yenadizze
Danced at Hiawatha's wedding;
How the gentle Chibiabos,
He the sweetest of musicians,
Sang his songs of love and longing;
How Iagoo, the great boaster,
He the marvellous story-teller,
Told his tales of strange adventure,
That the feast might be more joyous,
That the time might pass more gayly,
And the guests be more contented.
   Sumptuous was the feast Nokomis
Made at Hiawatha's wedding;
All the bowls were made of bass-wood,
White and polished very smoothly,
All the spoons of horn of bison,
Black and polished very smoothly.
   She had sent through all the village
Messengers with wands of willow,
As a sign of invitation,
As a token of the feasting;
And the wedding guests assembled,
Clad in all their richest raiment,
Robes of fur and belts of wampum,
Splendid with their paint and plumage,

Beautiful with beads and tassels.

First they ate the sturgeon, Nahma,
And the pike, the Maskenozha,
Caught and cooked by old Nokomis;
Then on pemican they feasted,
Pemican and buffalo marrow,
Haunch of deer and hump of bison,
Yellow cakes of the Mondamin,
And the wild rice of the river.

But the gracious Hiawatha,
And the lovely Laughing Water,
And the careful old Nokomis,
Tasted not the food before them,
Only waited on the others,
Only served their guests in silence.

And when all the guests had finished,
Old Nokomis, brisk and busy,
From an ample pouch of otter,
Filled the red-stone pipes for smoking
With tobacco from the South-land,
Mixed with bark of the red willow,
And with herbs and leaves of fragrance.

Then she said, "O Pau-Puk-Keewis,
Dance for us your merry dances,
Dance the Beggar's Dance to please us,
That the feast may be more joyous,
That the time may pass more gayly,
And our guests be more contented!"

Then the handsome Pau-Puk-Keewis,
He the idle Yenadizze,
He the merry mischief-maker,
Whom the people called the Storm-Fool,

Rose among the guests assembled.
   Skilled was he in sports and pastimes,
In the merry dance of snow-shoes,
In the play of quoits and ball-play;
Skilled was he in games of hazard,
In all games of skill and hazard,
Pugasaing, the Bowl and Counters,
Kuntassoo, the Game of Plum-stones.
Though the warriors called him Faint-Heart,
Called him coward, Shaugodaya,
Idler, gambler, Yenadizze,
Little heeded he their jesting,
Little cared he for their insults,
For the women and the maidens
Loved the handsome Pau-Puk-Keewis.
   He was dressed in shirt of doeskin,
White and soft, and fringed with ermine,
All inwrought with beads of wampum;
He was dressed in deer-skin leggings,
Fringed with hedgehog quills and ermine,
And in moccasins of buck-skin,
Thick with quills and beads embroidered.
On his head were plumes of swan's down,
On his heels were tails of foxes,
In one hand a fan of feathers,
And a pipe was in the other.
   Barred with streaks of red and yellow,
Streaks of blue and bright vermilion,
Shone the face of Pau-Puk-Keewis.
From his forehead fell his tresses,
Smooth, and parted like a woman's,
Shining bright with oil, and plaited,

Hung with braids of scented grasses,
As among the guests assembled,
To the sound of flutes and singing,
To the sound of drums and voices,
Rose the handsome Pau-Puk-Keewis,
And began his mystic dances.

   First he danced a solemn measure,
Very slow in step and gesture,
In and out among the pine-trees,
Through the shadows and the sunshine,
Treading softly like a panther.
Then more swiftly and still swifter,
Whirling, spinning round in circles,
Leaping o'er the guests assembled,
Eddying round and round the wigwam,
Till the leaves went whirling with him,
Till the dust and wind together
Swept in eddies round about him.

   Then along the sandy margin
Of the lake, the Big-Sea-Water,
On he sped with frenzied gestures,
Stamped upon the sand, and tossed it
Wildly in the air around him;
Till the wind became a whirlwind,
Till the sand was blown and sifted
Like great snowdrifts o'er the landscape,
Heaping all the shores with Sand Dunes,
Sand Hills of the Nagow Wudjoo!

   Thus the merry Pau-Puk-Keewis
Danced his Beggar's Dance to please them,
And, returning, sat down laughing
There among the guests assembled,

Sat and fanned himself serenely
With his fan of turkey-feathers.
   Then they said to Chibiabos,
To the friend of Hiawatha,
To the sweetest of all singers,
To the best of all musicians,
"Sing to us, O Chibiabos!
Songs of love and songs of longing,
That the feast may be more joyous,
That the time may pass more gayly,
And our guests be more contented!"
   And the gentle Chibiabos
Sang in accents sweet and tender,
Sang in tones of deep emotion,
Songs of love and songs of longing;
Looking still at Hiawatha,
Looking at fair Laughing Water,
Sang he softly, sang in this wise:
   "Onaway! Awake, beloved!
Thou the wild-flower of the forest!
Thou the wild-bird of the prairie!
Thou with eyes so soft and fawn-like!
   "If thou only lookest at me,
I am happy, I am happy,
As the lilies of the prairie,
When they feel the dew upon them!
   "Sweet thy breath is as the fragrance
Of the wild-flowers in the morning,
As their fragrance is at evening,
In the Moon when leaves are falling.
   "Does not all the blood within me
Leap to meet thee, leap to meet thee,

As the springs to meet the sunshine,
In the Moon when nights are brightest?
   "Onaway! my heart sings to thee,
Sings with joy when thou art near me,
As the sighing, singing branches
In the pleasant Moon of Strawberries!
   "When thou art not pleased, beloved,
Then my heart is sad and darkened,
As the shining river darkens
When the clouds drop shadows on it!
   "When thou smilest, my beloved,
Then my troubled heart is brightened,
As in sunshine gleam the ripples
That the cold wind makes in rivers.
   "Smiles the earth, and smile the waters,
Smile the cloudless skies above us,
But I lose the way of smiling
When thou art no longer near me!
   "I myself, myself! behold me!
Blood of my beating heart, behold me!
Oh awake, awake, beloved!
Onaway! awake, beloved!"
   Thus the gentle Chibiabos
Sang his song of love and longing;
And Iagoo, the great boaster,
He the marvellous story-teller,
He the friend of old Nokomis,
Jealous of the sweet musician,
Jealous of the applause they gave him,
Saw in all the eyes around him,
Saw in all their looks and gestures,
That the wedding guests assembled

Longed to hear his pleasant stories,
His immeasurable falsehoods.

Very boastful was Iagoo;
Never heard he an adventure
But himself had met a greater;
Never any deed of daring
But himself had done a bolder;
Never any marvellous story
But himself could tell a stranger.

Would you listen to his boasting,
Would you only give him credence,
No one ever shot an arrow
Half so far and high as he had;
Ever caught so many fishes,
Ever killed so many reindeer,
Ever trapped so many beaver!

None could run so fast as he could,
None could dive so deep as he could,
None could swim so far as he could;
None had made so many journeys,
None had seen so many wonders,
As this wonderful Iagoo,
As this marvellous story-teller!

Thus his name became a by-word
And a jest among the people;
And whene'er a boastful hunter
Praised his own address too highly,
Or a warrior, home returning,
Talked too much of his achievements,
All his hearers cried, "Iagoo!
Here's Iagoo come among us!"

He it was who carved the cradle

Of the little Hiawatha,
Carved its framework out of linden,
Bound it strong with reindeer sinews;
He it was who taught him later
How to make his bows and arrows,
How to make the bows of ash-tree,
And the arrows of the oak-tree.
So among the guests assembled
At my Hiawatha's wedding
Sat Iagoo, old and ugly,
Sat the marvellous story-teller.
   And they said, "O good Iagoo,
Tell us now a tale of wonder,
Tell us of some strange adventure,
That the feast may be more joyous,
That the time may pass more gayly,
And our guests be more contented!"
   And Iagoo answered straightway,
"You shall hear a tale of wonder,
You shall hear the strange adventures
Of Osseo, the Magician,
From the Evening Star descended."

XII
The Son of the Evening Star

Can it be the sun descending
O'er the level plain of water?
Or the Red Swan floating, flying,
Wounded by the magic arrow,
Staining all the waves with crimson,
With the crimson of its life-blood,

Filling all the air with splendor,
With the splendor of its plumage?
  Yes; it is the sun descending,
Sinking down into the water;
All the sky is stained with purple,
All the water flushed with crimson!
No; it is the Red Swan floating,
Diving down beneath the water;
To the sky its wings are lifted,
With its blood the waves are reddened!
  Over it the Star of Evening
Melts and trembles through the purple,
Hangs suspended in the twilight.
No; it is a bead of wampum
On the robes of the Great Spirit
As he passes through the twilight,
Walks in silence through the heavens.
  This with joy beheld Iagoo
And he said in haste: "Behold it!
See the sacred Star of Evening!
You shall hear a tale of wonder,
Hear the story of Osseo,
Son of the Evening Star, Osseo!
  "Once, in days no more remembered,
Ages nearer the beginning,
When the heavens were closer to us,
And the Gods were more familiar,
In the North-land lived a hunter,
With ten young and comely daughters,
Tall and lithe as wands of willow;
Only Oweenee, the youngest,
She the wilful and the wayward,

She the silent, dreamy maiden,
Was the fairest of the sisters.
   "All these women married warriors,
Married brave and haughty husbands;
Only Oweenee, the youngest,
Laughed and flouted all her lovers,
All her young and handsome suitors,
And then married old Osseo,
Old Osseo, poor and ugly,
Broken with age and weak with coughing,
Always coughing like a squirrel.
   "Ah, but beautiful within him
Was the spirit of Osseo,
From the Evening Star descended,
Star of Evening, Star of Woman,
Star of tenderness and passion!
All its fire was in his bosom,
All its beauty in his spirit,
All its mystery in his being,
All its splendor in his language!
   "And her lovers, the rejected,
Handsome men with belts of wampum,
Handsome men with paint and feathers,
Pointed at her in derision,
Followed her with jest and laughter.
But she said: 'I care not for you,
Care not for your belts of wampum,
Care not for your paint and feathers,
Care not for your jests and laughter;
I am happy with Osseo!'
   "Once to some great feast invited,
Through the damp and dusk of evening,

Walked together the ten sisters,
Walked together with their husbands;
Slowly followed old Osseo,
With fair Oweenee beside him;
All the others chatted gayly,
These two only walked in silence.
  "At the western sky Osseo
Gazed intent, as if imploring,
Often stopped and gazed imploring
At the trembling Star of Evening,
At the tender Star of Woman;
And they heard him murmur softly,
'Ah, showain nemeshin, Nosa!
Pity, pity me, my Father!'
  " 'Listen!' said the eldest sister,
'He is praying to his father!
What a pity that the old man
Does not stumble in the pathway,
Does not break his neck by falling!'
And they laughed till all the forest
Rang with their unseemly laughter.
  "On their pathway through the woodlands
Lay an oak, by storms uprooted,
Lay the great trunk of an oak-tree,
Buried half in leaves and mosses,
Mouldering, crumbling, huge and hollow.
And Osseo, when he saw it,
Gave a shout, a cry of anguish,
Leaped into its yawning cavern,
At one end went in an old man,
Wasted, wrinkled, old, and ugly;
From the other came a young man,

Tall and straight and strong and handsome.
  "Thus Osseo was transfigured,
Thus restored to youth and beauty;
But, alas for good Osseo,
And for Oweenee, the faithful!
Strangely, too, was she transfigured.
Changed into a weak old woman,
With a staff she tottered onward,
Wasted, wrinkled, old, and ugly!
And the sisters and their husbands
Laughed until the echoing forest
Rang with their unseemly laughter.
  "But Osseo turned not from her,
Walked with slower step beside her,
Took her hand, as brown and withered
As an oak-leaf is in Winter,
Called her sweetheart, Nenemoosha,
Soothed her with soft words of kindness,
Till they reached the lodge of feasting,
Till they sat down in the wigwam,
Sacred to the Star of Evening,
To the tender Star of Woman.
  "Wrapt in visions, lost in dreaming,
At the banquet sat Osseo;
All were merry, all were happy,
All were joyous but Osseo.
Neither food nor drink he tasted,
Neither did he speak nor listen,
But as one bewildered sat he,
Looking dreamily and sadly,
First at Oweenee, then upward
At the gleaming sky above them.

"Then a voice was heard, a whisper,
Coming from the starry distance,
Coming from the empty vastness,
Low, and musical, and tender;
And the voice said: 'O Osseo!
O my son, my best beloved!
Broken are the spells that bound you,
All the charms of the magician,
All the magic powers of evil;
Come to me; ascend, Osseo!

" 'Taste the food that stands before you:
It is blessed and enchanted,
It has magic virtues in it,
It will change you to a spirit.
All your bowls and all your kettles
Shall be wood and clay no longer;
But the bowls be changed to wampum,
And the kettles shall be silver;
They shall shine like shells of scarlet,
Like the fire shall gleam and glimmer.

" 'And the women shall no longer
Bear the dreary doom of labor,
But be changed to birds, and glisten
With the beauty of the starlight,
Painted with the dusky splendors
Of the skies and clouds of evening!'

"What Osseo heard as whispers,
What as words he comprehended,
Was but music to the others,
Music as of birds afar off,
Of the whippoorwill afar off,
Of the lonely Wawonaissa

Singing in the darksome forest.
  "Then the lodge began to tremble,
Straight began to shake and tremble,
And they felt it rising, rising,
Slowly through the air ascending,
From the darkness of the tree-tops
Forth into the dewy starlight,
Till it passed the topmost branches;
And behold! the wooden dishes
All were changed to shells of scarlet!
And behold! the earthen kettles
All were changed to bowls of silver!
And the roof-poles of the wigwam
Were as glittering rods of silver,
And the roof of bark upon them
As the shining shards of beetles.
  "Then Osseo gazed around him,
And he saw the nine fair sisters,
All the sisters and their husbands,
Changed to birds of various plumage.
Some were jays and some were magpies,
Others thrushes, others blackbirds;
And they hopped, and sang, and twittered,
Perked and fluttered all their feathers,
Strutted in their shining plumage,
And their tails like fans unfolded.
  "Only Oweenee, the youngest,
Was not changed, but sat in silence,
Wasted, wrinkled, old, and ugly,
Looking sadly at the others;
Till Osseo, gazing upward,
Gave another cry of anguish,

Such a cry as he had uttered
By the oak-tree in the forest.
  "Then returned her youth and beauty,
And her soiled and tattered garments
Were transformed to robes of ermine,
And her staff became a feather,
Yes, a shining silver feather!
  "And again the wigwam trembled,
Swayed and rushed through airy currents,
Through transparent cloud and vapor,
And amid celestial splendors
On the Evening Star alighted,
As a snow-flake falls on snow-flake,
As a leaf drops on a river,
As the thistle-down on water.
  "Forth with cheerful words of welcome
Came the father of Osseo,
He with radiant locks of silver,
He with eyes serene and tender.
And he said: 'My son, Osseo,
Hang the cage of birds you bring there,
Hang the cage with rods of silver,
And the birds with glistening feathers,
At the doorway of my wigwam.'
  "At the door he hung the bird-cage,
And they entered in and gladly
Listened to Osseo's father,
Ruler of the Star of Evening,
As he said: 'O my Osseo!
I have had compassion on you,
Given you back your youth and beauty,
Into birds of various plumage

Changed your sisters and their husbands;
Changed them thus because they mocked
     you
In the figure of the old man,
In that aspect sad and wrinkled,
Could not see your heart of passion,
Could not see your youth immortal;
Only Oweenee, the faithful,
Saw your naked heart and loved you.
   " 'In the lodge that glimmers yonder,
In the little star that twinkles
Through the vapors, on the left hand,
Lives the envious Evil Spirit,
The Wabeno, the magician,
Who transformed you to an old man.
Take heed lest his beams fall on you,
For the rays he darts around him
Are the power of his enchantment,
Are the arrows that he uses.'
   "Many years, in peace and quiet,
On the peaceful Star of Evening
Dwelt Osseo with his father;
Many years, in song and flutter,
At the doorway of the wigwam,
Hung the cage with rods of silver,
And fair Oweenee, the faithful,
Bore a son unto Osseo,
With the beauty of his mother,
With the courage of his father.
   "And the boy grew up and prospered,
And Osseo, to delight him,
Made him little bows and arrows,

Opened the great cage of silver,
And let loose his aunts and uncles,
All those birds with glossy feathers,
For his little son to shoot at.
  "Round and round they wheeled and
    darted,
Filled the Evening Star with music,
With their songs of joy and freedom;
Filled the Evening Star with splendor,
With the fluttering of their plumage;
Till the boy, the little hunter,
Bent his bow and shot an arrow,
Shot a swift and fatal arrow,
And a bird, with shining feathers,
At his feet fell wounded sorely.
  "But, O wondrous transformation!
'T was no bird he saw before him,
'T was a beautiful young woman,
With the arrow in her bosom!
  "When her blood fell on the planet,
On the sacred Star of Evening,
Broken was the spell of magic,
Powerless was the strange enchantment,
And the youth, the fearless bowman,
Suddenly felt himself descending,
Held by unseen hands, but sinking
Downward through the empty spaces,
Downward through the clouds and vapors,
Till he rested on an island,
On an island, green and grassy,
Yonder in the Big-Sea-Water.
  "After him he saw descending

All the birds with shining feathers,
Fluttering, falling, wafted downward,
Like the painted leaves of Autumn;
And the lodge with poles of silver,
With its roof like wings of beetles,
Like the shining shards of beetles,
By the winds of heaven uplifted,
Slowly sank upon the island,
Bringing back the good Osseo,
Bringing Oweenee, the faithful.

"Then the birds, again transfigured,
Reassumed the shape of mortals,
Took their shape, but not their stature;
They remained as Little People,
Like the pygmies, the Puk-Wudjies,
And on pleasant nights of Summer,
When the Evening Star was shining,
Hand in hand they danced together
On the island's craggy headlands,
On the sand-beach low and level.

"Still their glittering lodge is seen there,
On the tranquil Summer evenings,
And upon the shore the fisher
Sometimes hears their happy voices,
Sees them dancing in the starlight!"

When the story was completed,
When the wondrous tale was ended,
Looking round upon his listeners,
Solemnly Iagoo added:
'There are great men, I have known such,
Whom their people understand not,
Whom they even make a jest of,

Scoff and jeer at in derision.
From the story of Osseo
Let us learn the fate of jesters!"
 All the wedding guests delighted
Listened to the marvellous story,
Listened laughing and applauding,
And they whispered to each other:
"Does he mean himself, I wonder?
And are we the aunts and uncles?"
 Then again sang Chibiabos,
Sang a song of love and longing,
In those accents sweet and tender,
In those tones of pensive sadness,
Sang a maiden's lamentation
For her lover, her Algonquin.
 "When I think of my beloved,
Ah me! think of my beloved,
When my heart is thinking of him,
O my sweetheart, my Algonquin!
 "Ah me! when I parted from him,
Round my neck he hung the wampum,
As a pledge, the snow-white wampum,
O my sweetheart, my Algonquin!
 "I will go with you, he whispered,
Ah me! to your native country;
Let me go with you, he whispered,
O my sweetheart, my Algonquin!
 "Far away, away, I answered,
Very far away, I answered,
Ah me! is my native country,
O my sweetheart, my Algonquin!
 "When I looked back to behold him,

Where we parted, to behold him,
After me he still was gazing,
O my sweetheart, my Algonquin!
  "By the tree he still was standing,
By the fallen tree was standing,
That had dropped into the water,
O my sweetheart, my Algonquin!
  "When I think of my beloved,
Ah me! think of my beloved,
When my heart is thinking of him,
O my sweetheart, my Algonquin!"
  Such was Hiawatha's Wedding,
Such the dance of Pau-Puk-Keewis,
Such the story of Iagoo,
Such the songs of Chibiabos;
Thus the wedding banquet ended,
And the wedding guests departed,
Leaving Hiawatha happy
With the night and Minnehaha.

XIII
Blessing the Cornfields

Sing, O Song of Hiawatha,
Of the happy days that followed,
In the land of the Ojibways,
In the pleasant land and peaceful!
Sing the mysteries of Mondamin,
Sing the Blessing of the Cornfields!
  Buried was the bloody hatchet,
Buried was the dreadful war-club,
Buried were all warlike weapons,

And the war-cry was forgotten.
There was peace among the nations;
Unmolested roved the hunters,
Built the birch canoe for sailing,
Caught the fish in lake and river,
Shot the deer and trapped the beaver;
Unmolested worked the women,
Made their sugar from the maple,
Gathered wild rice in the meadows,
Dressed the skins of deer and beaver.
   All around the happy village
Stood the maize-fields, green and shining,
Waved the green plumes of Mondamin,
Waved his soft and sunny tresses,
Filling all the land with plenty.
'T was the women who in Spring-time
Planted the broad fields and fruitful,
Buried in the earth Mondamin;
'T was the women who in Autumn
Stripped the yellow husks of harvest,
Stripped the garments from Mondamin,
Even as Hiawatha taught them.
   Once, when all the maize was planted,
Hiawatha, wise and thoughtful,
Spake and said to Minnehaha,
To his wife, the Laughing Water:
"You shall bless to-night the cornfields,
Draw a magic circle round them,
To protect them from destruction,
Blast of mildew, blight of insect,
Wagemin, the thief of cornfields,
Paimosaid, who steals the maize-ear!

"In the night, when all is silence,
In the night, when all is darkness,
When the Spirit of Sleep, Nepahwin,
Shuts the doors of all the wigwams,
So that not an ear can hear you,
So that not an eye can see you,
Rise up from your bed in silence,
Lay aside your garments wholly,
Walk around the fields you planted,
Round the borders of the cornfields,
Covered by your tresses only,
Robed with darkness as a garment.
   "Thus the fields shall be more fruitful,
And the passing of your footsteps
Draw a magic circle round them,
So that neither blight nor mildew,
Neither burrowing worm nor insect,
Shall pass o'er the magic circle;
Not the dragon-fly, Kwo-ne-she,
Nor the spider, Subbekashe,
Nor the grasshopper, Pah-puk-keena,
Nor the mighty caterpillar,
Way-muk-kwana, with the bear-skin,
King of all the caterpillars!"
   On the tree-tops near the cornfields
Sat the hungry crows and ravens,
Kahgahgee, the King of Ravens,
With his band of black marauders.
And they laughed at Hiawatha,
Till the tree-tops shook with laughter,
With their melancholy laughter,
At the words of Hiawatha.

"Hear him!" said they; "hear the Wise Man,
Hear the plots of Hiawatha!"
　　When the noiseless night descended
Broad and dark o'er field and forest,
When the mournful Wawonaissa,
Sorrowing sang among the hemlocks,
And the Spirit of Sleep, Nepahwin,
Shut the doors of all the wigwams,
From her bed rose Laughing Water,
Laid aside her garments wholly,
And with darkness clothed and guarded,
Unashamed and unaffrighted,
Walked securely round the cornfields,
Drew the sacred, magic circle
Of her footprints round the cornfields.
　　No one but the Midnight only
Saw her beauty in the darkness,
No one but the Wawonaissa
Heard the panting of her bosom;
Guskewau, the darkness, wrapped her
Closely in his sacred mantle,
So that none might see her beauty,
So that none might boast, "I saw her!"
　　On the morrow, as the day dawned,
Kahgahgee, the King of Ravens,
Gathered all his black marauders,
Crows and blackbirds, jays and ravens,
Clamorous on the dusky tree-tops,
And descended, fast and fearless,
On the fields of Hiawatha,
On the grave of the Mondamin.
　　"We will drag Mondamin," said they,

"From the grave where he is buried,
Spite of all the magic circles
Laughing Water draws around it,
Spite of all the sacred footprints
Minnehaha stamps upon it!"
　But the wary Hiawatha,
Ever thoughtful, careful, watchful,
Had o'erheard the scornful laughter
When they mocked him from the tree-tops.
"Kaw!" he said, "my friends the ravens!
Kahgahgee, my King of Ravens!
I will teach you all a lesson
That shall not be soon forgotten!"
　He had risen before the daybreak,
He had spread o'er all the cornfields
Snares to catch the black marauders,
And was lying now in ambush
In the neighboring grove of pine-trees,
Waiting for the crows and blackbirds,
Waiting for the jays and ravens.
　Soon they came with caw and clamor,
Rush of wings and cry of voices,
To their work of devastation,
Settling down upon the cornfields,
Delving deep with beak and talon,
For the body of Mondamin.
And with all their craft and cunning,
All their skill in wiles of warfare,
They perceived no danger near them,
Till their claws became entangled,
Till they found themselves imprisoned
In the snares of Hiawatha.

From his place of ambush came he,
Striding terrible among them,
And so awful was his aspect
That the bravest quailed with terror.
Without mercy he destroyed them
Right and left, by tens and twenties,
And their wretched, lifeless bodies
Hung aloft on poles for scarecrows
Round the consecrated cornfields,
As a signal of his vengeance,
As a warning to marauders.

Only Kahgahgee, the leader,
Kahgahgee, the King of Ravens,
He alone was spared among them
As a hostage for his people.
With his prisoner-string he bound him,
Led him captive to his wigwam,
Tied him fast with cords of elm-bark
To the ridge-pole of his wigwam.

"Kahgahgee, my raven!" said he,
"You the leader of the robbers,
You the plotter of this mischief,
The contriver of this outrage,
I will keep you, I will hold you,
As a hostage for your people,
As a pledge of good behavior!"

And he left him, grim and sulky,
Sitting in the morning sunshine
On the summit of the wigwam,
Croaking fiercely his displeasure,
Flapping his great sable pinions,
Vainly struggling for his freedom,

Vainly calling on his people!
　Summer passed, and Shawondasee
Breathed his sighs o'er all the landscape,
From the South-land sent his ardors,
Wafted kisses warm and tender;
And the maize-field grew and ripened,
Till it stood in all the splendor
Of its garments green and yellow,
Of its tassels and its plumage,
And the maize-ears full and shining
Gleamed from bursting sheaths of verdure.
　Then Nokomis, the old woman,
Spake, and said to Minnehaha:
" 'T is the Moon when leaves are falling;
All the wild rice has been gathered,
And the maize is ripe and ready;
Let us gather in the harvest,
Let us wrestle with Mondamin,
Strip him of his plumes and tassels,
Of his garments green and yellow!"
　And the merry Laughing Water
Went rejoicing from the Wigwam,
With Nokomis, old and wrinkled,
And they called the women round them,
Called the young men and the maidens,
To the harvest of the cornfields,
To the husking of the maize-ear.
　On the border of the forest,
Underneath the fragrant pine-trees,
Sat the old men and the warriors
Smoking in the pleasant shadow.
In uninterrupted silence

Looked they at the gamesome labor
Of the young men and the women;
Listened to their noisy talking,
To their laughter and their singing,
Heard them chattering like the magpies,
Heard them laughing like the blue-jays,
Heard them singing like the robins.
    And whene'er some lucky maiden
Found a red ear in the husking,
Found a maize-ear red as blood is,
"Nushka!" cried they all together,
"Nushka! you shall have a sweetheart,
You shall have a handsome husband!"
"Ugh!" the old men all responded
From their seats beneath the pine-trees.
    And whene'er a youth or maiden
Found a crooked ear in husking,
Found a maize-ear in the husking
Blighted, mildewed, or misshapen,
Then they laughed and sang together,
Crept and limped about the cornfields,
Mimicked in their gait and gestures
Some old man, bent almost double,
Singing singly or together:
"Wagemin, the thief of cornfields!
Paimosaid, who steals the maize-ear!"
    Till the cornfields rang with laughter,
Till from Hiawatha's wigwam
Kahgahgee, the King of Ravens,
Screamed and quivered in his anger,
And from all the neighboring tree-tops
Cawed and croaked the black marauders.

"Ugh!" the old men all responded,
From their seats beneath the pine-trees!

XIV
Picture-Writing

In those days said Hiawatha,
"Lo! how all things fade and perish!
From the memory of the old men
Pass away the great traditions,
The achievements of the warriors,
The adventures of the hunters,
All the wisdom of the Medas,
All the craft of the Wabenos,
All the marvellous dreams and visions
Of the Jossakeeds, the Prophets!
  "Great men die and are forgotten,
Wise men speak; their words of wisdom
Perish in the ears that hear them,
Do not reach the generations
That, as yet unborn, are waiting
In the great, mysterious darkness
Of the speechless days that shall be!
  "On the grave-posts of our fathers
Are no signs, no figures painted;
Who are in those graves we know not,
Only know they are our fathers.
Of what kith they are and kindred,
From what old, ancestral Totem,
Be it Eagle, Bear, or Beaver,
They descended, this we know not,
Only know they are our fathers.

"Face to face we speak together,
But we cannot speak when absent,
Cannot send our voices from us
To the friends that dwell afar off;
Cannot send a secret message,
But the bearer learns our secret,
May pervert it, may betray it,
May reveal it unto others."
    Thus said Hiawatha, walking
In the solitary forest,
Pondering, musing in the forest,
On the welfare of his people.
    From his pouch he took his colors,
Took his paints of different colors,
On the smooth bark of a birch-tree
Painted many shapes and figures,
Wonderful and mystic figures,
And each figure had a meaning,
Each some word or thought suggested.
    Gitche Manito the Mighty,
He, the Master of Life, was painted
As an egg, with points projecting
To the four winds of the heavens.
Everywhere is the Great Spirit,
Was the meaning of this symbol.
    Mitche Manito the Mighty,
He the dreadful Spirit of Evil,
As a serpent was depicted,
As Kenabeek, the great serpent.
Very crafty, very cunning,
Is the creeping Spirit of Evil,
Was the meaning of this symbol.

Life and Death he drew as circles,
Life was white, but Death was darkened;
Sun and moon and stars he painted,
Man and beast, and fish and reptile,
Forests, mountains, lakes, and rivers.

For the earth he drew a straight line,
For the sky a bow above it;
White the space between for daytime,
Filled with little stars for night-time;
On the left a point for sunrise,
On the right a point for sunset,
On the top a point for noontide,
And for rain and cloudy weather
Waving lines descending from it.

Footprints pointing towards a wigwam
Were a sign of invitation,
Were a sign of guests assembling;
Bloody hands with palms uplifted
Were a symbol of destruction,
Were a hostile sign and symbol.

All these things did Hiawatha
Show unto his wondering people,
And interpreted their meaning,
And he said: "Behold, your grave-posts
Have no mark, no sign, nor symbol.
Go and paint them all with figures;
Each one with its household symbol,
With its own ancestral Totem;
So that those who follow after
May distinguish them and know them."

And they painted on the grave-posts
On the graves yet unforgotten,

Each his own ancestral Totem,
Each the symbol of his household;
Figures of the Bear and Reindeer,
Of the Turtle, Crane, and Beaver,
Each inverted as a token
That the owner was departed,
That the chief who bore the symbol
Lay beneath in dust and ashes.
  And the Jossakeeds, the Prophets,
The Wabenos, the Magicians,
And the Medicine-men, the Medas,
Painted upon bark and deer-skin
Figures for the songs they chanted,
For each song a separate symbol,
Figures mystical and awful,
Figures strange and brightly colored;
And each figure had its meaning,
Each some magic song suggested.
  The Great Spirit, the Creator,
Flashing light through all the heaven;
The Great Serpent, the Kenabeek,
With his bloody crest erected,
Creeping, looking into heaven;
In the sky the sun, that listens,
And the moon eclipsed and dying;
Owl and eagle, crane and hen-hawk,
And the cormorant, bird of magic;
Headless men, that walk the heavens,
Bodies lying pierced with arrows,
Bloody hands of death uplifted,
Flags on graves, and great war-captains
Grasping both the earth and heaven!

Such as these the shapes they painted
On the birch-bark and the deer-skin;
Songs of war and songs of hunting,
Songs of medicine and of magic,
All were written in these figures,
For each figure had its meaning,
Each its separate song recorded.

Nor forgotten was the Love-Song,
The most subtle of all medicines,
The most potent spell of magic,
Dangerous more than war or hunting!
Thus the Love-Song was recorded,
Symbol and interpretation.

First a human figure standing,
Painted in the brightest scarlet;
'T is the lover, the musician,
And the meaning is, "My painting
Makes me powerful over others."

Then the figure seated, singing,
Playing on a drum of magic,
And the interpretation, "Listen!
'T is my voice you hear, my singing!"

Then the same red figure seated
In the shelter of a wigwam,
And the meaning of the symbol,
"I will come and sit beside you
In the mystery of my passion!"

Then two figures, man and woman,
Standing hand in hand together
With their hands so clasped together
That they seemed in one united,
And the words thus represented

Are, "I see your heart within you,
And your cheeks are red with blushes!"
  Next the maiden on an island,
In the centre of an island;
And the song this shape suggested
Was, "Though you were at a distance,
Were upon some far-off island,
Such the spell I cast upon you,
Such the magic power of passion,
I could straightway draw you to me!"
  Then the figure of the maiden
Sleeping, and the lover near her,
Whispering to her in her slumbers,
Saying, "Though you were far from me
In the land of Sleep and Silence,
Still the voice of love would reach you!"
  And the last of all the figures
Was a heart within a circle,
Drawn within a magic circle;
And the image had this meaning:
"Naked lies your heart before me,
To your naked heart I whisper!"
  Thus it was that Hiawatha,
In his wisdom, taught the people
All the mysteries of painting,
All the art of Picture-Writing,
On the smooth bark of the birch-tree,
On the white skin of the reindeer,
On the grave-posts of the village.

XV
Hiawatha's Lamentation

In those days the Evil Spirits,
All the Manitos of mischief,
Fearing Hiawatha's wisdom,
And his love for Chibiabos,
Jealous of their faithful friendship,
And their noble words and actions,
Made at length a league against them,
To molest them and destroy them.
   Hiawatha, wise and wary,
Often said to Chibiabos,
"O my brother! do not leave me,
Lest the Evil Spirits harm you!"
Chibiabos, young and heedless,
Laughing shook his coal-black tresses,
Answered ever sweet and childlike,
"Do not fear for me, O brother!
Harm and evil come not near me!"
   Once when Peboan, the Winter,
Roofed with ice the Big-Sea-Water,
When the snow-flakes, whirling downward,
Hissed among the withered oak-leaves,
Changed the pine-trees into wigwams,
Covered all the earth with silence, —
Armed with arrows, shod with snow-shoes,
Heeding not his brother's warning,
Fearing not the Evil Spirits,
Forth to hunt the deer with antlers
All alone went Chibiabos.
Right across the Big-Sea-Water

Sprang with speed the deer before him.
With the wind and snow he followed,
O'er the treacherous ice he followed,
Wild with all the fierce commotion
And the rapture of the hunting.

But beneath, the Evil Spirits
Lay in ambush, waiting for him,
Broke the treacherous ice beneath him,
Dragged him downward to the bottom,
Buried in the sand his body.
Unktahee, the god of water,
He the god of the Dacotahs,
Drowned him in the deep abysses
Of the lake of Gitche Gumee.

From the headlands Hiawatha
Sent forth such a wail of anguish,
Such a fearful lamentation,
That the bison paused to listen,
And the wolves howled from the prairies,
And the thunder in the distance
Starting answered "Baim-wawa!"

Then his face with black he painted,
With his robe his head he covered,
In his wigwam sat lamenting,
Seven long weeks he sat lamenting,
Uttering still this moan of sorrow: —

"He is dead, the sweet musician!
He the sweetest of all singers!
He has gone from us forever,
He has moved a little nearer
To the Master of all music,
To the Master of all singing!

O my brother, Chibiabos!"
    And the melancholy fir-trees
Waved their dark green fans above him,
Waved their purple cones above him,
Sighing with him to console him,
Mingling with his lamentation
Their complaining, their lamenting.
    Came the Spring, and all the forest
Looked in vain for Chibiabos;
Sighed the rivulet, Sebowisha,
Sighed the rushes in the meadow.
    From the tree-tops sang the bluebird,
Sang the bluebird, the Owaissa,
"Chibiabos! Chibiabos!
He is dead, the sweet musician!"
    From the wigwam sang the robin,
Sang the robin, the Opechee,
"Chibiabos! Chibiabos!
He is dead, the sweetest singer!"
    And at night through all the forest
Went the whippoorwill complaining,
Wailing went the Wawonaissa,
"Chibiabos! Chibiabos!
He is dead, the sweet musician!
He the sweetest of all singers!"
    Then the medicine-men, the Medas,
The magicians, the Wabenos,
And the Jossakeeds, the Prophets,
Came to visit Hiawatha;
Built a Sacred Lodge beside him,
To appease him, to console him,
Walked in silent, grave procession,

Bearing each a pouch of healing,
Skin of beaver, lynx, or otter,
Filled with magic roots and simples,
Filled with very potent medicines.
　When he heard their steps approaching,
Hiawatha ceased lamenting,
Called no more on Chibiabos;
Naught he questioned, naught he answered,
But his mournful head uncovered,
From his face the mourning colors
Washed he slowly and in silence,
Slowly and in silence followed
Onward to the Sacred Wigwam.
　There a magic drink they gave him,
Made of Nahma-wusk, the spearmint,
And Wabeno-wusk, the yarrow,
Roots of power, and herbs of healing;
Beat their drums, and shook their rattles;
Chanted singly and in chorus,
Mystic songs like these, they chanted.
　"I myself, myself! behold me!
'T is the great Gray Eagle talking;
Come, ye white crows, come and hear him!
The loud-speaking thunder helps me;
All the unseen spirits help me;
I can hear their voices calling,
All around the sky I hear them!
I can blow you strong, my brother,
I can heal you, Hiawatha!"
　"Hi-au-ha!" replied the chorus,
"Way-ha-way!" the mystic chorus.
　"Friends of mine are all the serpents!

Hear me shake my skin of hen-hawk!
Mahng, the white loon, I can kill him;
I can shoot your heart and kill it!
I can blow you strong, my brother,
I can heal you, Hiawatha!"
  "Hi-au-ha!" replied the chorus.
"Way-ha-way!" the mystic chorus.
  "I myself, myself! the prophet!
When I speak the wigwam trembles,
Shakes the Sacred Lodge with terror,
Hands unseen begin to shake it!
When I walk, the sky I tread on
Bends and makes a noise beneath me!
I can blow you strong, my brother!
Rise and speak, O Hiawatha!"
  "Hi-au-ha!" replied the chorus,
"Way-ha-way!" the mystic chorus.
  Then they shook their medicine-pouches
O'er the head of Hiawatha,
Danced their medicine-dance around him;
And upstarting wild and haggard,
Like a man from dreams awakened,
He was healed of all his madness.
As the clouds are swept from heaven,
Straightway from his brain departed
All his moody melancholy;
As the ice is swept from rivers,
Straightway from his heart departed
All his sorrow and affliction.
  Then they summoned Chibiabos
From his grave beneath the waters,
From the sands of Gitche Gumee

Summoned Hiawatha's brother.
And so mighty was the magic
Of that cry and invocation,
That he heard it as he lay there
Underneath the Big-Sea-Water;
From the sand he rose and listened,
Heard the music and the singing,
Came, obedient to the summons,
To the doorway of the wigwam,
But to enter they forbade him.
   Through a chink a coal they gave him,
Through the door a burning fire-brand;
Ruler in the Land of Spirits,
Ruler o'er the dead, they made him,
Telling him a fire to kindle
For all those that died thereafter,
Camp-fires for their night encampments
On their solitary journey
To the kingdom of Ponemah,
To the land of the Hereafter.
   From the village of his childhood,
From the homes of those who knew him,
Passing silent through the forest,
Like a smoke-wreath wafted sideways,
Slowly vanished Chibiabos!
Where he passed, the branches moved not,
Where he trod, the grasses bent not,
And the fallen leaves of last year
Made no sound beneath his footsteps.
   Four whole days he journeyed onward
Down the pathway of the dead men;
On the dead-man's strawberry feasted,

Crossed the melancholy river,
On the swinging log he crossed it,
Came unto the Lake of Silver,
In the Stone Canoe was carried
To the Islands of the Blessed,
To the land of ghosts and shadows.
  On that journey, moving slowly,
Many weary spirits saw he,
Panting under heavy burdens,
Laden with war-clubs, bows and arrows,
Robes of fur, and pots and kettles,
And with food that friends had given
For that solitary journey.
  "Ay! why do the living," said they,
"Lay such heavy burdens on us!
Better were it to go naked,
Better were it to go fasting,
Than to bear such heavy burdens
On our long and weary journey!"
  Forth then issued Hiawatha,
Wandered eastward, wandered westward,
Teaching men the use of simples
And the antidotes for poisons,
And the cure of all diseases.
Thus was first made known to mortals
All the mystery of Medamin,
All the sacred art of healing.

XVI
Pau-Puk-Keewis

You shall hear how Pau-Puk-Keewis

He, the handsome Yenadizze,
Whom the people called the Storm-Fool,
Vexed the village with disturbance;
You shall hear of all his mischief,
And his flight from Hiawatha,
And his wondrous transmigrations,
And the end of his adventures.
　　On the shores of Gitche Gumee,
On the dunes of Nagow Wudjoo,
By the shining Big-Sea-Water
Stood the lodge of Pau-Puk-Keewis.
It was he who in his frenzy
Whirled these drifting sands together,
On the dunes of Nagow Wudjoo,
When, among the guests assembled,
He so merrily and madly
Danced at Hiawatha's wedding,
Danced the Beggar's Dance to please them.
　　Now, in search of new adventures,
From his lodge went Pau-Puk-Keewis,
Came with speed into the village,
Found the young men all assembled
In the lodge of old Iagoo,
Listening to his monstrous stories,
To his wonderful adventures.
　　He was telling them the story
Of Ojeeg, the Summer-Maker,
How he made a hole in heaven,
How he climbed up into heaven,
And let out the summer-weather,
The perpetual, pleasant Summer;
How the Otter first essayed it;

How the Beaver, Lynx, and Badger
Tried in turn the great achievement,
From the summit of the mountain
Smote their fists against the heavens,
Smote against the sky their foreheads,
Cracked the sky, but could not break it;
How the Wolverine, uprising,
Made him ready for the encounter,
Bent his knees down, like a squirrel,
Drew his arms back, like a cricket.

"Once he leaped," said old Iagoo,
"Once he leaped, and lo! above him
Bent the sky, as ice in rivers
When the waters rise beneath it;
Twice he leaped, and lo! above him
Cracked the sky, as ice in rivers
When the freshet is at highest!
Thrice he leaped, and lo! above him
Broke the shattered sky asunder,
And he disappeared within it,
And Ojeeg, the Fisher Weasel,
With a bound went in behind him!"

"Hark you!" shouted Pau-Puk-Keewis
As he entered at the doorway;
"I am tired of all this talking,
Tired of old Iagoo's stories,
Tired of Hiawatha's wisdom.
Here is something to amuse you,
Better than this endless talking."

Then from out his pouch of wolf-skin
Forth he drew, with solemn manner,
All the game of Bowl and Counters,

Pugasaing, with thirteen pieces.
White on one side were they painted,
And vermilion on the other;
Two Kenabeeks or great serpents,
Two Ininewug or wedge-men,
One great war-club, Pugamaugun,
And one slender fish, the Keego,
Four round pieces, Ozawabeeks,
And three Sheshebwug or ducklings.
All were made of bone and painted,
All except the Ozawabeeks;
These were brass, on one side burnished,
And were black upon the other.

    In a wooden bowl he placed them,
Shook and jostled them together,
Threw them on the ground before him.
Thus exclaiming and explaining:
"Red side up are all the pieces,
And one great Kenabeek standing
On the bright side of a brass piece,
On a burnished Ozawabeek;
Thirteen tens and eight are counted."

    Then again he shook the pieces,
Shook and jostled them together,
Threw them on the ground before him,
Still exclaiming and explaining:
"White are both the great Kenabeeks,
White the Ininewug, the wedge-men,
Red are all the other pieces;
Five tens and an eight are counted."

    Thus he taught the game of hazard,
Thus displayed it and explained it,

Running through its various chances,
Various changes, various meanings:
Twenty curious eyes stared at him.
Full of eagerness stared at him.
  "Many games," said old Iagoo,
"Many games of skill and hazard
Have I seen in different nations,
Have I played in different countries.
He who plays with old Iagoo
Must have very nimble fingers;
Though you think yourself so skilful
I can beat you, Pau-Puk-Keewis,
I can even give you lessons
In your game of Bowl and Counters!"
  So they sat and played together,
All the old men and the young men,
Played for dresses, weapons, wampum,
Played till midnight, played till morning,
Played until the Yenadizze,
Till the cunning Pau-Puk-Keewis,
Of their treasures had despoiled them,
Of the best of all their dresses,
Shirts of deer-skin, robes of ermine,
Belts of wampum, crests of feathers,
Warlike weapons, pipes and pouches.
Twenty eyes glared wildly at him,
Like the eyes of wolves glared at him.
  Said the lucky Pau-Puk-Keewis:
"In my wigwam I am lonely,
In my wanderings and adventures
I have need of a companion,
Fain would have a Meshinauwa,

An attendant and pipe-bearer.
I will venture all these winnings,
All these garments heaped about me,
All this wampum, all these feathers,
On a single throw will venture
All against the young man yonder!"
'T was a youth of sixteen summers,
'T was a nephew of Iagoo;
Face-in-a-Mist, the people called him.

   As the fire burns in a pipe-head
Dusky red beneath the ashes,
So beneath his shaggy eyebrows
Glowed the eyes of old Iagoo.
"Ugh!" he answered very fiercely;
"Ugh!" they answered all and each one.

   Seized the wooden bowl the old man,
Closely in his bony fingers
Clutched the fatal bowl, Onagon,
Shook it fiercely and with fury,
Made the pieces ring together
As he threw them down before him.

   Red were both the great Kenabeeks,
Red the Ininewug, the wedge-men,
Red the Sheshebwug, the ducklings,
Black the four brass Ozawabeeks,
White alone the fish, the Keego;
Only five the pieces counted!

   Then the smiling Pau-Puk-Keewis
Shook the bowl and threw the pieces;
Lightly in the air he tossed them,
And they fell about him scattered;
Dark and bright the Ozawabeeks,

Red and white the other pieces,
And upright among the others
One Ininewug was standing,
Even as crafty Pau-Puk-Keewis
Stood alone among the players,
Saying, "Five tens! mine the game is!"
　Twenty eyes glared at him fiercely,
Like the eyes of wolves glared at him,
As he turned and left the wigwam,
Followed by his Meshinauwa,
By the nephew of Iagoo,
By the tall and graceful stripling,
Bearing in his arms the winnings,
Shirts of deer-skin, robes of ermine,
Belts of wampum, pipes and weapons.
　"Carry them," said Pau-Puk-Keewis,
Pointing with his fan of feathers,
"To my wigwam far to eastward,
On the dunes of Nagow Wudjoo!"
　Hot and red with smoke and gambling
Were the eyes of Pau-Puk-Keewis
As he came forth to the freshness
Of the pleasant Summer morning.
All the birds were singing gayly,
All the streamlets flowing swiftly,
And the heart of Pau-Puk-Keewis
Sang with pleasure as the birds sing,
Beat with triumph like the streamlets,
As he wandered through the village,
In the early gray of morning,
With his fan of turkey-feathers,
With his plumes and tufts of swan's down,

Till he reached the farthest wigwam,
Reached the lodge of Hiawatha.
  Silent was it and deserted;
No one met him at the doorway,
No one came to bid him welcome;
But the birds were singing round it,
In and out and round the doorway,
Hopping, singing, fluttering, feeding,
And aloft upon the ridge-pole
Kahgahgee, the King of Ravens,
Sat with fiery eyes, and, screaming,
Flapped his wings at Pau-Puk-Keewis.
  "All are gone! the lodge is empty!"
Thus it was spake Pau-Puk-Keewis,
In his heart resolving mischief; —
"Gone is wary Hiawatha,
Gone the silly Laughing Water,
Gone Nokomis, the old woman,
And the lodge is left unguarded!"
  By the neck he seized the raven,
Whirled it round him like a rattle,
Like a medicine-pouch he shook it,
Strangled Kahgahgee, the raven,
From the ridge-pole of the wigwam
Left its lifeless body hanging,
As an insult to its master,
As a taunt to Hiawatha.
  With a stealthy step he entered,
Round the lodge in wild disorder
Threw the household things about him,
Piled together in confusion
Bowls of wood and earthen kettles,

Robes of buffalo and beaver,
Skins of otter, lynx, and ermine,
As an insult to Nokomis,
As a taunt to Minnehaha.
　　Then departed Pau-Puk-Keewis,
Whistling, singing through the forest,
Whistling gayly to the squirrels,
Who from hollow boughs above him
Dropped their acorn-shells upon him,
Singing gayly to the wood birds,
Who from out the leafy darkness
Answered with a song as merry.
　　Then he climbed the rocky headlands,
Looking o'er the Gitche Gumee,
Perched himself upon their summit,
Waiting full of mirth and mischief
The return of Hiawatha.
　　Stretched upon his back he lay there;
Far below him plashed the waters,
Plashed and washed the dreamy waters;
Far above him swam the heavens,
Swam the dizzy, dreamy heavens;
Round him hovered, fluttered, rustled,
Hiawatha's mountain chickens,
Flock-wise swept and wheeled about him,
Almost brushed him with their pinions.
　　And he killed them as he lay there,
Slaughtered them by tens and twenties,
Threw their bodies down the headland,
Threw them on the beach below him,
Till at length Kayoshk, the sea-gull,
Perched upon a crag above them,

Shouted: "It is Pau-Puk-Keewis!
He is slaying us by hundreds!
Send a message to our brother,
Tidings send to Hiawatha!"

Full of wrath was Hiawatha
When he came into the village,
Found the people in confusion,
Heard of all the misdemeanors,
All the malice and the mischief,
Of the cunning Pau-Puk-Keewis.
    Hard his breath came through his nostrils,
Through his teeth he buzzed and muttered
Words of anger and resentment,
Hot and humming, like a hornet.
"I will slay this Pau-Puk-Keewis,
Slay this mischief-maker!" said he.
"Not so long and wide the world is,
Not so rude and rough the way is,
That my wrath shall not attain him,
That my vengeance shall not reach him!"
    Then in swift pursuit departed
Hiawatha and the hunters
On the trail of Pau-Puk-Keewis,
Through the forest, where he passed it,
To the headlands where he rested;
But they found not Pau-Puk-Keewis,
Only in the trampled grasses,
In the whortleberry-bushes,

Found the couch where he had rested,
Found the impress of his body.
   From the lowlands far beneath them,
From the Muskoday, the meadow,
Pau-Puk-Keewis, turning backward,
Made a gesture of defiance,
Made a gesture of derision;
And aloud cried Hiawatha,
From the summit of the mountains:
"Not so long and wide the world is,
Not so rude and rough the way is,
But my wrath shall overtake you,
And my vengeance shall attain you!"
   Over rock and over river,
Thorough bush, and brake, and forest,
Ran the cunning Pau-Puk-Keewis;
Like an antelope he bounded,
Till he came unto a streamlet
In the middle of the forest,
To a streamlet still and tranquil,
That had overflowed its margin,
To a dam made by the beavers,
To a pond of quiet water,
Where knee-deep the trees were standing,
Where the water-lilies floated,
Where the rushes waved and whispered.
   On the dam stood Pau-Puk-Keewis,
On the dam of trunks and branches,
Through whose chinks the water spouted,
O'er whose summit flowed the streamlet.
From the bottom rose the beaver,
Looked with two great eyes of wonder,

Eyes that seemed to ask a question,
At the stranger, Pau-Puk-Keewis.
　On the dam stood Pau-Puk-Keewis,
O'er his ankles flowed the streamlet,
Flowed the bright and silvery water,
And he spake unto the beaver,
With a smile he spake in this wise:
　"O my friend Ahmeek, the beaver,
Cool and pleasant is the water;
Let me dive into the water,
Let me rest there in your lodges;
Change me, too, into a beaver!"
　Cautiously replied the beaver,
With reserve he thus made answer:
"Let me first consult the others,
Let me ask the other beavers."
Down he sank into the water,
Heavily sank he, as a stone sinks,
Down among the leaves and branches,
Brown and matted at the bottom.
　On the dam stood Pau-Puk-Keewis,
O'er his ankles flowed the streamlet,
Spouted through the chinks below him,
Dashed upon the stones beneath him,
Spread serene and calm before him,
And the sunshine and the shadows
Fell in flecks and gleams upon him,
Fell in little shining patches,
Through the waving, rustling branches.
　From the bottom rose the beavers,
Silently above the surface
Rose one head and then another,

Till the pond seemed full of beavers,
Full of black and shining faces.

To the beavers Pau-Puk-Keewis
Spake entreating, said in this wise:
"Very pleasant is your dwelling,
O my friends! and safe from danger;
Can you not with all your cunning,
All your wisdom and contrivance,
Change me, too, into a beaver?"

"Yes!" replied Ahmeek, the beaver,
He the King of all the beavers,
"Let yourself slide down among us,
Down into the tranquil water."

Down into the pond among them
Silently sank Pau-Puk-Keewis;
Black became his shirt of deer-skin,
Black his moccasins and leggings,
In a broad black tail behind him
Spread his fox-tails and his fringes;
He was changed into a beaver.

"Make me large," said Pau-Puk-Keewis,
"Make me large and make me larger,
Larger than the other beavers."
"Yes," the beaver chief responded,
"When our lodge below you enter,
In our wigwam we will make you
Ten times larger than the others."

Thus into the clear, brown water
Silently sank Pau-Puk-Keewis:
Found the bottom covered over
With the trunks of trees and branches,
Hoards of food against the winter,

Piles and heaps against the famine;
Found the lodge with arching doorway,
Leading into spacious chambers.
  Here they made him large and larger,
Made him largest of the beavers,
Ten times larger than the others.
"You shall be our ruler," said they;
"Chief and King of all the beavers."
  But not long had Pau-Puk-Keewis
Sat in state among the beavers,
When there came a voice of warning
From the watchman at his station
In the water-flags and lilies,
Saying, "Here is Hiawatha!
Hiawatha with his hunters!"
  Then they heard a cry above them,
Heard a shouting and a tramping,
Heard a crashing and a rushing,
And the water round and o'er them
Sank and sucked away in eddies,
And they knew their dam was broken.
  On the lodge's roof the hunters
Leaped, and broke it all asunder;
Streamed the sunshine through the crevice,
Sprang the beavers through the doorway,
Hid themselves in deeper water,
In the channel of the streamlet;
But the mighty Pau-Puk-Keewis
Could not pass beneath the doorway;
He was puffed with pride and feeding,
He was swollen like a bladder.
  Through the roof looked Hiawatha,

Cried aloud, "O Pau-Puk-Keewis!
Vain are all your craft and cunning,
Vain your manifold disguises!
Well I know you, Pau-Puk-Keewis!"
With their clubs they beat and bruised him,
Beat to death poor Pau-Puk-Keewis,
Pounded him as maize is pounded,
Till his skull was crushed to pieces.
   Six tall hunters, lithe and limber,
Bore him home on poles and branches,
Bore the body of the beaver;
But the ghost, the Jeebi in him,
Thought and felt as Pau-Puk-Keewis,
Still lived on as Pau-Puk-Keewis.
   And it fluttered, strove, and struggled,
Waving hither, waving thither,
As the curtains of a wigwam
Struggle with their thongs of deer-skin,
When the wintry wind is blowing;
Till it drew itself together,
Till it rose up from the body,
Till it took the form and features
Of the cunning Pau-Puk-Keewis
Vanishing into the forest.
   But the wary Hiawatha
Saw the figure ere it vanished,
Saw the form of Pau-Puk-Keewis
Glide into the soft blue shadow
Of the pine-trees of the forest;
Toward the squares of white beyond it,
Toward an opening in the forest,
Like a wind it rushed and panted,

Bending all the boughs before it,
And behind it, as the rain comes,
Came the steps of Hiawatha.
  To a lake with many islands
Came the breathless Pau-Puk-Keewis,
Where among the water-lilies
Pishnekuh, the brant, were sailing;
Through the tufts of rushes floating,
Steering through the reedy islands.
Now their broad black beaks they lifted,
Now they plunged beneath the water,
Now they darkened in the shadow,
Now they brightened in the sunshine.
  "Pishnekuh!" cried Pau-Puk-Keewis,
"Pishnekuh! my brothers!" said he,
"Change me to a brant with plumage,
With a shining neck and feathers,
Make me large, and make me larger,
Ten times larger than the others."
  Straightway to a brant they changed him,
With two huge and dusky pinions,
With a bosom smooth and rounded,
With a bill like two great paddles,
Made him larger than the others,
Ten times larger than the largest,
Just as, shouting from the forest,
On the shore stood Hiawatha.
  Up they rose with cry and clamor,
With a whir and beat of pinions,
Rose up from the reedy islands,
From the water-flags and lilies.
And they said to Pau-Puk-Keewis:

"In your flying, look not downward,
Take good heed, and look not downward,
Lest some strange mischance should happen,
Lest some great mishap befall you!"
    Fast and far they fled to northward,
Fast and far through mist and sunshine,
Fed among the moors and fen-lands,
Slept among the reeds and rushes.
    On the morrow as they journeyed,
Buoyed and lifted by the South-wind,
Wafted onward by the South-wind,
Blowing fresh and strong behind them,
Rose a sound of human voices,
Rose a clamor from beneath them,
From the lodges of a village,
From the people miles beneath them.
    For the people of the village
Saw the flock of brant with wonder,
Saw the wings of Pau-Puk-Keewis
Flapping far up in the ether,
Broader than two doorway curtains.
    Pau-Puk-Keewis heard the shouting,
Knew the voice of Hiawatha,
Knew the outcry of Iagoo,
And forgetful of the warning,
Drew his neck in, and looked downward,
And the wind that blew behind him
Caught his mighty fan of feathers,
Sent him wheeling, whirling downward!
    All in vain did Pau-Puk-Keewis
Struggle to regain his balance!
Whirling round and round and downward,

He beheld in turn the village
And in turn the flock above him,
Saw the village coming nearer,
And the flock receding farther,
Heard the voices growing louder,
Heard the shouting and the laughter;
Saw no more the flock above him,
Only saw the earth beneath him;
Dead out of the empty heaven,
Dead among the shouting people,
With a heavy sound and sullen,
Fell the brant with broken pinions.

But his soul, his ghost, his shadow,
Still survived as Pau-Puk-Keewis,
Took again the form and features
Of the handsome Yenadizze,
And again went rushing onward,
Followed fast by Hiawatha,
Crying: "Not so wide the world is,
Not so long and rough the way is,
But my wrath shall overtake you,
But my vengeance shall attain you!"

And so near he came, so near him,
That his hand was stretched to seize him,
His right hand to seize and hold him,
When the cunning Pau-Puk-Keewis
Whirled and spun about in circles,
Fanned the air into a whirlwind,
Danced the dust and leaves about him,
And amid the whirling eddies
Sprang into a hollow oak-tree,
Changed himself into a serpent,

Gliding out through root and rubbish.
  With his right hand Hiawatha
Smote amain the hollow oak-tree,
Rent it into shreds and splinters,
Left it lying there in fragments.
But in vain; for Pau-Puk-Keewis,
Once again in human figure,
Full in sight ran on before him,
Sped away in gust and whirlwind,
On the shores of Gitche Gumee,
Westward by the Big-Sea-Water,
Came unto the rocky headlands,
To the Pictured Rocks of sandstone,
Looking over lake and landscape.
  And the Old Man of the Mountain,
He the Manito of Mountains,
Opened wide his rocky doorways,
Opened wide his deep abysses,
Giving Pau-Puk-Keewis shelter
In his caverns dark and dreary,
Bidding Pau-Puk-Keewis welcome
To his gloomy lodge of sandstone.
  There without stood Hiawatha,
Found the doorways closed against him,
With his mittens, Minjekahwun,
Smote great caverns in the sandstone,
Cried aloud in tones of thunder,
"Open! I am Hiawatha!"
But the Old Man of the Mountain
Opened not, and made no answer
From the silent crags of sandstone,
From the gloomy rock abysses.

Then he raised his hands to heaven,
Called imploring on the tempest,
Called Waywassimo, the lightning,
And the thunder, Annemeekee;
And they came with night and darkness,
Sweeping down the Big-Sea-Water
From the distant Thunder Mountains;
And the trembling Pau-Puk-Keewis
Heard the footsteps of the thunder,
Saw the red eyes of the lightning,
Was afraid, and crouched and trembled.
    Then Waywassimo, the lightning,
Smote the doorways of the caverns,
With his war-club smote the doorways,
Smote the jutting crags of sandstone,
And the thunder, Annemeekee,
Shouted down into the caverns,
Saying, "Where is Pau-Puk-Keewis!"
And the crags fell, and beneath them
Dead among the rocky ruins
Lay the cunning Pau-Puk-Keewis,
Lay the handsome Yenadizze,
Slain in his own human figure.
    Ended were his wild adventures,
Ended were his tricks and gambols,
Ended all his craft and cunning,
Ended all his mischief-making,
All his gambling and his dancing,
All his wooing of the maidens.
    Then the noble Hiawatha
Took his soul, his ghost, his shadow,
Spake and said: "O Pau-Puk-Keewis,

Never more in human figure
Shall you search for new adventures;
Never more with jest and laughter
Dance the dust and leaves in whirlwinds;
But above there in the heavens
You shall soar and sail in circles;
I will change you to an eagle,
To Keneu, the great war-eagle,
Chief of all the fowls with feathers,
Chief of Hiawatha's chickens."
  And the name of Pau-Puk-Keewis
Lingers still among the people,
Lingers still among the singers,
And among the story-tellers;
And in Winter, when the snow-flakes
Whirl in eddies round the lodges,
When the wind in gusty tumult
O'er the smoke-flue pipes and whistles,
"There," they cry, "comes Pau-Puk-Keewis;
He is dancing through the village,
He is gathering in his harvest!"

XVIII
The Death of Kwasind

Far and wide among the nations
Spread the name and fame of Kwasind;
No man dared to strive with Kwasind,
No man could compete with Kwasind.
But the mischievous Puk-Wudjies,
They the envious Little People,
They the fairies and the pygmies,

Plotted and conspired against him.
  "If this hateful Kwasind," said they,
"If this great, outrageous fellow
Goes on thus a little longer,
Tearing everything he touches,
Rending everything to pieces,
Filling all the world with wonder,
What becomes of the Puk-Wudjies?
Who will care for the Puk-Wudjies?
He will tread us down like mushrooms,
Drive us all into the water,
Give our bodies to be eaten
By the wicked Nee-ba-naw-baigs,
By the Spirits of the water!"
  So the angry Little People
All conspired against the Strong Man,
All conspired to murder Kwasind,
Yes, to rid the world of Kwasind,
The audacious, overbearing,
Heartless, haughty, dangerous Kwasind!
  Now this wondrous strength of Kwasind
In his crown alone was seated;
In his crown too was his weakness;
There alone could he be wounded,
Nowhere else could weapon pierce him,
Nowhere else could weapon harm him.
  Even there the only weapon
That could wound him, that could slay him,
Was the seed-cone of the pine-tree,
Was the blue cone of the fir-tree.
This was Kwasind's fatal secret,
Known to no man among mortals;

But the cunning Little People,
The Puk-Wudjees, knew the secret,
Knew the only way to kill him.
  So they gathered cones together,
Gathered seed-cones of the pine-tree,
Gathered blue cones of the fir-tree,
In the woods by Taquamenaw,
Brought them to the river's margin,
Heaped them in great piles together,
Where the red rocks from the margin
Jutting overhang the river.
There they lay in wait for Kwasind,
The malicious Little People.
  'T was an afternoon in Summer;
Very hot and still the air was,
Very smooth the gliding river,
Motionless the sleeping shadows:
Insects glistened in the sunshine,
Insects skated on the water,
Filled the drowsy air with buzzing,
With a far resounding war-cry.
  Down the river came the Strong Man,
In his birch canoe came Kwasind,
Floating slowly down the current
Of the sluggish Taquamenaw,
Very languid with the weather,
Very sleepy with the silence.
  From the overhanging branches,
From the tassels of the birch-trees,
Soft the Spirit of Sleep descended;
By his airy hosts surrounded,
His invisible attendants,

Came the Spirit of Sleep, Nepahwin;
Like the burnished Dush-kwo-ne-she,
Like a dragon-fly, he hovered
O'er the drowsy head of Kwasind.
  To his ear there came a murmur
As of waves upon a sea-shore,
As of far-off tumbling waters,
As of winds among the pine-trees;
And he felt upon his forehead
Blows of little airy war-clubs,
Wielded by the slumbrous legions
Of the Spirit of Sleep, Nepahwin,
As of some one breathing on him.
  At the first blow of their war-clubs,
Fell a drowsiness on Kwasind;
At the second blow they smote him,
Motionless his paddle rested;
At the third, before his vision
Reeled the landscape into darkness,
Very sound asleep was Kwasind.
  So he floated down the river,
Like a blind man seated upright,
Floated down the Taquamenaw,
Underneath the trembling birch-trees,
Underneath the wooded headlands,
Underneath the war encampment
Of the pygmies, the Puk-Wudjies.
  There they stood, all armed and waiting,
Hurled the pine-cones down upon him,
Struck him on his brawny shoulders,
On his crown defenceless struck him.
"Death to Kwasind!" was the sudden

War-cry of the Little People.
    And he sideways swayed and tumbled,
Sideways fell into the river,
Plunged beneath the sluggish water
Headlong, as an otter plunges;
And the birch canoe, abandoned,
Drifted empty down the river,
Bottom upward swerved and drifted:
Nothing more was seen of Kwasind.
    But the memory of the Strong Man
Lingered long among the people,
And whenever through the forest
Raged and roared the wintry tempest,
And the branches, tossed and troubled,
Creaked and groaned and split asunder,
"Kwasind!" cried they; "that is Kwasind!
He is gathering in his fire-wood!"

XIX
The Ghosts

Never stoops the soaring vulture
On his quarry in the desert,
On the sick or wounded bison,
But another vulture, watching
From his high aerial look-out,
Sees the downward plunge, and follows;
And a third pursues the second,
Coming from the invisible ether,
First a speck, and then a vulture,
Till the air is dark with pinions.
    So disasters come not singly;

But as if they watched and waited,
Scanning one another's motions,
When the first descends, the others
Follow, follow, gathering flock-wise
Round their victim, sick and wounded,
First a shadow, then a sorrow,
Till the air is dark with anguish.

Now, o'er all the dreary North-land,
Mighty Peboan, the Winter,
Breathing on the lakes and rivers,
Into stone had changed their waters.
From his hair he shook the snow-flakes,
Till the plains were strewn with whiteness,
One uninterrupted level,
As if, stooping, the Creator
With his hand had smoothed them over.

Through the forest, wide and wailing,
Roamed the hunter on his snow-shoes;
In the village worked the women,
Pounded maize, or dressed the deer-skin;
And the young men played together
On the ice the noisy ball-play,
On the plain the dance of snow-shoes.

One dark evening, after sundown,
In her wigwam Laughing Water
Sat with old Nokomis, waiting
For the steps of Hiawatha
Homeward from the hunt returning.

On their faces gleamed the fire-light,
Painting them with streaks of crimson,
In the eyes of old Nokomis
Glimmered like the watery moonlight,

In the eyes of Laughing Water
Glistened like the sun in water;
And behind them crouched their shadows
In the corners of the wigwam,
And the smoke in wreaths above them
Climbed and crowded through the smoke-
    flue.
    Then the curtain of the doorway
From without was slowly lifted;
Brighter glowed the fire a moment,
And a moment swerved the smoke-wreath,
As two women entered softly,
Passed the doorway uninvited,
Without word of salutation,
Without sign of recognition,
Sat down in the farthest corner,
Crouching low among the shadows.
    From their aspect and their garments,
Strangers seemed they in the village;
Very pale and haggard were they,
As they sat there sad and silent,
Trembling, cowering with the shadows.
    Was it the wind above the smoke-flue,
Muttering down into the wigwam?
Was it the owl, the Koko-koho,
Hooting from the dismal forest?
Sure a voice said in the silence:
"These are corpses clad in garments,
These are ghosts that come to haunt you,
From the kingdom of Ponemah,
From the land of the Hereafter!"
    Homeward now came Hiawatha

From his hunting in the forest,
With the snow upon his tresses,
And the red deer on his shoulders.
At the feet of Laughing Water
Down he threw his lifeless burden;
Nobler, handsomer she thought him,
Than when first he came to woo her,
First threw down the deer before her,
As a token of his wishes,
As a promise of the future.

Then he turned and saw the strangers,
Cowering, crouching with the shadows;
Said within himself, "Who are they?
What strange guests has Minnehaha?"
But he questioned not the strangers,
Only spake to bid them welcome
To his lodge, his food, his fireside.

When the evening meal was ready,
And the deer had been divided,
Both the pallid guests, the strangers,
Springing from among the shadows,
Seized upon the choicest portions,
Seized the white fat of the roebuck,
Set apart for Laughing Water,
For the wife of Hiawatha;
Without asking, without thanking,
Eagerly devoured the morsels,
Flitted back among the shadows
In the corner of the wigwam.

Not a word spake Hiawatha,
Not a motion made Nokomis,
Not a gesture Laughing Water;

Not a change came o'er their features;
Only Minnehaha softly
Whispered, saying, "They are famished;
Let them do what best delights them;
Let them eat, for they are famished."
   Many a daylight dawned and darkened,
Many a night shook off the daylight
As the pine shakes off the snow-flakes
From the midnight of its branches;
Day by day the guests unmoving
Sat there silent in the wigwam;
But by night, in storm or starlight,
Forth they went into the forest,
Bringing fire-wood to the wigwam,
Bringing pine-cones for the burning,
Always sad and always silent.
   And whenever Hiawatha
Came from fishing or from hunting,
When the evening meal was ready,
And the food had been divided,
Gliding from their darksome corner,
Came the pallid guests, the strangers,
Seized upon the choicest portions
Set aside for Laughing Water,
And without rebuke or question
Flitted back among the shadows.
   Never once had Hiawatha
By a word or look reproved them;
Never once had old Nokomis
Made a gesture of impatience;
Never once had Laughing Water
Shown resentment at the outrage.

All had they endured in silence,
That the rights of guest and stranger,
That the virtue of free-giving,
By a look might not be lessened,
By a word might not be broken.

Once at midnight Hiawatha,
Ever wakeful, ever watchful,
In the wigwam, dimly lighted
By the brands that still were burning,
By the glimmering, flickering fire-light,
Heard a sighing, oft repeated,
Heard a sobbing, as of sorrow.

From his couch rose Hiawatha,
From his shaggy hides of bison,
Pushed aside the deer-skin curtain,
Saw the pallid guests, the shadows,
Sitting upright on their couches,
Weeping in the silent midnight.

And he said: "O guests! why is it
That your hearts are so afflicted,
That you sob so in the midnight?
Has perchance the old Nokomis,
Has my wife, my Minnehaha,
Wronged or grieved you by unkindness,
Failed in hospitable duties?"

Then the shadows ceased from weeping,
Ceased from sobbing and lamenting,
And they said, with gentle voices:
"We are ghosts of the departed,
Souls of those who once were with you.
From the realms of Chibiabos
Hither have we come to try you,

Hither have we come to warn you.
  "Cries of grief and lamentation
Reach us in the Blessed Islands;
Cries of anguish from the living,
Calling back their friends departed,
Sadden us with useless sorrow.
Therefore have we come to try you;
No one knows us, no one heeds us.
We are but a burden to you,
And we see that the departed
Have no place among the living.
  "Think of this, O Hiawatha!
Speak of it to all the people,
That henceforward and forever
They no more with lamentations
Sadden the souls of the departed
In the Islands of the Blessed.
  "Do not lay such heavy burdens
In the graves of those you bury,
Not such weight of furs and wampum,
Not such weight of pots and kettles,
For the spirits faint beneath them.
Only give them food to carry,
Only give them fire to light them.
  "Four days is the spirit's journey
To the land of ghosts and shadows,
Four its lonely night encampments;
Four times must their fires be lighted.
Therefore, when the dead are buried,
Let a fire, as night approaches,
Four times on the grave be kindled,
That the soul upon its journey

May not lack the cheerful fire-light,
May not grope about in darkness.
 "Farewell, noble Hiawatha!
We have put you to the trial,
To the proof have put your patience,
By the insult of our presence,
By the outrage of our actions.
We have found you great and noble.
Fail not in the greater trial,
Faint not in the harder struggle."
 When they ceased, a sudden darkness
Fell and filled the silent wigwam.
Hiawatha heard a rustle
As of garments trailing by him,
Heard the curtain of the doorway
Lifted by a hand he saw not,
Felt the cold breath of the night air,
For a moment saw the star-light;
But he saw the ghosts no longer,
Saw no more the wandering spirits
From the kingdom of Ponemah,
From the land of the Hereafter.

XX
The Famine

Oh, the long and dreary Winter!
Oh, the cold and cruel Winter!
Ever thicker, thicker, thicker
Froze the ice on lake and river,
Ever deeper, deeper, deeper
Fell the snow o'er all the landscape,

Fell the covering snow, and drifted
Through the forest, round the village.
 Hardly from his buried wigwam
Could the hunter force a passage;
With his mittens and his snow-shoes
Vainly walked he through the forest,
Sought for bird or beast and found none,
Saw no track of deer or rabbit,
In the snow beheld no footprints,
In the ghastly, gleaming forest
Fell, and could not rise from weakness,
Perished there from cold and hunger.
 Oh the famine and the fever!
Oh the wasting of the famine!
Oh the blasting of the fever!
Oh the wailing of the children!
Oh the anguish of the women!
 All the earth was sick and famished;
Hungry was the air around them,
Hungry was the sky above them,
And the hungry stars in heaven
Like the eyes of wolves glared at them!
 Into Hiawatha's wigwam
Came two other guests, as silent
As the ghosts were, and as gloomy,
Waited not to be invited,
Did not parley at the doorway,
Sat there without word of welcome
In the seat of Laughing Water;
Looked with haggard eyes and hollow
At the face of Laughing Water.
 And the foremost said: "Behold me!

I am Famine, Bukadawin!"
And the other said: "Behold me!
I am Fever, Ahkosewin!"
   And the lovely Minnehaha
Shuddered as they looked upon her,
Shuddered at the words they uttered,
Lay down on her bed in silence,
Hid her face, but made no answer;
Lay there trembling, freezing, burning
At the looks they cast upon her,
At the fearful words they uttered.
   Forth into the empty forest
Rushed the maddened Hiawatha;
In his heart was deadly sorrow,
In his face a stony firmness;
On his brow the sweat of anguish
Started, but it froze and fell not.
   Wrapped in furs and armed for hunting,
With his mighty bow of ash-tree,
With his quiver full of arrows,
With his mittens, Minjekahwun,
Into the vast and vacant forest
On his snow-shoes strode he forward.
   "Gitche Manito, the Mighty!"
Cried he with his face uplifted
In that bitter hour of anguish,
"Give your children food, O father!
Give us food, or we must perish!
Give me food for Minnehaha,
For my dying Minnehaha!"
   Through the far-resounding forest,
Through the forest vast and vacant

Rang that cry of desolation,
But there came no other answer
Than the echo of his crying,
Than the echo of the woodlands,
"Minnehaha! Minnehaha!"
　　All day long roved Hiawatha
In that melancholy forest,
Through the shadow of whose thickets,
In the pleasant days of Summer,
Of that ne'er forgotten Summer,
He had brought his young wife homeward
From the land of the Dacotahs;
When the birds sang in the thickets,
And the streamlets laughed and glistened,
And the air was full of fragrance,
And the lovely Laughing Water
Said with voice that did not tremble,
"I will follow you, my husband!"
　　In the wigwam with Nokomis,
With those gloomy guests, that watched her,
With the Famine and the Fever,
She was lying, the Beloved,
She the dying Minnehaha.
　　"Hark!" she said; "I hear a rushing,
Hear a roaring and a rushing,
Hear the Falls of Minnehaha
Calling to me from a distance!"
"No, my child!" said old Nokomis,
" 'T is the night-wind in the pine-trees!"
　　"Look!" she said; "I see my father
Standing lonely at his doorway,
Beckoning to me from his wigwam

In the land of the Dacotahs!"
"No, my child!" said old Nokomis,
" 'T is the smoke, that waves and beckons!"
   "Ah!" said she, "the eyes of Pauguk
Glare upon me in the darkness,
I can feel his icy fingers
Clasping mine amid the darkness!
Hiawatha! Hiawatha!"
   And the desolate Hiawatha,
Far away amid the forest,
Miles away among the mountains,
Heard that sudden cry of anguish,
Heard the voice of Minnehaha
Calling to him in the darkness,
"Hiawatha! Hiawatha!"
   Over snow-fields waste and pathless,
Under snow-encumbered branches,
Homeward hurried Hiawatha,
Empty-handed, heavy-hearted,
Heard Nokomis moaning, wailing:
"Wahonowin! Wahonowin!
Would that I had perished for you,
Would that I were dead as you are!
Wahonowin! Wahonowin!"
   And he rushed into the wigwam,
Saw the old Nokomis slowly
Rocking to and fro and moaning,
Saw his lovely Minnehaha
Lying dead and cold before him,
And his bursting heart within him
Uttered such a cry of anguish,
That the forest moaned and shuddered,

That the very stars in heaven
Shook and trembled with his anguish.
  Then he sat down, still and speechless,
On the bed of Minnehaha,
At the feet of Laughing Water,
At those willing feet, that never
More would lightly run to meet him,
Never more would lightly follow.
  With both hands his face he covered,
Seven long days and nights he sat there,
As if in a swoon he sat there,
Speechless, motionless, unconscious
Of the daylight or the darkness.
  Then they buried Minnehaha;
In the snow a grave they made her,
In the forest deep and darksome,
Underneath the moaning hemlocks;
Clothed her in her richest garments,
Wrapped her in her robes of ermine,
Covered her with snow, like ermine;
Thus they buried Minnehaha.
  And at night a fire was lighted,
On her grave four times was kindled,
For her soul upon its journey
To the Islands of the Blessed.
From his doorway Hiawatha
Saw it burning in the forest,
Lighting up the gloomy hemlocks;
From his sleepless bed uprising,
From the bed of Minnehaha,
Stood and watched it at the doorway,
That it might not be extinguished,

Might not leave her in the darkness.
  "Farewell!" said he, "Minnehaha!
Farewell, O my Laughing Water!
All my heart is buried with you,
All my thoughts go onward with you!
Come not back again to labor,
Come not back again to suffer,
Where the Famine and the Fever
Wear the heart and waste the body.
Soon my task will be completed,
Soon your footsteps I shall follow
To the Islands of the Blessed,
To the Kingdom of Ponemah,
To the land of the Hereafter!"

XXI
The White Man's Foot

In his lodge beside a river,
Close beside a frozen river,
Sat an old man, sad and lonely.
White his hair was as a snow-drift;
Dull and low his fire was burning,
And the old man shook and trembled,
Folded in his Waubewyon,
In his tattered white-skin-wrapper,
Hearing nothing but the tempest
As it roared along the forest,
Seeing nothing but the snow-storm,
As it whirled and hissed and drifted.
  All the coals were white with ashes,
And the fire was slowly dying,

As a young man, walking lightly,
At the open doorway entered.
Red with blood of youth his cheeks were,
Soft his eyes, as stars in Spring-time,
Bound his forehead was with grasses;
Bound and plumed with scented grasses,
On his lips a smile of beauty,
Filling all the lodge with sunshine,
In his hand a bunch of blossoms
Filling all the lodge with sweetness.

"Ah, my son!" exclaimed the old man,
"Happy are my eyes to see you.
Sit here on the mat beside me,
Sit here by the dying embers,
Let us pass the night together.
Tell me of your strange adventures,
Of the lands where you have travelled;
I will tell you of my prowess,
Of my many deeds of wonder."

From his pouch he drew his peace-pipe,
Very old and strangely fashioned;
Made of red stone was the pipe-head,
And the stem a reed with feathers;
Filled the pipe with bark of willow,
Placed a burning coal upon it,
Gave it to his guest, the stranger,
And began to speak in this wise:
"When I blow my breath about me,
When I breathe upon the landscape,
Motionless are all the rivers,
Hard as stone becomes the water!"

And the young man answered, smiling:

"When I blow my breath about me,
When I breathe upon the landscape,
Flowers spring up o'er all the meadows,
Singing, onward rush the rivers!"

  "When I shake my hoary tresses,"
Said the old man darkly frowning,
"All the land with snow is covered;
All the leaves from all the branches
Fall and fade and die and wither,
For I breathe, and lo! they are not.
From the waters and the marshes
Rise the wild goose and the heron,
Fly away to distant regions,
For I speak, and lo! they are not.
And where'er my footsteps wander,
All the wild beasts of the forest
Hide themselves in holes and caverns,
And the earth becomes as flintstone!"

  "When I shake my flowing ringlets,"
Said the young man, softly laughing,
"Showers of rain fall warm and welcome,
Plants lift up their heads rejoicing,
Back into their lakes and marshes
Come the wild goose and the heron,
Homeward shoots the arrowy swallow,
Sing the bluebird and the robin,
And where'er my footsteps wander,
All the meadows wave with blossoms,
All the woodlands ring with music,
All the trees are dark with foliage!"

  While they spake, the night departed:
From the distant realms of Wabun,

From his shining lodge of silver,
Like a warrior robed and painted,
Came the sun, and said, "Behold me!
Gheezis, the great sun, behold me!"
  Then the old man's tongue was speechless
And the air grew warm and pleasant,
And upon the wigwam sweetly
Sang the bluebird and the robin,
And the stream began to murmur,
And a scent of growing grasses
Through the lodge was gently wafted.
  And Segwun, the youthful stranger,
More distinctly in the daylight
Saw the icy face before him;
It was Peboan, the Winter!
  From his eyes the tears were flowing,
As from melting lakes the streamlets,
And his body shrunk and dwindled
As the shouting sun ascended,
Till into the air it faded,
Till into the ground it vanished,
And the young man saw before him,
On the hearth-stone of the wigwam,
Where the fire had smoked and smouldered,
Saw the earliest flower of Spring-time,
Saw the Beauty of the Spring-time,
Saw the Miskodeed in blossom.
  Thus it was that in the North-land
After that unheard-of coldness,
That intolerable Winter,
Came the Spring with all its splendor,
All its birds and all its blossoms,

All its flowers and leaves and grasses.
  Sailing on the wind to northward,
Flying in great flocks, like arrows,
Like huge arrows shot through heaven,
Passed the swan, the Mahnahbezee,
Speaking almost as a man speaks;
And in long lines waving, bending
Like a bow-string snapped asunder,
Came the white goose, Waw-be-wawa;
And in pairs, or singly flying,
Mahng the loon, with clangorous pinions,
The blue heron, the Shuh-shuh-gah,
And the grouse, the Mushkodasa.
  In the thickets and the meadows
Piped the bluebird, the Owaissa,
On the summit of the lodges
Sang the robin, the Opechee,
In the covert of the pine-trees
Cooed the pigeon, the Omemee,
And the sorrowing Hiawatha,
Speechless in his infinite sorrow,
Heard their voices calling to him,
Went forth from his gloomy doorway,
Stood and gazed into the heaven,
Gazed upon the earth and waters.
  From his wanderings far to eastward,
From the regions of the morning,
From the shining land of Wabun,
Homeward now returned Iagoo,
The great traveller, the great boaster,
Full of new and strange adventures,
Marvels many and many wonders.

And the people of the village
Listened to him as he told them
Of his marvellous adventures,
Laughing answered him in this wise:
"Ugh! it is indeed Iagoo!
No one else beholds such wonders!"
   He had seen, he said, a water
Bigger than the Big-Sea-Water,
Broader than the Gitche Gumee,
Bitter so that none could drink it!
At each other looked the warriors,
Looked the women at each other,
Smiled, and said, "It cannot be so!
Kaw!" they said, "it cannot be so!"
   O'er it, said he, o'er this water
Came a great canoe with pinions,
A canoe with wings came flying,
Bigger than a grove of pine-trees,
Taller than the tallest tree-tops!
And the old men and the women
Looked and tittered at each other;
"Kaw!" they said, "we don't believe it!"
   From its mouth, he said, to greet him,
Came Waywassimo, the lightning,
Came the thunder, Annemeekee!
And the warriors and the women
Laughed aloud at poor Iagoo;
"Kaw!" they said, "what tales you tell us!"
   In it, said he, came a people,
In the great canoe with pinions
Came, he said, a hundred warriors;
Painted white were all their faces

And with hair their chins were covered!
And the warriors and the women
Laughed and shouted in derision,
Like the ravens on the tree-tops,
Like the crows upon the hemlocks.
"Kaw!" they said, "what lies you tell us!
Do not think that we believe them!"
    Only Hiawatha laughed not,
But he gravely spake and answered
To their jeering and their jesting:
"True is all Iagoo tells us;
I have seen it in a vision,
Seen the great canoe with pinions,
Seen the people with white faces,
Seen the coming of this bearded
People of the wooden vessel
From the regions of the morning,
From the shining land of Wabun.
    "Gitche Manito, the Mighty,
The Great Spirit, the Creator,
Sends them hither on his errand,
Sends them to us with his message.
Wheresoe'er they move, before them
Swarms the stinging fly, the Ahmo,
Swarms the bee, the honey-maker;
Wheresoe'er they tread, beneath them
Springs a flower unknown among us,
Springs the White-man's Foot in blossom.
    "Let us welcome, then, the strangers,
Hail them as our friends and brothers,
And the heart's right hand of friendship
Give them when they come to see us.

Gitche Manito, the Mighty,
Said this to me in my vision.
  "I beheld, too, in that vision
All the secrets of the future,
Of the distant days that shall be.
I beheld the westward marches
Of the unknown, crowded nations.
All the land was full of people,
Restless, struggling, toiling, striving,
Speaking many tongues, yet feeling
But one heart-beat in their bosoms.
In the woodlands rang their axes,
Smoked their towns in all the valleys,
Over all the lakes and rivers
Rushed their great canoes of thunder.
  "Then a darker, drearier vision
Passed before me, vague and cloud-like;
I beheld our nation scattered,
All forgetful of my counsels,
Weakened, warring with each other:
Saw the remnants of our people
Sweeping westward, wild and woful,
Like the cloud-rack of a tempest,
Like the withered leaves of Autumn!"

XXII
Hiawatha's Departure

By the shore of Gitche Gumee,
By the shining Big-Sea-Water,
At the doorway of his wigwam,
In the pleasant Summer morning,

Hiawatha stood and waited.
All the air was full of freshness,
All the earth was bright and joyous,
And before him, through the sunshine,
Westward toward the neighboring forest
Passed in golden swarms the Ahmo,
Passed the bees, the honey-makers,
Burning, singing in the sunshine.

Bright above him shone the heavens,
Level spread the lake before him;
From its bosom leaped the sturgeon,
Sparkling, flashing in the sunshine;
On its margin the great forest
Stood reflected in the water,
Every tree-top had its shadow,
Motionless beneath the water.

From the brow of Hiawatha
Gone was every trace of sorrow,
As the fog from off the water,
As the mist from off the meadow.
With a smile of joy and triumph,
With a look of exultation,
As of one who in a vision
Sees what is to be, but is not,
Stood and waited Hiawatha.

Toward the sun his hands were lifted,
Both the palms spread out against it,
And between the parted fingers
Fell the sunshine on his features,
Flecked with light his naked shoulders,
As it falls and flecks on oak-tree
Through the rifted leaves and branches.

O'er the water floating, flying,
Something in the hazy distance,
Something in the mists of morning,
Loomed and lifted from the water,
Now seemed floating, now seemed flying,
Coming nearer, nearer, nearer.
    Was it Shingebis the diver?
Or the pelican, the Shada?
Or the heron, the Shuh-shuh-gah?
Or the white goose, Waw-be-wawa,
With the water dripping, flashing,
From its glossy neck and feathers?
    It was neither goose nor diver,
Neither pelican nor heron,
O'er the water floating, flying,
Through the shining mist of morning,
But a birch canoe with paddles,
Rising, sinking on the water,
Dripping, flashing in the sunshine;
And within it came a people
From the distant land of Wabun,
From the farthest realms of morning
Came the Black-Robe chief, the Prophet,
He the Priest of Prayer, the Pale-face,
With his guides and his companions.
    And the noble Hiawatha,
With his hands aloft extended,
Held aloft in sign of welcome,
Waited, full of exultation,
Till the birch canoe with paddles
Grated on the shining pebbles,
Stranded on the sandy margin,

Till the Black-Robe chief, the Pale-face,
With the cross upon his bosom,
Landed on the sandy margin.
　　Then the joyous Hiawatha
Cried aloud and spake in this wise:
"Beautiful is the sun, O strangers,
When you come so far to see us!
All our town in peace awaits you,
All our doors stand open for you;
You shall enter all our wigwams,
For the heart's right hand we give you.
　　"Never bloomed the earth so gayly,
Never shone the sun so brightly,
As to-day they shine and blossom
When you come so far to see us!
Never was our lake so tranquil,
Nor so free from rocks and sand-bars;
For your birch canoe in passing
Has removed both rock and sand-bar.
　　"Never before had our tobacco
Such a sweet and pleasant flavor,
Never the broad leaves of our cornfields
Were so beautiful to look on,
As they seem to us this morning,
When you come so far to see us!"
　　And the Black-Robe chief made answer,
Stammered in his speech a little,
Speaking words yet unfamiliar:
"Peace be with you, Hiawatha,
Peace be with you and your people,
Peace of prayer, and peace of pardon,
Peace of Christ, and joy of Mary!"

Then the generous Hiawatha
Led the strangers to his wigwam,
Seated them on skins of bison,
Seated them on skins of ermine,
And the careful old Nokomis
Brought them food in bowls of basswood,
Water brought in birchen dippers,
And the calumet, the peace-pipe,
Filled and lighted for their smoking.
   All the old men of the village,
All the warriors of the nation,
All the Jossakeeds, the Prophets,
The magicians, the Wabenos,
And the medicine-men, the Medas,
Came to bid the strangers welcome;
"It is well," they said, "O brothers,
That you come so far to see us!"
   In a circle round the doorway,
With their pipes they sat in silence,
Waiting to behold the strangers,
Waiting to receive their message;
Till the Black-Robe chief, the Pale-face,
From the wigwam came to greet them,
Stammering in his speech a little,
Speaking words yet unfamiliar;
"It is well," they said, "O brother,
That you come so far to see us!"
   Then the Black-Robe chief, the Prophet,
Told his message to the people,
Told the purport of his mission,
Told them of the Virgin Mary,
And her blessed Son, the Saviour,

How in distant lands and ages
He had lived on earth as we do;
How he fasted, prayed, and labored;
How the Jews, the tribe accursed,
Mocked him, scourged him, crucified him;
How he rose from where they laid him,
Walked again with his disciples,
And ascended into heaven.
　　And the chiefs made answer, saying:
"We have listened to your message,
We have heard your words of wisdom,
We will think on what you tell us.
It is well for us, O brothers,
That you come so far to see us!"
　　Then they rose up and departed
Each one homeward to his wigwam,
To the young men and the women
Told the story of the strangers
Whom the Master of Life had sent them
From the shining land of Wabun.
　　Heavy with the heat and silence
Grew the afternoon of Summer;
With a drowsy sound the forest
Whispered round the sultry wigwam,
With a sound of sleep the water
Rippled on the beach below it;
From the cornfields shrill and ceaseless
Sang the grasshopper, Pah-puk-keena;
And the guests of Hiawatha,
Weary with the heat of Summer,
Slumbered in the sultry wigwam.
　　Slowly o'er the simmering landscape

Fell the evening's dusk and coolness,
And the long and level sunbeams
Shot their spears into the forest,
Breaking through its shields of shadow,
Rushed into each secret ambush,
Searched each thicket, dingle, hollow;
Still the guests of Hiawatha
Slumbered in the silent wigwam.
   From his place rose Hiawatha,
Bade farewell to old Nokomis,
Spake in whispers, spake in this wise,
Did not wake the guests, that slumbered:
   "I am going, O Nokomis,
On a long and distant journey,
To the portals of the Sunset,
To the regions of the home-wind,
Of the Northwest-Wind, Keewaydin.
But these guests I leave behind me,
In your watch and ward I leave them;
See that never harm comes near them,
See that never fear molests them,
Never danger nor suspicion,
Never want of food or shelter,
In the lodge of Hiawatha!"
   Forth into the village went he,
Bade farewell to all the warriors,
Bade farewell to all the young men,
Spake persuading, spake in this wise:
   "I am going, O my people,
On a long and distant journey;
Many moons and many winters
Will have come, and will have vanished,

Ere I come again to see you.
But my guests I leave behind me;
Listen to their words of wisdom,
Listen to the truth they tell you,
For the Master of Life has sent them
From the land of light and morning!"

On the shore stood Hiawatha,
Turned and waved his hand at parting;
On the clear and luminous water
Launched his birch canoe for sailing,
From the pebbles of the margin
Shoved it forth into the water;
Whispered to it, "Westward! westward!"
And with speed it darted forward.

And the evening sun descending
Set the clouds on fire with redness,
Burned the broad sky, like a prairie,
Left upon the level water
One long track and trail of splendor,
Down whose stream, as down a river,
Westward, westward Hiawatha
Sailed into the fiery sunset,
Sailed into the purple vapors,
Sailed into the dusk of evening.

And the people from the margin
Watched him floating, rising, sinking,
Till the birch canoe seemed lifted
High into that sea of splendor,
Till it sank into the vapors
Like the new moon slowly, slowly
Sinking in the purple distance.

And they said, "Farewell forever!"

Said, "Farewell, O Hiawatha!"
And the forests, dark and lonely,
Moved through all their depths of darkness,
Sighed, "Farewell, O Hiawatha!"
And the waves upon the margin
Rising, rippling on the pebbles,
Sobbed, "Farewell, O Hiawatha!"
And the heron, the Shuh-shuh-gah,
From her haunts among the fen-lands,
Screamed, "Farewell, O Hiawatha!"
  Thus departed Hiawatha,
Hiawatha the Beloved,
In the glory of the sunset,
In the purple mists of evening,
To the regions of the home-wind,
Of the Northwest-Wind, Keewaydin,
To the Islands of the Blessed,
To the kingdom of Ponemah,
To the land of the Hereafter!

The Courtship of Miles Standish and Other Poems

The Courtship of Miles Standish

I.
Miles Standish.

In the Old Colony days, in Plymouth the
   land of the Pilgrims,
To and fro in a room of his simple and primi-
   tive dwelling,
Clad in doublet and hose, and boots of
   Cordovan leather,
Strode, with a martial air, Miles Standish the
   Puritan Captain.
Buried in thought he seemed, with his hands
   behind him, and pausing
Ever and anon to behold his glittering weap-
   ons of warfare,
Hanging in shining array along the walls of
   the chamber, —
Cutlass and corselet of steel, and his trusty
   sword of Damascus,
Curved at the point and inscribed with its

mystical Arabic sentence,
While underneath, in a corner, were fowling-
piece, musket, and matchlock.
Short of stature he was, but strongly built
and athletic,
Broad in the shoulders, deep-chested, with
muscles and sinews of iron;
Brown as a nut was his face, but his russet
beard was already
Flaked with patches of snow, as hedges
sometimes in November.
Near him was seated John Alden, his friend,
and household companion,
Writing with diligent speed at a table of pine
by the window;
Fair-haired, azure-eyed, with delicate Saxon
complexion,
Having the dew of his youth, and the beauty
thereof, as the captives
Whom Saint Gregory saw, and exclaimed,
"Not Angles, but Angels."
Youngest of all was he of the men who came
in the Mayflower.

Suddenly breaking the silence, the diligent
scribe interrupting,
Spake, in the pride of his heart, Miles
Standish the Captain of Plymouth.
"Look at these arms," he said, "the warlike
weapons that hang here
Burnished and bright and clean, as if for

parade or inspection!

This is the sword of Damascus I fought with in Flanders; this breastplate,

Well I remember the day! once saved my life in a skirmish;

Here in front you can see the very dint of the bullet

Fired point-blank at my heart by a Spanish arcabucero.

Had it not been of sheer steel, the forgotten bones of Miles Standish

Would at this moment be mould, in their grave in the Flemish morasses."

Thereupon answered John Alden, but looked not up from his writing:

"Truly the breath of the Lord hath slackened the speed of the bullet;

He in his mercy preserved you, to be our shield and our weapon!"

Still the Captain continued, unheeding the words of the stripling:

"See, how bright they are burnished, as if in an arsenal hanging;

That is because I have done it myself, and not left it to others.

Serve yourself, would you be well served, is an excellent adage;

So I take care of my arms, as you of your pens and your inkhorn.

Then, too, there are my soldiers, my great, invincible army,

Twelve men, all equipped, having each his

rest and his matchlock,
Eighteen shillings a month, together with diet
    and pillage,
And, like Cæsar, I know the name of each of
    my soldiers!"
This he said with a smile, that danced in his
    eyes, as the sunbeams
Dance on the waves of the sea, and vanish
    again in a moment.
Alden laughed as he wrote, and still the
    Captain continued:
"Look! you can see from this window my
    brazen howitzer planted
High on the roof of the church, a preacher
    who speaks to the purpose,
Steady, straightforward, and strong, with ir-
    resistible logic,
Orthodox, flashing conviction right into the
    hearts of the heathen.
Now we are ready, I think, for any assault of
    the Indians;
Let them come, if they like, and the sooner
    they try it the better, —
Let them come, if they like, be it sagamore,
    sachem, or powwow,
Aspinet, Samoset, Corbitant, Squanto, or
    Tokamahamon!"

  Long at the window he stood, and wistfully
    gazed on the landscape,
Washed with a cold gray mist, the vapory
    breath of the east-wind,

Forest and meadow and hill, and the steel-
blue rim of the ocean,
Lying silent and sad, in the afternoon shad-
ows and sunshine.
Over his countenance flitted a shadow like
those on the landscape,
Gloom intermingled with light; and his voice
was subdued with emotion,
Tenderness, pity, regret, as after a pause he
proceeded:
"Yonder there, on the hill by the sea, lies
buried Rose Standish;
Beautiful rose of love, that bloomed for me
by the wayside!
She was the first to die of all who came in
the Mayflower!
Green above her is growing the field of wheat
we have sown there,
Better to hide from the Indian scouts the
graves of our people,
Lest they should count them and see how
many already have perished!"
Sadly his face he averted, and strode up and
down, and was thoughtful.

Fixed to the opposite wall was a shelf of
books, and among them
Prominent three, distinguished alike for bulk
and for binding;
Bariffe's Artillery Guide, and the Com-
mentaries of Cæsar
Out of the Latin translated by Arthur Gol-

dinge of London,
And, as if guarded by these, between them
was standing the Bible.
Musing a moment before them, Miles
Standish paused, as if doubtful
Which of the three he should choose for his
consolation and comfort,
Whether the wars of the Hebrews, the famous
campaigns of the Romans,
Or the Artillery practice, designed for bel-
ligerent Christians.
Finally down from its shelf he dragged the
ponderous Roman,
Seated himself at the window, and opened
the book, and in silence
Turned o'er the well-worn leaves, where
thumb-marks thick on the margin,
Like the trample of feet, proclaimed the
battle was hottest.
Nothing was heard in the room but the hur-
rying pen of the stripling,
Busily writing epistles important, to go by
the Mayflower,
Ready to sail on the morrow, or next day at
latest, God willing!
Homeward bound with the tidings of all that
terrible winter,
Letters written by Alden, and full of the
name of Priscilla!
Full of the name and the fame of the Puritan
maiden Priscilla!

II.
Love and Friendship.

Nothing was heard in the room but the hur-
 rying pen of the stripling,
Or an occasional sigh from the laboring heart
 of the Captain,
Reading the marvellous words and achieve-
 ments of Julius Cæsar.
After a while he exclaimed, as he smote with
 his hand, palm downwards,
Heavily on the page: "A wonderful man was
 this Cæsar!
You are a writer, and I am a fighter, but here
 is a fellow
Who could both write and fight, and in both
 was equally skilful!"
Straightway answered and spake John Alden,
 the comely, the youthful:
"Yes, he was equally skilled, as you say, with
 his pen and his weapons.
Somewhere have I read, but where I forget,
 he could dictate
Seven letters at once, at the same time writ-
 ing his memoirs."
"Truly," continued the Captain, not heeding
 or hearing the other,
"Truly a wonderful man was Caius Julius
 Cæsar!
Better be first, he said, in a little Iberian vil-
 lage,
Than be second in Rome, and I think he was

right when he said it.
Twice was he married before he was twenty,
and many times after;
Battles five hundred he fought, and a thou-
sand cities he conquered;
He, too, fought in Flanders, as he himself
has recorded;
Finally he was stabbed by his friend, the ora-
tor Brutus!
Now, do you know what he did on a certain
occasion in Flanders,
When the rear-guard of his army retreated,
the front giving way too,
And the immortal Twelfth Legion was
crowded so closely together
There was no room for their swords? Why,
he seized a shield from a soldier,
Put himself straight at the head of his troops,
and commanded the captains,
Calling on each by his name, to order forward
the ensigns;
Then to widen the ranks, and give more
room for their weapons;
So he won the day, the battle of something-
or-other.
That's what I always say; if you wish a thing
to be well done,
You must do it yourself, you must not leave
it to others!"

All was silent again; the Captain continued
his reading.

Nothing was heard in the room but the hur-
rying pen of the stripling
Writing epistles important to go next day by
the Mayflower,
Filled with the name and the fame of the
Puritan maiden Priscilla;
Every sentence began or closed with the
name of Priscilla,
Till the treacherous pen, to which he con-
fided the secret,
Strove to betray it by singing and shouting
the name of Priscilla!
Finally closing his book, with a bang of the
ponderous cover,
Sudden and loud as the sound of a soldier
grounding his musket,
Thus to the young man spake Miles Standish
the Captain of Plymouth:
"When you have finished your work, I have
something important to tell you.
Be not however in haste; I can wait; I shall
not be impatient!"
Straightway Alden replied, as he folded the
last of his letters,
Pushing his papers aside, and giving respect-
ful attention:
"Speak; for whenever you speak, I am always
ready to listen,
Always ready to hear whatever pertains to
Miles Standish."
Thereupon answered the Captain, embar-
rassed, and culling his phrases:

" 'T is not good for a man to be alone, say the Scriptures.
This I have said before, and again and again I repeat it;
Every hour in the day, I think it, and feel it, and say it.
Since Rose Standish died, my life has been weary and dreary;
Sick at heart have I been, beyond the healing of friendship;
Oft in my lonely hours have I thought of the maiden Priscilla.
She is alone in the world; her father and mother and brother
Died in the winter together; I saw her going and coming,
Now to the grave of the dead, and now to the bed of the dying,
Patient, courageous, and strong, and said to myself, that if ever
There were angels on earth, as there are angels in heaven,
Two have I seen and known; and the angel whose name is Priscilla
Holds in my desolate life the place which the other abandoned.
Long have I cherished the thought, but never have dared to reveal it,
Being a coward in this, though valiant enough for the most part.
Go to the damsel Priscilla, the loveliest maiden of Plymouth,

Say that a blunt old Captain, a man not of
    words but of actions,
Offers his hand and his heart, the hand and
    heart of a soldier.
Not in these words, you know, but this in
    short is my meaning;
I am a maker of war, and not a maker of
    phrases.
You, who are bred as a scholar, can say it in
    elegant language,
Such as you read in your books of the plead-
    ings and wooings of lovers,
Such as you think best adapted to win the
    heart of a maiden."

  When he had spoken, John Alden, the fair-
    haired, taciturn stripling,
All aghast at his words, surprised, embar-
    rassed, bewildered,
Trying to mask his dismay by treating the
    subject with lightness,
Trying to smile, and yet feeling his heart
    stand still in his bosom,
Just as a timepiece stops in a house that is
    stricken by lightning,
Thus made answer and spake, or rather stam-
    mered than answered:
"Such a message as that, I am sure I should
    mangle and mar it;
If you would have it well done, — I am only
    repeating your maxim, —
You must do it yourself, you must not leave

it to others!"

But with the air of a man whom nothing can
turn from his purpose,

Gravely shaking his head, made answer the
Captain of Plymouth:

"Truly the maxim is good, and I do not mean
to gainsay it;

But we must use it discreetly, and not waste
powder for nothing.

Now, as I said before, I was never a maker of
phrases.

I can march up to a fortress and summon
the place to surrender,

But march up to a woman with such a
proposal, I dare not.

I'm not afraid of bullets, nor shot from the
mouth of a cannon,

But of a thundering 'No!' point-blank from
the mouth of a woman,

That I confess I'm afraid of, nor am I
ashamed to confess it!

So you must grant my request, for you are
an elegant scholar,

Having the graces of speech, and skill in the
turning of phrases."

Taking the hand of his friend, who still was
reluctant and doubtful,

Holding it long in his own, and pressing it
kindly, he added:

"Though I have spoken thus lightly, yet deep
is the feeling that prompts me;

Surely you cannot refuse what I ask in the

name of our friendship!"

Then made answer John Alden: "The name
  of friendship is sacred;

What you demand in that name, I have not
  the power to deny you!"

So the strong will prevailed, subduing and
  moulding the gentler,

Friendship prevailed over love, and Alden
  went on his errand.

III.

The Lover's Errand.

So the strong will prevailed, and Alden went
  on his errand,

Out of the street of the village, and into the
  paths of the forest,

Into the tranquil woods, where bluebirds and
  robins were building

Towns in the populous trees, with hanging
  gardens of verdure,

Peaceful, aerial cities of joy and affection and
  freedom.

All around him was calm, but within him
  commotion and conflict,

Love contending with friendship, and self
  with each generous impulse.

To and fro in his breast his thoughts were
  heaving and dashing,

As in a foundering ship, with every roll of
  the vessel,

Washes the bitter sea, the merciless surge of

the ocean!

"Must I relinquish it all," he cried with a wild lamentation, —

"Must I relinquish it all, the joy, the hope, the illusion?

Was it for this I have loved, and waited, and worshipped in silence?

Was it for this I have followed the flying feet and the shadow

Over the wintry sea, to the desolate shores of New England?

Truly the heart is deceitful, and out of its depths of corruption

Rise, like an exhalation, the misty phantoms of passion;

Angels of light they seem, but are only delusions of Satan.

All is clear to me now; I feel it, I see it distinctly!

This is the hand of the Lord; it is laid upon me in anger,

For I have followed too much the heart's desires and devices,

Worshipping Astaroth blindly, and impious idols of Baal.

This is the cross I must bear; the sin and the swift retribution."

So through the Plymouth woods John Alden went on his errand;

Crossing the brook at the ford, where it brawled over pebble and shallow,

Gathering still, as he went, the May-flowers blooming around him,
Fragrant, filling the air with a strange and wonderful sweetness,
Children lost in the woods, and covered with leaves in their slumber.
"Puritan flowers," he said, "and the type of Puritan maidens,
Modest and simple and sweet, the very type of Priscilla!
So I will take them to her; to Priscilla the Mayflower of Plymouth,
Modest and simple and sweet, as a parting gift will I take them;
Breathing their silent farewells, as they fade and wither and perish,
Soon to be thrown away as is the heart of the giver."
So through the Plymouth woods John Alden went on his errand;
Came to an open space, and saw the disk of the ocean,
Sailless, sombre and cold with the comfort-less breath of the east-wind;
Saw the new-built house, and people at work in a meadow;
Heard, as he drew near the door, the musical voice of Priscilla
Singing the hundredth Psalm, the grand old Puritan anthem,
Music that Luther sang to the sacred words of the Psalmist,

Full of the breath of the Lord, consoling and
comforting many.
Then, as he opened the door, he beheld the
form of the maiden
Seated beside her wheel, and the carded wool
like a snow-drift
Piled at her knee, her white hands feeding
the ravenous spindle,
While with her foot on the treadle she guided
the wheel in its motion.
Open wide on her lap lay the well-worn
psalm-book of Ainsworth,
Printed in Amsterdam, the words and the
music together,
Rough-hewn, angular notes, like stones in
the wall of a churchyard,
Darkened and overhung by the running vine
of the verses.
Such was the book from whose pages she
sang the old Puritan anthem,
She, the Puritan girl, in the solitude of the
forest,
Making the humble house and the modest
apparel of homespun
Beautiful with her beauty, and rich with the
wealth of her being!
Over him rushed, like a wind that is keen
and cold and relentless,
Thoughts of what might have been, and the
weight and woe of his errand;
All the dreams that had faded, and all the
hopes that had vanished,

All his life henceforth a dreary and tenant-
less mansion,
Haunted by vain regrets, and pallid, sorrow-
ful faces.
Still he said to himself; and almost fiercely
he said it,
"Let not him that putteth his hand to the
plough look backwards;
Though the ploughshare cut through the
flowers of life to its fountains,
Though it pass o'er the graves of the dead
and the hearths of the living,
It is the will of the Lord; and his mercy en-
dureth forever!"

So he entered the house: and the hum of
the wheel and the singing
Suddenly ceased; for Priscilla, aroused by his
step on the threshold,
Rose as he entered, and gave hint her hand,
in signal of welcome,
Saying, "I knew it was you, when I heard
your step in the passage;
For I was thinking of you, as I sat there sing-
ing and spinning."
Awkward and dumb with delight, that a
thought of him had been mingled
Thus in the sacred psalm, that came from
the heart of the maiden,
Silent before her he stood, and gave her the
flowers for an answer,
Finding no words for his thought. He remem-

bered that day in the winter,
After the first great snow, when he broke a
path from the village,
Reeling and plunging along through the
drifts that encumbered the doorway,
Stamping the snow from his feet as he
entered the house, and Priscilla
Laughed at his snowy locks, and gave him a
seat by the fireside,
Grateful and pleased to know he had thought
of her in the snow-storm.
Had he but spoken then! perhaps not in vain
had he spoken;
Now it was all too late; the golden moment
had vanished!
So he stood there abashed, and gave her the
flowers for an answer.

Then they sat down and talked of the birds
and the beautiful Spring-time,
Talked of their friends at home, and the
Mayflower that sailed on the morrow.
"I have been thinking all day," said gently
the Puritan maiden,
"Dreaming all night, and thinking all day, of
the hedge-rows of England, —
They are in blossom now, and the country is
all like a garden;
Thinking of lanes and fields, and the song of
the lark and the linnet,
Seeing the village street, and familiar faces of
neighbors

Going about as of old, and stopping to gos-
  sip together,
And, at the end of the street, the village
  church, with the ivy
Climbing the old gray tower, and the quiet
  graves in the churchyard.
Kind are the people I live with, and dear to
  me my religion;
Still my heart is so sad, that I wish myself
  back in Old England.
You will say it is wrong, but I cannot help it:
  I almost
Wish myself back in Old England, I feel so
  lonely and wretched."

  Thereupon answered the youth: "Indeed I
    do not condemn you;
Stouter hearts than a woman's have quailed
  in this terrible winter.
Yours is tender and trusting, and needs a
  stronger to lean on;
So I have come to you now, with an offer
  and proffer of marriage
Made by a good man and true, Miles
  Standish the Captain of Plymouth!"

  Thus he delivered his message, the dexter-
    ous writer of letters, —
Did not embellish the theme, nor array it in
  beautiful phrases,
But came straight to the point, and blurted it
  out like a school-boy;

Even the Captain himself could hardly have
    said it more bluntly.
Mute with amazement and sorrow, Priscilla
    the Puritan maiden
Looked into Alden's face, her eyes dilated
    with wonder,
Feeling his words like a blow, that stunned
    her and rendered her speechless;
Till at length she exclaimed, interrupting the
    ominous silence:
"If the great Captain of Plymouth is so very
    eager to wed me,
Why does he not come himself and take the
    trouble to woo me?
If I am not worth the wooing, I surely am
    not worth the winning!"
Then John Alden began explaining and
    smoothing the matter,
Making it worse as he went, by saying the
    Captain was busy, —
Had no time for such things; — such things!
    the words grating harshly
Fell on the ear of Priscilla; and swift as a
    flash she made answer:
"Has he no time for such things, as you call
    it, before he is married,
Would he be likely to find it, or make it, after
    the wedding?
That is the way with you men; you don't
    understand us, you cannot.
When you have made up your minds, after
    thinking of this one and that one,

Choosing, selecting, rejecting, comparing
one with another,
Then you make known your desire, with
abrupt and sudden avowal,
And are offended and hurt, and indignant
perhaps, that a woman
Does not respond at once to a love that she
never suspected,
Does not attain at a bound the height to
which you have been climbing.
This is not right nor just: for surely a wom-
an's affection
Is not a thing to be asked for, and had for
only the asking.
When one is truly in love, one not only says
it, but shows it.
Had he but waited awhile, had he only
showed that he loved me,
Even this Captain of yours — who knows?
— at last might have won me,
Old and rough as he is; but now it never can
happen."

Still John Alden went on, unheeding the
words of Priscilla,
Urging the suit of his friend, explaining,
persuading, expanding;
Spoke of his courage and skill, and of all his
battles in Flanders,
How with the people of God he had chosen
to suffer affliction;
How, in return for his zeal, they had made

him Captain of Plymouth;
He was a gentleman born, could trace his
pedigree plainly
Back to Hugh Standish of Duxbury Hall, in
Lancashire, England,
Who was the son of Ralph, and the grandson
of Thurston de Standish;
Heir unto vast estates, of which he was basely
defrauded,
Still bore the family arms, and had for his
crest a cock argent
Combed and wattled gules, and all the rest
of the blazon.
He was a man of honor, of noble and gener-
ous nature;
Though he was rough, he was kindly; she
knew how during the winter
He had attended the sick, with a hand as
gentle as woman's;
Somewhat hasty and hot, he could not deny
it, and headstrong,
Stern as a soldier might be, but hearty, and
placable always,
Not to be laughed at and scorned, because
he was little of stature;
For he was great of heart, magnanimous,
courtly, courageous;
Any woman in Plymouth, nay, any woman in
England,
Might be happy and proud to be called the
wife of Miles Standish!

But as he warmed and glowed, in his simple
  and eloquent language,
Quite forgetful of self, and full of the praise
  of his rival,
Archly the maiden smiled, and, with eyes
  overrunning with laughter,
Said, in a tremulous voice, "Why don't you
  speak for yourself, John?"

IV.
John Alden.

Into the open air John Alden, perplexed
  and bewildered,
Rushed like a man insane, and wandered
  alone by the sea-side;
Paced up and down the sands, and bared his
  head to the east-wind,
Cooling his heated brow, and the fire and
  fever within him.
Slowly as out of the heavens, with apocalyp-
  tical splendors,
Sank the City of God, in the vision of John
  the Apostle,
So, with its cloudy walls of chrysolite, jasper,
  and sapphire,
Sank the broad red sun, and over its turrets
  uplifted
Glimmered the golden reed of the angel who
  measured the city.

"Welcome, O wind of the East!" he ex-

claimed in his wild exultation,
"Welcome, O wind of the East, from the
caves of the misty Atlantic!
Blowing o'er fields of dulse, and measureless
meadows of sea-grass,
Blowing o'er rocky wastes, and the grottos
and gardens of ocean!
Lay thy cold, moist hand on my burning
forehead, and wrap me
Close in thy garments of mist, to allay the
fever within me!"

Like an awakened conscience, the sea was
moaning and tossing,
Beating remorseful and loud the mutable
sands of the seashore.
Fierce in his soul was the struggle and tumult
of passions contending;
Love triumphant and crowned, and friend-
ship wounded and bleeding,
Passionate cries of desire, and importunate
pleadings of duty!
"Is it my fault," he said, "that the maiden
has chosen between us?
Is it my fault that he failed, — my fault that I
am the victor?"
Then within him there thundered a voice,
like the voice of the Prophet:
"It hath displeased the Lord!" — and he
thought of David's transgression,
Bathsheba's beautiful face, and his friend in
the front of the battle!

Shame and confusion of guilt, and abasement and self-condemnation,
Overwhelmed him at once; and he cried in the deepest contrition:
"It hath displeased the Lord! It is the temptation of Satan!"

Then, uplifting his head, he looked at the sea, and beheld there
Dimly the shadowy form of the Mayflower riding at anchor,
Rocked on the rising tide, and ready to sail on the morrow;
Heard the voices of men through the mist, the rattle of cordage
Thrown on the deck, the shouts of the mate, and the sailors' "Ay, ay, Sir!"
Clear and distinct, but not loud, in the dripping air of the twilight
Still for a moment he stood, and listened, and stared at the vessel,
Then went hurriedly on, as one who, seeing a phantom,
Stops, then quickens his pace, and follows the beckoning shadow.
"Yes, it is plain to me now," he murmured; "the hand of the Lord is
Leading me out of the land of darkness, the bondage of error,
Through the sea, that shall lift the walls of its waters around me,
Hiding me, cutting me off, from the cruel

thoughts that pursue me.

Back will I go o'er the ocean, this dreary land
will abandon,

Her whom I may not love, and him whom
my heart has offended.

Better to be in my grave in the green old
churchyard in England,

Close by my mother's side, and among the
dust of my kindred;

Better be dead and forgotten, than living in
shame and dishonor;

Sacred and safe and unseen, in the dark of
the narrow chamber

With me my secret shall lie, like a buried
jewel that glimmers

Bright on the hand that is dust, in the
chambers of silence and darkness, —

Yes, as the marriage ring of the great espousal
hereafter!"

Thus as he spake, he turned, in the strength
of his strong resolution,

Leaving behind him the shore, and hurried
along in the twilight,

Through the congenial gloom of the forest
silent and sombre,

Till he beheld the lights in the seven houses
of Plymouth,

Shining like seven stars in the dusk and mist
of the evening.

Soon he entered his door, and found the
redoubtable Captain

Sitting alone, and absorbed in the martial
pages of Cæsar,
Fighting some great campaign in Hainault or
Brabant or Flanders.
"Long have you been on your errand," he
said with a cheery demeanor,
Even as one who is waiting an answer, and
fears not the issue.
"Not far off is the house, although the woods
are between us;
But you have lingered so long, that while you
were going and coming
I have fought ten battles and sacked and
demolished a city.
Come, sit down, and in order relate to me all
that has happened."

Then John Alden spake, and related the
wondrous adventure,
From beginning to end, minutely, just as it
happened;
How he had seen Priscilla, and how he had
sped in his courtship,
Only smoothing a little, and softening down
her refusal.
But when he came at length to the words
Priscilla had spoken,
Words so tender and cruel: "Why don't you
speak for yourself, John?"
Up leaped the Captain of Plymouth, and
stamped on the floor, till his armor
Clanged on the wall, where it hung, with a

sound of sinister omen.
All his pent-up wrath burst forth in a sudden
explosion,
E'en as a hand-grenade, that scatters destruc-
tion around it.
Wildly he shouted, and loud: "John Alden!
you have betrayed me!
Me, Miles Standish, your friend! have sup-
planted, defrauded, betrayed me!
One of my ancestors ran his sword through
the heart of Wat Tyler;
Who shall prevent me from running my own
through the heart of a traitor?
Yours is the greater treason, for yours is a
treason to friendship!
You, who lived under my roof, whom I
cherished and loved as a brother;
You, who have fed at my board, and drunk at
my cup, to whose keeping
I have intrusted my honor, my thoughts the
most sacred and secret, —
You too, Brutus! ah woe to the name of
friendship hereafter!
Brutus was Cæsar's friend, and you were
mine, but henceforward
Let there be nothing between us save war,
and implacable hatred!"

So spake the Captain of Plymouth, and
strode about in the chamber,
Chafing and choking with rage; like cords
were the veins on his temples.

But in the midst of his anger a man appeared
    at the doorway,
Bringing in uttermost haste a message of
    urgent importance,
Rumors of danger and war and hostile incur-
    sions of Indians
Straightway the Captain paused, and, without
    further question or parley,
Took from the nail on the wall his sword with
    its scabbard of iron,
Buckled the belt round his waist, and, frown-
    ing fiercely, departed.
Alden was left alone. He heard the clank of
    the scabbard
Growing fainter and fainter, and dying away
    in the distance.
Then he arose from his seat, and looked forth
    into the darkness,
Felt the cool air blow on his cheek, that was
    hot with the insult,
Lifted his eyes to the heavens, and, folding
    his hands as in childhood,
Prayed in the silence of night to the Father
    who seeth in secret.

  Meanwhile the choleric Captain strode
    wrathful away to the council,
Found it already assembled, impatiently wait-
    ing his coming;
Men in the middle of life, austere and grave
    in deportment,
Only one of them old, the hill that was near-

est to heaven,
Covered with snow, but erect, the excellent Elder of Plymouth.
God had sifted three kingdoms to find the wheat for this planting,
Then had sifted the wheat, as the living seed of a nation;
So say the chronicles old, and such is the faith of the people!
Near them was standing an Indian, in attitude stern and defiant,
Naked down to the waist, and grim and ferocious in aspect;
While on the table before them was lying unopened a Bible,
Ponderous, bound in leather, brass studded, printed in Holland,
And beside it outstretched the skin of a rattlesnake glittered,
Filled, like a quiver, with arrows; a signal and challenge of warfare,
Brought by the Indian, and speaking with arrowy tongues of defiance.
This Miles Standish beheld, as he entered, and heard them debating
What were an answer befitting the hostile message and menace,
Talking of this and of that, contriving, suggesting, objecting;
One voice only for peace, and that the voice of the Elder,
Judging it wise and well that some at least

were converted,
Rather than any were slain, for this was but
Christian behavior!
Then out spake Miles Standish, the stalwart
Captain of Plymouth,
Muttering deep in his throat, for his voice
was husky with anger,
"What! do you mean to make war with milk
and the water of roses?
Is it to shoot red squirrels you have your
howitzer planted
There on the roof of the church, or is it to
shoot red devils?
Truly the only tongue that is understood by
a savage
Must be the tongue of fire that speaks from
the mouth of the cannon!"
Thereupon answered and said the excellent
Elder of Plymouth,
Somewhat amazed and alarmed at this ir-
reverent language:
"Not so thought St. Paul, nor yet the other
Apostles;
Not from the cannon's mouth were the
tongues of fire they spake with!"
But unheeded fell this mild rebuke on the
Captain,
Who had advanced to the table, and thus
continued discoursing:
"Leave this matter to me, for to me by right
it pertaineth.
War is a terrible trade; but in the cause that

is righteous,
Sweet is the smell of powder; and thus I
answer the challenge!"

Then from the rattlesnake's skin, with a
sudden, contemptuous gesture,
Jerking the Indian arrows, he filled it with
powder and bullets
Full to the very jaws, and handed it back to
the savage,
Saying, in thundering tones: "Here, take it!
this is your answer!"
Silently out of the room then glided the
glistening savage,
Bearing the serpent's skin, and seeming
himself like a serpent,
Winding his sinuous way in the dark to the
depths of the forest.

V.
The Sailing of the Mayflower.

Just in the gray of the dawn, as the mists
uprose from the meadows,
There was a stir and a sound in the slumber-
ing village of Plymouth;
Clanging and clicking of arms, and the order
imperative, "Forward!"
Given in tone suppressed, a tramp of feet,
and then silence.
Figures ten, in the mist, marched slowly out
of the village.

Standish the stalwart it was, with eight of his
valorous army,
Led by their Indian guide, by Hobomok,
friend of the white men,
Northward marching to quell the sudden
revolt of the savage.
Giants they seemed in the mist, or the mighty
men of King David;
Giants in heart they were, who believed in
God and the Bible, —
Ay, who believed in the smiting of Midian-
ites and Philistines.
Over them gleamed far off the crimson ban-
ners of morning;
Under them loud on the sands, the serried
billows, advancing,
Fired along the line, and in regular order
retreated.

Many a mile had they marched, when at
length the village of Plymouth
Woke from its sleep, and arose, intent on its
manifold labors.
Sweet was the air and soft; and slowly the
smoke from the chimneys
Rose over roofs of thatch, and pointed
steadily eastward;
Men came forth from the doors, and paused
and talked of the weather,
Said that the wind had changed, and was
blowing fair for the Mayflower;
Talked of their Captain's departure, and all

the dangers that menaced,
He being gone, the town, and what should
be done in his absence.
Merrily sang the birds, and the tender voices
of women
Consecrated with hymns the common cares
of the household.
Out of the sea rose the sun, and the billows
rejoiced at his coming;
Beautiful were his feet on the purple tops of
the mountains;
Beautiful on the sails of the Mayflower riding
at anchor,
Battered and blackened and worn by all the
storms of the winter.
Loosely against her masts was hanging and
flapping her canvas,
Rent by so many gales, and patched by the
hands of the sailors.
Suddenly from her side, as the sun rose over
the ocean,
Darted a puff of smoke, and floated seaward;
anon rang
Loud over field and forest the cannon's roar,
and the echoes
Heard and repeated the sound, the signal-
gun of departure!
Ah! but with louder echoes replied the hearts
of the people!
Meekly, in voices subdued, the chapter was
read from the Bible,
Meekly the prayer was begun, but ended in

fervent entreaty!

Then from their houses in haste came forth
the Pilgrims of Plymouth,

Men and women and children, all hurrying
down to the seashore,

Eager, with tearful eyes, to say farewell to the
Mayflower,

Homeward bound o'er the sea, and leaving
them here in the desert.

Foremost among them was Alden. All night
he had lain without slumber,

Turning and tossing about in the heat and
unrest of his fever.

He had beheld Miles Standish, who came
back late from the council,

Stalking into the room, and heard him mut-
ter and murmur,

Sometimes it seemed a prayer, and some-
times it sounded like swearing.

Once he had come to the bed, and stood
there a moment in silence;

Then he had turned away, and said: "I will
not awake him;

Let him sleep on, it is best; for what is the
use of more talking!"

Then he extinguished the light, and threw
himself down on his pallet,

Dressed as he was, and ready to start at the
break of the morning, —

Covered himself with the cloak he had worn
in his campaigns in Flanders, —

Slept as a soldier sleeps in his bivouac, ready
for action.
But with the dawn he arose; in the twilight
Alden beheld him
Put on his corselet of steel, and all the rest of
his armor,
Buckle about his waist his trusty blade of
Damascus,
Take from the corner his musket, and so
stride out of the chamber.
Often the heart of the youth had burned and
yearned to embrace him,
Often his lips had essayed to speak, implor-
ing for pardon;
All the old friendship came back, with its
tender and grateful emotions;
But his pride overmastered the nobler nature
within him, —
Pride, and the sense of his wrong, and the
burning fire of the insult.
So he beheld his friend departing in anger,
but spake not,
Saw him go forth to danger, perhaps to
death, and he spake not!
Then he arose from his bed, and heard what
the people were saying,
Joined in the talk at the door, with Stephen
and Richard and Gilbert,
Joined in the morning prayer, and in the
reading of Scripture,
And, with the others, in haste went hurrying
down to the sea-shore,

Down to the Plymouth Rock, that had been
to their feet as a doorstep
Into a world unknown, — the corner-stone
of a nation!

There with his boat was the Master, already
a little impatient
Lest he should lose the tide, or the wind
might shift to the eastward,
Square-built, hearty, and strong, with an
odor of ocean about him,
Speaking with this one and that, and cram-
ming letters and parcels
Into his pockets capacious, and messages
mingled together
Into his narrow brain, till at last he was
wholly bewildered.
Nearer the boat stood Alden, with one foot
placed on the gunwale,
One still firm on the rock, and talking at
times with the sailors,
Seated erect on the thwarts, all ready and
eager for starting.
He too was eager to go, and thus put an end
to his anguish,
Thinking to fly from despair, that swifter
than keel is or canvas,
Thinking to drown in the sea the ghost that
would rise and pursue him.
But as he gazed on the crowd, he beheld the
form of Priscilla
Standing dejected among them, unconscious

of all that was passing.

Fixed were her eyes upon his, as if she divined his intention,

Fixed with a look so sad, so reproachful, imploring, and patient,

That with a sudden revulsion his heart recoiled from its purpose,

As from the verge of a crag, where one step more is destruction.

Strange is the heart of man, with its quick, mysterious instincts!

Strange is the life of man, and fatal or fated are moments,

Whereupon turn, as on hinges, the gates of the wall adamantine!

"Here I remain!" he exclaimed, as he looked at the heavens above him,

Thanking the Lord whose breath had scattered the mist and the madness,

Wherein, blind and lost, to death he was staggering headlong.

"Yonder snow-white cloud, that floats in the ether above me,

Seems like a hand that is pointing and beckoning over the ocean.

There is another hand, that is not so spectral and ghost-like,

Holding me, drawing me back, and clasping mine for protection.

Float, O hand of cloud, and vanish away in the ether!

Roll thyself up like a fist, to threaten and

daunt me; I heed not
Either your warning or menace, or any omen
    of evil!
There is no land so sacred, no air so pure
    and so wholesome,
As is the air she breathes, and the soil that is
    pressed by her footsteps.
Here for her sake will I stay, and like an invis-
    ible presence
Hover around her forever, protecting, sup-
    porting her weakness;
Yes! as my foot was the first that stepped on
    this rock at the landing,
So, with the blessing of God, shall it be the
    last at the leaving!"

  Meanwhile the Master alert, but with digni-
    fied air and important,
Scanning with watchful eye the tide and the
    wind and the weather,
Walked about on the sands, and the people
    crowded around him
Saying a few last words, and enforcing his
    careful remembrance.
Then, taking each by the hand, as if he were
    grasping a tiller,
Into the boat he sprang, and in haste shoved
    off to his vessel,
Glad in his heart to get rid of all this worry
    and flurry,
Glad to be gone from a land of sand and
    sickness and sorrow,

Short allowance of victual, and plenty of
nothing but Gospel!
Lost in the sound of the oars was the last
farewell of the Pilgrims.
O strong hearts and true! not one went back
in the Mayflower!
No, not one looked back, who had set his
hand to this ploughing!

Soon were heard on board the shouts and
songs of the sailors
Heaving the windlass round, and hoisting
the ponderous anchor.
Then the yards were braced, and all sails set
to the west-wind,
Blowing steady and strong; and the May-
flower sailed from the harbor,
Rounded the point of the Gurnet, and leav-
ing far to the southward
Island and cape of sand, and the Field of the
First Encounter,
Took the wind on her quarter, and stood for
the open Atlantic,
Borne on the send of the sea, and the swell-
ing hearts of the Pilgrims.

Long in silence they watched the receding
sail of the vessel,
Much endeared to them all, as something
living and human;
Then, as if filled with the spirit, and wrapt in
a vision prophetic,

417

Baring his hoary head, the excellent Elder of
  Plymouth
Said, "Let us pray!" and they prayed, and
  thanked the Lord and took courage.
Mournfully sobbed the waves at the base of
  the rock, and above them
Bowed and whispered the wheat on the hill
  of death, and their kindred
Seemed to awake in their graves, and to join
  in the prayer that they uttered.
Sun-illumined and white, on the eastern
  verge of the ocean
Gleamed the departing sail, like a marble slab
  in a graveyard;
Buried beneath it lay forever all hope of
  escaping.
Lo! as they turned to depart, they saw the
  form of an Indian,
Watching them from the hill; but while they
  spake with each other,
Pointing with outstretched hands, and say-
  ing, "Look!" he had vanished.
So they returned to their homes; but Alden
  lingered a little,
Musing alone on the shore, and watching the
  wash of the billows
Round the base of the rock, and the sparkle
  and flash of the sunshine,
Like the spirit of God, moving visibly over
  the waters.

VI.
Priscilla.

Thus for a while he stood, and mused by the
    shore of the ocean,
Thinking of many things, and most of all of
    Priscilla;
And as if thought had the power to draw to
    itself, like the loadstone,
Whatsoever it touches, by subtile laws of its
    nature,
Lo! as he turned to depart, Priscilla was
    standing beside him.

  "Are you so much offended, you will not
    speak to me?" said she.
"Am I so much to blame, that yesterday,
    when you were pleading
Warmly the cause of another, my heart,
    impulsive and wayward,
Pleaded your own, and spake out, forgetful
    perhaps of decorum?
Certainly you can forgive me for speaking so
    frankly, for saying
What I ought not to have said, yet now I can
    never unsay it;
For there are moments in life, when the heart
    is so full of emotion,
That if by chance it be shaken, or into its
    depths like a pebble
Drops some careless word, it overflows, and
    its secret,

Spilt on the ground like water, can never be
    gathered together.
Yesterday I was shocked, when I heard you
    speak of Miles Standish,
Praising his virtues, transforming his very
    defects into virtues,
Praising his courage and strength, and even
    his fighting in Flanders,
As if by fighting alone you could win the
    heart of a woman,
Quite overlooking yourself and the rest, in
    exalting your hero.
Therefore I spake as I did, by an irresistible
    impulse.
You will forgive me, I hope, for the sake of
    the friendship between us,
Which is too true and too sacred to be so
    easily broken!"
Thereupon answered John Alden, the scholar,
    the friend of Miles Standish:
"I was not angry with you, with myself alone
    I was angry,
Seeing how badly I managed the matter I
    had in my keeping."
"No!" interrupted the maiden, with answer
    prompt and decisive;
"No; you were angry with me, for speaking
    so frankly and freely.
It was wrong, I acknowledge; for it is the fate
    of a woman
Long to be patient and silent, to wait like a
    ghost that is speechless,

Till some questioning voice dissolves the
  spell of its silence.
Hence is the inner life of so many suffering
  women
Sunless and silent and deep, like subter-
  ranean rivers
Running through caverns of darkness, un-
  heard, unseen, and unfruitful,
Chafing their channels of stone, with endless
  and profitless murmurs."
Thereupon answered John Alden, the young
  man, the lover of women:
"Heaven forbid it, Priscilla; and truly they
  seem to me always
More like the beautiful rivers that watered
  the garden of Eden,
More like the river Euphrates, through
  deserts of Havilah flowing,
Filling the land with delight, and memories
  sweet of the garden!"
"Ah, by these words, I can see," again inter-
  rupted the maiden,
"How very little you prize me, or care for
  what I am saying.
When from the depths of my heart, in pain
  and with secret misgiving,
Frankly I speak to you, asking for sympathy
  only and kindness,
Straightway you take up my words, that are
  plain and direct and in earnest,
Turn them away from their meaning, and
  answer with flattering phrases.

This is not right, is not just, is not true to
the best that is in you;
For I know and esteem you, and feel that
your nature is noble,
Lifting mine up to a higher, a more ethereal
level.
Therefore I value your friendship, and feel it
perhaps the more keenly
If you say aught that implies I am only as
one among many,
If you make use of those common and
complimentary phrases
Most men think so fine, in dealing and
speaking with women,
But which women reject as insipid, if not as
insulting."

Mute and amazed was Alden; and listened
and looked at Priscilla,
Thinking he never had seen her more fair,
more divine in her beauty.
He who but yesterday pleaded so glibly the
cause of another,
Stood there embarrassed and silent, and
seeking in vain for an answer.
So the maiden went on, and little divined or
imagined
What was at work in his heart, that made
him so awkward and speechless.
"Let us, then, be what we are, and speak
what we think, and in all things
Keep ourselves loyal to truth, and the sacred

professions of friendship.

It is no secret I tell you, nor am I ashamed to declare it:

I have liked to be with you, to see you, to speak with you always.

So I was hurt at your words, and a little affronted to hear you

Urge me to marry your friend, though he were the Captain Miles Standish.

For I must tell you the truth: much more to me is your friendship

Than all the love he could give, were he twice the hero you think him."

Then she extended her hand, and Alden, who eagerly grasped it,

Felt all the wounds in his heart, that were aching and bleeding so sorely,

Healed by the touch of that hand, and he said, with a voice full of feeling:

"Yes, we must ever be friends; and of all who offer you friendship

Let me be ever the first, the truest, the nearest and dearest!"

Casting a farewell look at the glimmering sail of the Mayflower,

Distant, but still in sight, and sinking below the horizon,

Homeward together they walked, with a strange, indefinite feeling,

That all the rest had departed and left them alone in the desert.

But, as they went through the fields in the
　blessing and smile of the sunshine,
Lighter grew their hearts, and Priscilla said
　very archly:
"Now that our terrible Captain has gone in
　pursuit of the Indians,
Where he is happier far than he would be
　commanding a household,
You may speak boldly, and tell me of all that
　happened between you,
When you returned last night, and said how
　ungrateful you found me."
Thereupon answered John Alden, and told
　her the whole of the story, —
Told her his own despair, and the direful
　wrath of Miles Standish.
Whereat the maiden smiled, and said be-
　tween laughing and earnest,
"He is a little chimney, and heated hot in a
　moment!"
But as he gently rebuked her, and told her
　how he had suffered, —
How he had even determined to sail that day
　in the Mayflower,
And had remained for her sake, on hearing
　the dangers that threatened, —
All her manner was changed, and she said
　with a faltering accent,
"Truly I thank you for this: how good you
　have been to me always!"

Thus, as a pilgrim devout, who toward

Jerusalem journeys,
Taking three steps in advance, and one
reluctantly backward,
Urged by importunate zeal, and withheld by
pangs of contrition;
Slowly but steadily onward, receding yet ever
advancing,
Journeyed this Puritan youth to the Holy
Land of his longings,
Urged by the fervor of love, and withheld by
remorseful misgivings.

VII.
The March of Miles Standish.

Meanwhile the stalwart Miles Standish was
marching steadily northward,
Winding through forest and swamp, and
along the trend of the sea-shore,
All day long, with hardly a halt, the fire of
his anger
Burning and crackling within, and the sul-
phurous odor of powder
Seeming more sweet to his nostrils than all
the scents of the forest.
Silent and moody he went, and much he
revolved his discomfort;
He who was used to success, and to easy
victories always,
Thus to be flouted, rejected, and laughed to
scorn by a maiden,
Thus to be mocked and betrayed by the

friend whom most he had trusted!
Ah! 't was too much to be borne, and he fret-
ted and chafed in his armor!

"I alone am to blame," he muttered, "for
mine was the folly.
What has a rough old soldier, grown grim
and gray in the harness,
Used to the camp and its ways, to do with
the wooing of maidens?
'T was but a dream, — let it pass, — let it
vanish like so many others!
What I thought was a flower, is only a weed,
and is worthless;
Out of my heart will I pluck it, and throw it
away, and henceforward
Be but a fighter of battles, a lover and wooer
of dangers!"
Thus he revolved in his mind his sorry defeat
and discomfort,
While he was marching by day or lying at
night in the forest,
Looking up at the trees, and the constella-
tions beyond them.

After a three days' march he came to an
Indian encampment
Pitched on the edge of a meadow, between
the sea and the forest;
Women at work by the tents, and warriors,
horrid with war-paint,
Seated about a fire, and smoking and talking

together;

Who, when they saw from afar the sudden
    approach of the white men,

Saw the flash of the sun on breastplate and
    sabre and musket,

Straightway leaped to their feet, and two,
    from among them advancing,

Came to parley with Standish, and offer him
    furs as a present;

Friendship was in their looks, but in their
    hearts there was hatred.

Braves of the tribe were these, and brothers,
    gigantic in stature,

Huge as Goliath of Gath, or the terrible Og,
    king of Bashan;

One was Pecksuot named, and the other was
    called Wattawamat.

Round their necks were suspended their
    knives in scabbards of wampum,

Two-edged, trenchant knives, with points as
    sharp as a needle.

Other arms had they none, for they were
    cunning and crafty.

"Welcome, English!" they said, — these
    words they had learned from the traders

Touching at times on the coast, to barter and
    chaffer for peltries.

Then in their native tongue they began to
    parley with Standish,

Through his guide and interpreter,
    Hobomok, friend of the white man,

Begging for blankets and knives, but mostly

for muskets and powder,
Kept by the white man, they said, concealed,
with the plague, in his cellars,
Ready to be let loose, and destroy his brother
the red man!
But when Standish refused, and said he
would give them the Bible,
Suddenly changing their tone, they began to
boast and to bluster.
Then Wattawamat advanced with a stride in
front of the other,
And, with a lofty demeanor, thus vauntingly
spake to the Captain:
"Now Wattawamat can see, by the fiery eyes
of the Captain,
Angry is he in his heart; but the heart of the
brave Wattawamat
Is not afraid at the sight. He was not born of
a woman,
But on a mountain at night, from an oak-
tree riven by lightning,
Forth he sprang at a bound, with all his
weapons about him,
Shouting, 'Who is there here to fight with
the brave Wattawamat?' "
Then he unsheathed his knife, and, whetting
the blade on his left hand,
Held it aloft and displayed a woman's face
on the handle;
Saying, with bitter expression and look of
sinister meaning:
"I have another at home, with the face of a

man on the handle;
By and by they shall marry; and there will be
plenty of children!"

Then stood Pecksuot forth, self-vaunting,
insulting Miles Standish:
While with his fingers he patted the knife
that hung at his bosom,
Drawing it half from its sheath, and plunging
it back, as he muttered,
"By and by it shall see; it shall eat; ah, ha!
but shall speak not!
This is the mighty Captain the white men
have sent to destroy us!
He is a little man; let him go and work with
the women!"

Meanwhile Standish had noted the faces
and figures of Indians
Peeping and creeping about from bush to
tree in the forest,
Feigning to look for game, with arrows set
on their bowstrings,
Drawing about him still closer and closer the
net of their ambush.
But undaunted he stood, and dissembled and
treated them smoothly;
So the old chronicles say, that were writ in
the days of the fathers.
But when he heard their defiance, the boast,
the taunt, and the insult,
All the hot blood of his race, of Sir Hugh

and of Thurston de Standish,
Boiled and beat in his heart, and swelled in
the veins of his temples.
Headlong he leaped on the boaster, and,
snatching his knife from its scabbard,
Plunged it into his heart, and, reeling back-
ward, the savage
Fell with his face to the sky, and a fiendlike
fierceness upon it.
Straight there arose from the forest the awful
sound of the war-whoop,
And, like a flurry of snow on the whistling
wind of December,
Swift and sudden and keen came a flight of
feathery arrows.
Then came a cloud of smoke, and out of the
cloud came the lightning,
Out of the lightning thunder; and death
unseen ran before it.
Frightened the savages fled for shelter in
swamp and in thicket,
Hotly pursued and beset; but their sachem,
the brave Wattawamat,
Fled not; he was dead. Unswerving and swift
had a bullet
Passed through his brain, and he fell with
both hands clutching the greensward,
Seeming in death to hold back from his foe
the land of his fathers.

There on the flowers of the meadow the
warriors lay, and above them,

Silent, with folded arms, stood Hobomok, friend of the white man.
Smiling at length he exclaimed to the stalwart Captain of Plymouth: —
"Pecksuot bragged very loud, of his courage, his strength, and his stature, —
Mocked the great Captain, and called him a little man; but I see now
Big enough have you been to lay him speechless before you!"

Thus the first battle was fought and won by the stalwart Miles Standish.
When the tidings thereof were brought to the village of Plymouth,
And as a trophy of war the head of the brave Wattawamat
Scowled from the roof of the fort, which at once was a church and a fortress,
All who beheld it rejoiced, and praised the Lord, and took courage.
Only Priscilla averted her face from this spectre of terror,
Thanking God in her heart that she had not married Miles Standish;
Shrinking, fearing almost, lest, coming home from his battles,
He should lay claim to her hand, as the prize and reward of his valor.

VIII.
The Spinning-Wheel.

Month after month passed away, and in
    Autumn the ships of the merchants
Came with kindred and friends, with cattle
    and corn for the Pilgrims.
All in the village was peace; the men were
    intent on their labors,
Busy with hewing and building, with garden-
    plot and with merestead,
Busy with breaking the glebe, and mowing
    the grass in the meadows,
Searching the sea for its fish, and hunting
    the deer in the forest.
All in the village was peace; but at times the
    rumor of warfare
Filled the air with alarm, and the apprehen-
    sion of danger.
Bravely the stalwart Standish was scouring
    the land with his forces,
Waxing valiant in fight and defeating the
    alien armies,
Till his name had become a sound of fear to
    the nations.
Anger was still in his heart, but at times the
    remorse and contrition
Which in all noble natures succeed the pas-
    sionate outbreak,
Came like a rising tide, that encounters the
    rush of a river,
Staying its current awhile, but making it bit-

ter and brackish.

Meanwhile Alden at home had built him a new habitation,
Solid, substantial, of timber rough-hewn from the firs of the forest.
Wooden-barred was the door, and the roof was covered with rushes;
Latticed the windows were, and the window-panes were of paper,
Oiled to admit the light, while wind and rain were excluded.
There too he dug a well, and around it planted an orchard:
Still may be seen to this day some trace of the well and the orchard.
Close to the house was the stall, where, safe and secure from annoyance,
Raghorn, the snow-white bull, that had fallen to Alden's allotment
In the division of cattle, might ruminate in the night-time
Over the pastures he cropped, made fragrant by sweet pennyroyal.

Oft when his labor was finished, with eager feet would the dreamer
Follow the pathway that ran through the woods to the house of Priscilla,
Led by illusions romantic and subtile deceptions of fancy,
Pleasure disguised as duty, and love in the

semblance of friendship.
Ever of her he thought, when he fashioned
the walls of his dwelling;
Ever of her he thought, when he delved in
the soil of his garden;
Ever of her he thought, when he read in his
Bible on Sunday
Praise of the virtuous woman, as she is
described in the Proverbs, —
How the heart of her husband doth safely
trust in her always,
How all the days of her life she will do him
good, and not evil,
How she seeketh the wool and the flax and
worketh with gladness,
How she layeth her hand to the spindle and
holdeth the distaff;
How she is not afraid of the snow for herself
or her household,
Knowing her household are clothed with the
scarlet cloth of her weaving!

So as she sat at her wheel one afternoon in
the Autumn,
Alden, who opposite sat, and was watching
her dexterous fingers,
As if the thread she was spinning were that
of his life and his fortune,
After a pause in their talk, thus spake to the
sound of the spindle.
"Truly, Priscilla," he said, "when I see you
spinning and spinning,

Never idle a moment, but thrifty and
thoughtful of others,
Suddenly you are transformed, are visibly
changed in a moment;
You are no longer Priscilla, but Bertha the
Beautiful Spinner."
Here the light foot on the treadle grew swifter
and swifter; the spindle
Uttered an angry snarl, and the thread
snapped short in her fingers;
While the impetuous speaker, not heeding
the mischief, continued:
"You are the beautiful Bertha, the spinner,
the queen of Helvetia;
She whose story I read at a stall in the streets
of Southampton,
Who, as she rode on her palfrey, o'er valley
and meadow and mountain,
Ever was spinning her thread from a distaff
fixed to her saddle.
She was so thrifty and good, that her name
passed into a proverb.
So shall it be with your own, when the
spinning-wheel shall no longer
Hum in the house of the farmer, and fill its
chambers with music.
Then shall the mothers, reproving, relate how
it was in their childhood,
Praising the good old times, and the days of
Priscilla the spinner!"
Straight uprose from her wheel the beautiful
Puritan maiden,

Pleased with the praise of her thrift from him
    whose praise was the sweetest,
Drew from the reel on the table a snowy
    skein of her spinning,
Thus making answer, meanwhile, to the flat-
    tering phrases of Alden:
"Come, you must not be idle; if I am a pat-
    tern for housewives,
Show yourself equally worthy of being the
    model of husbands.
Hold this skein on your hands, while I wind
    it, ready for knitting;
Then who knows but hereafter, when fash-
    ions have changed and the manners,
Fathers may talk to their sons of the good
    old times of John Alden!"
Thus, with a jest and a laugh, the skein on
    his hands she adjusted,
He sitting awkwardly there, with his arms
    extended before him,
She standing graceful, erect, and winding the
    thread from his fingers,
Sometimes chiding a little his clumsy man-
    ner of holding,
Sometimes touching his hands, as she disen-
    tangled expertly
Twist or knot in the yarn, unawares — for
    how could she help it? —
Sending electrical thrills through every nerve
    in his body.

Lo! in the midst of this scene, a breathless

messenger entered,
Bringing in hurry and heat the terrible news
from the village.
Yes; Miles Standish was dead! — an Indian
had brought them the tidings, —
Slain by a poisoned arrow, shot down in the
front of the battle,
Into an ambush beguiled, cut off with the
whole of his forces;
All the town would be burned, and all the
people be murdered!
Such were the tidings of evil that burst on
the hearts of the hearers.
Silent and statue-like stood Priscilla, her face
looking backward
Still at the face of the speaker, her arms
uplifted in horror;
But John Alden, upstarting, as if the barb of
the arrow
Piercing the heart of his friend had struck
his own, and had sundered
Once and forever the bonds that held him
bound as a captive
Wild with excess of sensation, the awful
delight of his freedom,
Mingled with pain and regret, unconscious
of what he was doing,
Clasped, almost with a groan, the motionless
form of Priscilla,
Pressing her close to his heart, as forever his
own, and exclaiming:
"Those whom the Lord hath united, let no

man put them asunder!"

Even as rivulets twain, from distant and separate sources,
Seeing each other afar, as they leap from the rocks, and pursuing
Each one its devious path, but drawing nearer and nearer,
Rush together at last, at their trysting-place in the forest;
So these lives that had run thus far in separate channels,
Coming in sight of each other, then swerving and flowing asunder,
Parted by barriers strong, but drawing nearer and nearer,
Rushed together at last, and one was lost in the other.

IX.
The Wedding-Day.

Forth from the curtain of clouds, from the tent of purple and scarlet,
Issued the sun, the great High-Priest, in his garments resplendent,
Holiness unto the Lord, in letters of light, on his forehead,
Round the hem of his robe the golden bells and pomegranates.
Blessing the world he came, and the bars of vapor beneath him

Gleamed like a grate of brass, and the sea at his feet was a laver!

This was the wedding morn of Priscilla the Puritan maiden.
Friends were assembled together; the Elder and Magistrate also
Graced the scene with their presence, and stood like the Law and the Gospel,
One with the sanction of earth and one with the blessing of heaven.
Simple and brief was the wedding, as that of Ruth and of Boaz.
Softly the youth and the maiden repeated the words of betrothal,
Taking each other for husband and wife in the Magistrate's presence,
After the Puritan way, and the laudable custom of Holland.
Fervently then, and devoutly, the excellent Elder of Plymouth
Prayed for the hearth and the home, that were founded that day in affection,
Speaking of life and of death, and imploring Divine benedictions.

Lo! when the service was ended, a form appeared on the threshold,
Clad in armor of steel, a sombre and sorrowful figure!
Why does the bridegroom start and stare at the strange apparition?

Why does the bride turn pale, and hide her face on his shoulder?

Is it a phantom of air, — a bodiless, spectral illusion?

Is it a ghost from the grave, that has come to forbid the betrothal?

Long had it stood there unseen, a guest uninvited, unwelcomed;

Over its clouded eyes there had passed at times an expression

Softening the gloom and revealing the warm heart hidden beneath them,

As when across the sky the driving rack of the rain-cloud

Grows for a moment thin, and betrays the sun by its brightness.

Once it had lifted its hand, and moved its lips, but was silent,

As if an iron will had mastered the fleeting intention,

But when were ended the troth and the prayer and the last benediction,

Into the room it strode, and the people beheld with amazement

Bodily there in his armor Miles Standish, the Captain of Plymouth!

Grasping the bridegroom's hand, he said with emotion, "Forgive me!

I have been angry and hurt, — too long have I cherished the feeling;

I have been cruel and hard, but now, thank God! it is ended.

Mine is the same hot blood that leaped in
the veins of Hugh Standish,
Sensitive, swift to resent, but as swift in aton-
ing for error.
Never so much as now was Miles Standish
the friend of John Alden."
Thereupon answered the bridegroom: "Let
all be forgotten between us, —
All save the dear, old friendship, and that
shall grow older and dearer!"
Then the Captain advanced, and, bowing,
saluted Priscilla,
Gravely, and after the manner of old-
fashioned gentry in England,
Something of camp and of court, of town
and of country, commingled,
Wishing her joy of her wedding, and loudly
lauding her husband.
Then he said with a smile: "I should have
remembered the adage, —
If you would be well served, you must serve
yourself; and moreover,
No man can gather cherries in Kent at the
season of Christmas!"

Great was the people's amazement, and
greater yet their rejoicing,
Thus to behold once more the sunburnt face
of their Captain,
Whom they had mourned as dead; and they
gathered and crowded about him,
Eager to see him and hear him, forgetful of

bride and of bridegroom,
Questioning, answering, laughing, and each
interrupting the other,
Till the good Captain declared, being quite
overpowered and bewildered,
He had rather by far break into an Indian
encampment,
Than come again to a wedding to which he
had not been invited.

Meanwhile the bridegroom went forth and
stood with the bride at the doorway,
Breathing the perfumed air of that warm and
beautiful morning.
Touched with autumnal tints, but lonely and
sad in the sunshine,
Lay extended before them the land of toil
and privation;
There were the graves of the dead, and the
barren waste of the sea-shore,
There the familiar fields, the groves of pine,
and the meadows;
But to their eyes transfigured, it seemed as
the Garden of Eden,
Filled with the presence of God, whose voice
was the sound of the ocean.

Soon was their vision disturbed by the
noise and stir of departure,
Friends coming forth from the house, and
impatient of longer delaying,
Each with his plan for the day, and the work

that was left uncompleted.
Then from a stall near at hand, amid excla-
mations of wonder,
Alden the thoughtful, the careful, so happy,
so proud of Priscilla,
Brought out his snow-white bull, obeying the
hand of its master,
Led by a cord that was tied to an iron ring in
its nostrils,
Covered with crimson cloth, and a cushion
placed for a saddle.
She should not walk, he said, through the
dust and heat of the noonday;
Nay, she should ride like a queen, not plod
along like a peasant.
Somewhat alarmed at first, but reassured by
the others,
Placing her hand on the cushion, her foot in
the hand of her husband,
Gayly, with joyous laugh, Priscilla mounted
her palfrey.
"Nothing is wanting now," he said with a
smile, "but the distaff;
Then you would be in truth my queen, my
beautiful Bertha!"

Onward the bridal procession now moved
to their new habitation,
Happy husband and wife, and friends con-
versing together.
Pleasantly murmured the brook, as they
crossed the ford in the forest,

Pleased with the image that passed, like a dream of love through its bosom,
Tremulous, floating in air, o'er the depths of the azure abysses.
Down through the golden leaves the sun was pouring his splendors,
Gleaming on purple grapes, that, from branches above them suspended,
Mingled their odorous breath with the balm of the pine and the fir-tree,
Wild and sweet as the clusters that grew in the valley of Eschol.
Like a picture it seemed of the primitive, pastoral ages,
Fresh with the youth of the world, and recalling Rebecca and Isaac,
Old and yet ever new, and simple and beautiful always,
Love immortal and young in the endless succession of lovers.
So through the Plymouth woods passed onward the bridal procession.

BIRDS OF PASSAGE

Black shadows fall
From the lindens tall,
That lift aloft their massive wall
  Against the southern sky;

And from the realms

Of the shadowy elms
A tide-like darkness overwhelms
　　The fields that round us lie.

But the night is fair,
And everywhere
A warm, soft vapor fills the air,
　　And distant sounds seem near;

And above, in the light
Of the star-lit night,
Swift birds of passage wing their flight
　　Through the dewy atmosphere.

I hear the beat
Of their pinions fleet,
As from the land of snow and sleet
　　They seek a southern lea.

I hear the cry
Of their voices high
Falling dreamily through the sky,
　　But their forms I cannot see.

Oh, say not so!
Those sounds that flow
In murmurs of delight and woe
　　Come not from wings of birds.

They are the throngs
Of the poet's songs,

Murmurs of pleasures, and pains, and
  wrongs,
   The sound of winged words.

This is the cry
Of souls, that high
On toiling, beating pinions, fly
   Seeking a warmer clime.

From their distant flight
Through realms of light
It falls into our world of night,
   With the murmuring sound of rhyme.

THE LADDER OF ST. AUGUSTINE

Saint Augustine! well hast thou said,
   That of our vices we can frame
A ladder, if we will but tread
   Beneath our feet each deed of shame!

All common things, each day's events,
   That with the hour begin and end,
Our pleasures and our discontents,
   Are rounds by which we may ascend.

The low desire, the base design,
   That makes another's virtues less;
The revel of the ruddy wine,
   And all occasions of excess;

The longing for ignoble things;
  The strife for triumph more than truth;
The hardening of the heart, that brings
  Irreverence for the dreams of youth;

All thoughts of ill; all evil deeds,
  That have their root in thoughts of ill;
Whatever hinders or impedes
  The action of the nobler will; —

All these must first be trampled down
  Beneath our feet, if we would gain
In the bright fields of fair renown
  The right of eminent domain.

We have not wings, we cannot soar;
  But we have feet to scale and climb
By slow degrees, by more and more,
  The cloudy summits of our time.

Thy mighty pyramids of stone
  That wedge-like cleave the desert airs,
When nearer seen, and better known,
  Are but gigantic flights of stairs.

The distant mountains, that uprear
  Their solid bastions to the skies,
Are crossed by pathways, that appear
  As we to higher levels rise.

The heights by great men reached and kept

Were not attained by sudden flight,
But they, while their companions slept,
    Were toiling upward in the night.

Standing on what too long we bore
    With shoulders bent and downcast eyes,
We may discern — unseen before —
    A path to higher destinies,

Nor deem the irrevocable Past
    As wholly wasted, wholly vain,
If, rising on its wrecks, at last
    To something nobler we attain.

THE PHANTOM SHIP

In Mather's Magnalia Christi,
    Of the old colonial time,
May be found in prose the legend
    That is here set down in rhyme.

A ship sailed from New Haven,
    And the keen and frosty airs,
That filled her sails at parting,
    Were heavy with good men's prayers.

"O Lord! if it be thy pleasure" —
    Thus prayed the old divine —
"To bury our friends in the ocean,
    Take them, for they are thine!"

But Master Lamberton muttered,
  And under his breath said he,
"This ship is so crank and walty,
  I fear our grave she will be!"

And the ships that came from England,
  When the winter months were gone,
Brought no tidings of this vessel
  Nor of Master Lamberton.

This put the people to praying
  That the Lord would let them hear
What in his greater wisdom
  He had done with friends so dear.

And at last their prayers were answered:
  It was in the month of June,
An hour before the sunset
  Of a windy afternoon,

When, steadily steering landward,
  A ship was seen below,
And they knew it was Lamberton, Master,
  Who sailed so long ago.

On she came, with a cloud of canvas,
  Right against the wind that blew,
Until the eye could distinguish
  The faces of the crew.

Then fell her straining topmasts,

Hanging tangled in the shrouds,
And her sails were loosened and lifted,
And blown away like clouds.

And the masts, with all their rigging,
Fell slowly, one by one,
And the hulk dilated and vanished,
As a sea-mist in the sun!

And the people who saw this marvel
Each said unto his friend,
That this was the mould of their vessel,
And thus her tragic end.

And the pastor of the village
Gave thanks to God in prayer,
That, to quiet their troubled spirits,
He had sent this Ship of Air.

THE WARDEN OF THE CINQUE PORTS

A mist was driving down the British Chan-
  nel,
  The day was just begun,
And through the window-panes, on floor and
  panel,
  Streamed the red autumn sun.

It glanced on flowing flag and rippling pen-
  non,
  And the white sails of ships;

And, from the frowning rampart, the black
   cannon
   Hailed it with feverish lips.

Sandwich and Romney, Hastings, Hithe, and
   Dover
   Were all alert that day,
To see the French war-steamers speeding
   over,
   When the fog cleared away.

Sullen and silent, and like couchant lions,
   Their cannon, through the night,
Holding their breath, had watched, in grim
   defiance,
   The sea-coast opposite.

And now they roared at drum-beat from their
   stations
   On every citadel;
Each answering each, with morning saluta-
   tions,
   That all was well.

And down the coast, all taking up the burden,
   Replied the distant forts,
As if to summon from his sleep the Warden
   And Lord of the Cinque Ports.

Him shall no sunshine from the fields of
   azure,

No drum-beat from the wall,
No morning gun from the black fort's embra-
   sure,
   Awaken with its call!

No more, surveying with an eye impartial
   The long line of the coast,
Shall the gaunt figure of the old Field Mar-
   shal
   Be seen upon his post!

For in the night, unseen, a single warrior,
   In sombre harness mailed,
Dreaded of man, and surnamed the De-
   stroyer,
   The rampart wall had scaled.

He passed into the chamber of the sleeper,
   The dark and silent room,
And as he entered, darker grew, and deeper,
   The silence and the gloom.

He did not pause to parley or dissemble,
   But smote the Warden hoar;
Ah! what a blow! that made all England
   tremble
   And groan from shore to shore.

Meanwhile, without, the surly cannon waited,
   The sun rose bright o'erhead;
Nothing in Nature's aspect intimated
   That a great man was dead.

HAUNTED HOUSES

All houses wherein men have lived and died
  Are haunted houses. Through the open
  doors
The harmless phantoms on their errands
  glide,
  With feet that make no sound upon the
  floors.

We meet them at the doorway, on the stair,
  Along the passages they come and go,
Impalpable impressions on the air,
  A sense of something moving to and fro.

There are more guests at table, than the hosts
  Invited; the illuminated hall
Is thronged with quiet, inoffensive ghosts,
  As silent as the pictures on the wall.

The stranger at my fireside cannot see
  The forms I see, nor hear the sounds I hear;
He but perceives what is; while unto me
  All that has been is visible and clear.

We have no title-deeds to house or lands;
  Owners and occupants of earlier dates
From graves forgotten stretch their dusty
  hands,
  And hold in mortmain still their old estates.

The spirit-world around this world of sense
  Floats like an atmosphere, and everywhere
Wafts through these earthly mists and vapors
    dense
  A vital breath of more ethereal air.

Our little lives are kept in equipoise
  By opposite attractions and desires;
The struggle of the instinct that enjoys,
  And the more noble instinct that aspires.

These perturbations, this perpetual jar
  Of earthly wants and aspirations high,
Come from the influence of an unseen star,
  An undiscovered planet in our sky.

And as the moon from some dark gate of
    cloud
  Throws o'er the sea a floating bridge of
    light,
Across whose trembling planks our fancies
    crowd
  Into the realm of mystery and night, —

So from the world of spirits there descends
  A bridge of light, connecting it with this,
O'er whose unsteady floor, that sways and
    bends,
  Wander our thoughts above the dark abyss.

In the Churchyard at Cambridge

In the village churchyard she lies,
Dust is in her beautiful eyes,
  No more she breathes, nor feels, nor stirs;
At her feet and at her head
Lies a slave to attend the dead,
  But their dust is white as hers.

Was she, a lady of high degree,
So much in love with the vanity
  And foolish pomp of this world of ours?
Or was it Christian charity,
And lowliness and humility,
  The richest and rarest of all dowers?

Who shall tell us? No one speaks;
No color shoots into those cheeks,
  Either of anger or of pride,
At the rude question we have asked;
Nor will the mystery be unmasked
  By those who are sleeping at her side.

Hereafter? — And do you think to look
On the terrible pages of that Book
  To find her failings, faults, and errors?
Ah, you will then have other cares,
In your own shortcomings and despairs,
  In your own secret sins and terrors!

THE EMPEROR'S BIRD'S-NEST

Once the Emperor Charles of Spain,
  With his swarthy, grave commanders,
I forget in what campaign,
Long besieged, in mud and rain,
  Some old frontier town of Flanders.

Up and down the dreary camp,
  In great boots of Spanish leather,
Striding with a measured tramp,
These Hidalgos, dull and damp,
  Cursed the Frenchmen, cursed the weather.

Thus as to and fro they went
  Over upland and through hollow,
Giving their impatience vent,
Perched upon the Emperor's tent,
  In her nest, they spied a swallow.

Yes, it was a swallow's nest,
  Built of clay and hair of horses,
Mane, or tail, or dragoon's crest,
Found on hedge-rows east and west,
  After skirmish of the forces.

Then an old Hidalgo said,
  As he twirled his gray mustachio,
"Sure this swallow overhead
Thinks the Emperor's tent a shed,
  And the Emperor but a Macho!"

Hearing his imperial name
  Coupled with those words of malice,
Half in anger, half in shame,
Forth the great campaigner came
  Slowly from his canvas palace.

"Let no hand the bird molest,"
  Said he solemnly, "nor hurt her!"
Adding then, by way of jest,
"Golondrina is my guest,
  'T is the wife of some deserter!"

Swift as bowstring speeds a shaft,
  Through the camp was spread the rumor,
And the soldiers, as they quaffed
Flemish beer at dinner, laughed
  At the Emperor's pleasant humor.

So unharmed and unafraid
  Sat the swallow still and brooded,
Till the constant cannonade
Through the walls a breach had made,
  And the siege was thus concluded.

Then the army, elsewhere bent,
  Struck its tents as if disbanding,
Only not the Emperor's tent,
For he ordered, ere he went,
  Very curtly, "Leave it standing!"

So it stood there all alone,
  Loosely flapping, torn and tattered,

Till the brood was fledged and flown,
Singing o'er those walls of stone
  Which the cannon-shot had shattered.

THE TWO ANGELS

Two angels, one of Life and one of Death,
  Passed o'er our village as the morning
    broke;
The dawn was on their faces, and beneath,
  The sombre houses hearsed with plumes of
    smoke.

Their attitude and aspect were the same,
  Alike their features and their robes of white;
But one was crowned with amaranth, as with
    flame,
  And one with asphodels, like flakes of light.

I saw them pause on their celestial way;
  Then said I, with deep fear and doubt op-
    pressed,
"Beat not so loud, my heart, lest thou betray
  The place where thy beloved are at rest!"

And he who wore the crown of asphodels,
  Descending, at my door began to knock,
And my soul sank within me, as in wells
  The waters sink before an earthquake's
    shock.

I recognized the nameless agony,
 The terror and the tremor and the pain,
That oft before had filled or haunted me,
 And now returned with threefold strength
 again.

The door I opened to my heavenly guest,
 And listened, for I thought I heard God's
 voice;
And, knowing whatsoe'er he sent was best,
 Dared neither to lament nor to rejoice.

Then with a smile, that filled the house with
 light,
 "My errand is not Death, but Life," he said;
And ere I answered, passing out of sight,
 On his celestial embassy he sped.

'T was at thy door, O friend! and not at mine,
 The angel with the amaranthine wreath,
Pausing, descended, and with voice divine
 Whispered a word that had a sound like
 Death.

Then fell upon the house a sudden gloom,
 A shadow on those features fair and thin;
And softly, from that hushed and darkened
 room,
 Two angels issued, where but one went in.

All is of God! If he but wave his hand,

The mists collect, the rain falls thick and
  loud,
Till, with a smile of light on sea and land,
  Lo! he looks back from the departing cloud.

Angels of Life and Death alike are his;
  Without his leave they pass no threshold
  o'er;
Who, then, would wish or dare, believing this,
  Against his messengers to shut the door?

DAYLIGHT AND MOONLIGHT

In broad daylight, and at noon,
Yesterday I saw the moon
Sailing high, but faint and white,
As a school-boy's paper kite.

In broad daylight, yesterday,
I read a Poet's mystic lay;
And it seemed to me at most
As a phantom, or a ghost.

But at length the feverish day
Like a passion died away,
And the night, serene and still,
Fell on village, vale, and hill.

Then the moon, in all her pride,
Like a spirit glorified,
Filled and overflowed the night

With revelations of her light.

And the Poet's song again
Passed like music through my brain;
Night interpreted to me
All its grace and mystery.

THE JEWISH CEMETERY AT NEWPORT

How strange it seems! These Hebrews in
   their graves,
   Close by the street of this fair seaport town,
Silent beside the never-silent waves,
   At rest in all this moving up and down!

The trees are white with dust, that o'er their
   sleep
   Wave their broad curtains in the south-
   wind's breath,
While underneath these leafy tents they keep
   The long, mysterious Exodus of Death.

And these sepulchral stones, so old and
   brown,
   That pave with level flags their burial-place,
Seem like the tablets of the Law, thrown
   down
   And broken by Moses at the mountain's
   base.

The very names recorded here are strange,

461

Of foreign accent, and of different climes;
  Alvares and Rivera interchange
  With Abraham and Jacob of old times.

"Blessed be God! for he created Death!"
  The mourners said, "and Death is rest and
    peace;"
Then added, in the certainty of faith,
  "And giveth Life that nevermore shall
    cease."

Closed are the portals of their Synagogue,
  No Psalms of David now the silence break,
No Rabbi reads the ancient Decalogue
  In the grand dialect the Prophets spake.

Gone are the living, but the dead remain,
  And not neglected; for a hand unseen,
Scattering its bounty, like a summer rain,
  Still keeps their graves and their remem-
    brance green.

How came they here? What burst of Chris-
    tian hate,
  What persecution, merciless and blind,
Drove o'er the sea — that desert desolate —
  These Ishmaels and Hagars of mankind?

They lived in narrow streets and lanes ob-
    scure,
  Ghetto and Judenstrass, in mirk and mire;

462

Taught in the school of patience to endure
  The life of anguish and the death of fire.

All their lives long, with the unleavened bread
  And bitter herbs of exile and its fears,
The wasting famine of the heart they fed,
  And slaked its thirst with marah of their
    tears.

Anathema maranatha! was the cry
  That rang from town to town, from street
    to street;
At every gate the accursed Mordecai
  Was mocked and jeered, and spurned by
    Christian feet.

Pride and humiliation hand in hand
  Walked with them through the world
    where'er they went;
Trampled and beaten were they as the sand,
  And yet unshaken as the continent.

For in the background figures vague and vast
  Of patriarchs and of prophets rose sublime,
And all the great traditions of the Past
  They saw reflected in the coming time.

And thus forever with reverted look
  The mystic volume of the world they read,
Spelling it backward, like a Hebrew book,
  Till life became a Legend of the Dead.

But ah! what once has been shall be no more!
  The groaning earth in travail and in pain
Brings forth its races, but does not restore,
  And the dead nations never rise again.

MY LOST YOUTH

Often I think of the beautiful town
  That is seated by the sea;
Often in thought go up and down
The pleasant streets of that dear old town,
  And my youth comes back to me.
  And a verse of a Lapland song
  Is haunting my memory still:
  "A boy's will is the wind's will,
And the thoughts of youth are long, long
  thoughts."

I can see the shadowy lines of its trees,
  And catch, in sudden gleams,
The sheen of the far-surrounding seas,
And islands that were the Hesperides
  Of all my boyish dreams.
  And the burden of that old song,
  It murmurs and whispers still:
  "A boy's will is the wind's will,
And the thoughts of youth are long, long
  thoughts."

I remember the black wharves and the slips,
  And the sea-tides tossing free;

And Spanish sailors with bearded lips,
And the beauty and mystery of the ships,
  And the magic of the sea.
  And the voice of that wayward song
  Is singing and saying still:
  "A boy's will is the wind's will,
And the thoughts of youth are long, long
    thoughts."

I remember the bulwarks by the shore,
  And the fort upon the hill;
The sunrise gun, with its hollow roar,
The drum-beat repeated o'er and o'er,
  And the bugle wild and shrill.
  And the music of that old song
  Throbs in my memory still:
  "A boy's will is the wind's will,
And the thoughts of youth are long, long
    thoughts."

I remember the sea-fight far away,
  How it thundered o'er the tide!
And the dead captains, as they lay
In their graves, o'erlooking the tranquil bay,
  Where they in battle died.
  And the sound of that mournful song
  Goes through me with a thrill:
  "A boy's will is the wind's will,
And the thoughts of youth are long, long
    thoughts."

I can see the breezy dome of groves,
  The shadows of Deering's Woods;
And the friendships old and the early loves
Come back with a Sabbath sound, as of doves
  In quiet neighborhoods.
  And the verse of that sweet old song,
  It flutters and murmurs still:
  "A boy's will is the wind's will,
And the thoughts of youth are long, long
  thoughts."

I remember the gleams and glooms that dart
  Across the school-boy's brain;
The song and the silence in the heart,
That in part are prophecies, and in part
  Are longings wild and vain.
  And the voice of that fitful song
  Sings on, and is never still:
  "A boy's will is the wind's will,
And the thoughts of youth are long, long
  thoughts."

There are things of which I may not speak;
  There are dreams that cannot die;
There are thoughts that make the strong
  heart weak,
And bring a pallor into the cheek,
  And a mist before the eye.
  And the words of that fatal song
  Come over me like a chill:
  "A boy's will is the wind's will,
And the thoughts of youth are long, long

thoughts."

Strange to me now are the forms I meet
  When I visit the dear old town;
But the native air is pure and sweet,
And the trees that o'ershadow each well-
    known street,
  As they balance up and down,
  Are singing the beautiful song,
  Are sighing and whispering still:
"A boy's will is the wind's will,
And the thoughts of youth are long, long
    thoughts."

And Deering's Woods are fresh and fair,
  And with joy that is almost pain
My heart goes back to wander there,
And among the dreams of the days that were,
  I find my lost youth again.
  And the strange and beautiful song,
  The groves are repeating it still:
"A boy's will is the wind's will,
And the thoughts of youth are long, long
    thoughts."

THE ROPEWALK

In that building, long and low,
With its windows all a-row,
  Like the port-holes of a hulk,
Human spiders spin and spin,

Backward down their threads so thin
  Dropping, each a hempen bulk.

At the end, an open door;
Squares of sunshine on the floor
  Light the long and dusky lane;
And the whirring of a wheel,
Dull and drowsy, makes me feel
  All its spokes are in my brain.

As the spinners to the end
Downward go and reascend,
  Gleam the long threads in the sun;
While within this brain of mine
Cobwebs brighter and more fine
  By the busy wheel are spun.

Two fair maidens in a swing,
Like white doves upon the wing,
  First before my vision pass;
Laughing, as their gentle hands
Closely clasp the twisted strands,
  At their shadow on the grass.

Then a booth of mountebanks,
With its smell of tan and planks,
  And a girl poised high in air
On a cord, in spangled dress,
With a faded loveliness,
  And a weary look of care.

Then a homestead among farms,
And a woman with bare arms
　　Drawing water from a well;
As the bucket mounts apace,
With it mounts her own fair face,
　　As at some magician's spell.

Then an old man in a tower,
Ringing loud the noontide hour,
　　While the rope coils round and round
Like a serpent at his feet,
And again, in swift retreat,
　　Nearly lifts him from the ground.

Then within a prison-yard,
Faces fixed, and stern, and hard,
　　Laughter and indecent mirth;
Ah! it is the gallows-tree!
Breath of Christian charity,
　　Blow, and sweep it from the earth!

Then a school-boy, with his kite
Gleaming in a sky of light,
　　And an eager, upward look;
Steeds pursued through lane and field;
Fowlers with their snares concealed;
　　And an angler by a brook.

Ships rejoicing in the breeze,
Wrecks that float o'er unknown seas,
　　Anchors dragged through faithless sand;
Sea-fog drifting overhead,

And, with lessening line and lead,
  Sailors feeling for the land.

All these scenes do I behold,
These, and many left untold,
  In that building long and low;
While the wheel goes round and round,
With a drowsy, dreamy sound,
  And the spinners backward go.

DAYBREAK

A wind came up out of the sea,
And said, "O mists, make room for me."

It hailed the ships, and cried, "Sail on,
Ye mariners, the night is gone."

And hurried landward far away,
Crying, "Awake! it is the day."

It said unto the forest, "Shout!
Hang all your leafy banners out!"

It touched the wood-bird's folded wing,
And said, "O bird, awake and sing."

And o'er the farms, "O chanticleer,
Your clarion blow; the day is near."

It whispered to the fields of corn,

"Bow down, and hail the coming morn."

It shouted through the belfry-tower,
"Awake, O bell! proclaim the hour."

It crossed the churchyard with a sigh,
And said, "Not yet! in quiet lie."

THE FIFTIETH BIRTHDAY OF AGASSIZ

May 28, 1857

It was fifty years ago
  In the pleasant month of May,
In the beautiful Pays de Vaud,
  A child in its cradle lay.

And Nature, the old nurse, took
  The child upon her knee,
Saying: "Here is a story-book
  Thy Father has written for thee."

"Come, wander with me," she said,
  "Into regions yet untrod;
And read what is still unread
  In the manuscripts of God."

And he wandered away and away
  With Nature, the dear old nurse,
Who sang to him night and day
  The rhymes of the universe.

And whenever the way seemed long,
  Or his heart began to fail,
She would sing a more wonderful song,
  Or tell a more marvellous tale.

So she keeps him still a child,
  And will not let him go,
Though at times his heart beats wild
  For the beautiful Pays de Vaud;

Though at times he hears in his dreams
  The Ranz des Vaches of old,
And the rush of mountain streams
  From glaciers clear and cold;

And the mother at home says, "Hark!
  For his voice I listen and yearn;
It is growing late and dark,
  And my boy does not return!"

CHILDREN

Come to me, O ye children!
  For I hear you at your play,
And the questions that perplexed me
  Have vanished quite away.

Ye open the eastern windows,
  That look towards the sun,
Where thoughts are singing swallows
  And the brooks of morning run.

In your hearts are the birds and the sunshine,
  In your thoughts the brooklet's flow,
But in mine is the wind of Autumn
  And the first fall of the snow.

Ah! what would the world be to us
  If the children were no more?
We should dread the desert behind us
  Worse than the dark before.

What the leaves are to the forest,
  With light and air for food,
Ere their sweet and tender juices
  Have been hardened into wood, —

That to the world are children;
  Through them it feels the glow
Of a brighter and sunnier climate
  Than reaches the trunks below.

Come to me, O ye children!
  And whisper in my ear
What the birds and the winds are singing
  In your sunny atmosphere.

For what are all our contrivings,
  And the wisdom of our books,
When compared with your caresses,
  And the gladness of your looks?

Ye are better than all the ballads

That ever were sung or said;
For ye are living poems,
  And all the rest are dead.

SANDALPHON

Have you read in the Talmud of old,
In the Legends the Rabbins have told
  Of the limitless realms of the air,
Have you read it, — the marvellous story
Of Sandalphon, the Angel of Glory,
  Sandalphon, the Angel of Prayer?

How, erect, at the outermost gates
Of the City Celestial he waits,
  With his feet on the ladder of light,
That, crowded with angels unnumbered,
By Jacob was seen, as he slumbered
  Alone in the desert at night?

The Angels of Wind and of Fire
Chant only one hymn, and expire
  With the song's irresistible stress;
Expire in their rapture and wonder,
As harp-strings are broken asunder
  By music they throb to express.

But serene in the rapturous throng,
Unmoved by the rush of the song,
  With eyes unimpassioned and slow,
Among the dead angels, the deathless

Sandalphon stands listening breathless
  To sounds that ascend from below; —

From the spirits on earth that adore,
From the souls that entreat and implore
  In the fervor and passion of prayer;
From the hearts that are broken with losses,
And weary with dragging the crosses
  Too heavy for mortals to bear.

And he gathers the prayers as he stands,
And they change into flowers in his hands,
  Into garlands of purple and red;
And beneath the great arch of the portal,
Through the streets of the City Immortal
  Is wafted the fragrance they shed.

It is but a legend, I know, —
A fable, a phantom, a show,
  Of the ancient Rabbinical lore;
Yet the old mediæval tradition,
The beautiful, strange superstition,
  But haunts me and holds me the more.

When I look from my window at night,
And the welkin above is all white,
  All throbbing and panting with stars,
Among them majestic is standing
Sandalphon the angel, expanding
  His pinions in nebulous bars.

And the legend, I feel, is a part
Of the hunger and thirst of the heart,
  The frenzy and fire of the brain,
That grasps at the fruitage forbidden,
The golden pomegranates of Eden,
  To quiet its fever and pain.

POEMS 1859–1863

THE CHILDREN'S HOUR

Between the dark and the daylight,
  When the night is beginning to lower,
Comes a pause in the day's occupations,
  That is known as the Children's Hour.

I hear in the chamber above me
  The patter of little feet,
The sound of a door that is opened,
  And voices soft and sweet.

From my study I see in the lamplight,
  Descending the broad hall stair,
Grave Alice, and laughing Allegra,
  And Edith with golden hair.

A whisper, and then a silence:
  Yet I know by their merry eyes
They are plotting and planning together
  To take me by surprise.

A sudden rush from the stairway,
  A sudden raid from the hall!
By three doors left unguarded
  They enter my castle wall!

They climb up into my turret
  O'er the arms and back of my chair;
If I try to escape, they surround me;
  They seem to be everywhere.

They almost devour me with kisses,
  Their arms about me entwine,
Till I think of the Bishop of Bingen
  In his Mouse-Tower on the Rhine!

Do you think, O blue-eyed banditti,
  Because you have scaled the wall,
Such an old mustache as I am
  Is not a match for you all!

I have you fast in my fortress,
  And will not let you depart,
But put you down into the dungeon
  In the round-tower of my heart.

And there will I keep you forever,
  Yes, forever and a day,
Till the walls shall crumble to ruin,
  And moulder in dust away!

ENCELADUS

Under Mount Etna he lies,
  It is slumber, it is not death;
For he struggles at times to arise
And above him the lurid skies
  Are hot with his fiery breath.

The crags are piled on his breast,
  The earth is heaped on his head;
But the groans of his wild unrest,
Though smothered and half suppressed,
  Are heard, and he is not dead.

And the nations far away
  Are watching with eager eyes;
They talk together and say,
"To-morrow, perhaps to-day,
  Enceladus will arise!"

And the old gods, the austere
  Oppressors in their strength,
Stand aghast and white with fear
At the ominous sounds they hear,
  And tremble, and mutter, "At length!"

All me! for the land that is sown
  With the harvest of despair!
Where the burning cinders, blown
From the lips of the overthrown
  Enceladus, fill the air.

Where ashes are heaped in drifts
  Over vineyard and field and town,
Whenever he starts and lifts
His head through the blackened rifts
  Of the crags that keep him down.

See, see! the red light shines!
  'T is the glare of his awful eyes!
  And the storm-wind shouts through the
  pines
Of Alps and of Apennines,
  "Enceladus, arise!"

THE CUMBERLAND

At anchor in Hampton Roads we lay,
  On board of the Cumberland, sloop-of-
  war;
And at times from the fortress across the bay
  The alarum of drums swept past,
  Or a bugle blast
From the camp on the shore.

Then far away to the south uprose
  A little feather of snow-white smoke,
And we knew that the iron ship of our foes
  Was steadily steering its course
  To try the force
Of our ribs of oak.

Down upon us heavily runs,

Silent and sullen, the floating fort;
Then comes a puff of smoke from her guns,
  And leaps the terrible death,
  With fiery breath,
  From each open port.

We are not idle, but send her straight
  Defiance back in a full broadside!
As hail rebounds from a roof of slate,
  Rebounds our heavier hail
  From each iron scale
  Of the monster's hide.

"Strike your flag!" the rebel cries,
  In his arrogant old plantation strain.
"Never!" our gallant Morris replies;
  "It is better to sink than to yield!"
  And the whole air pealed
  With the cheers of our men.

Then, like a kraken huge and black,
  She crushed our ribs in her iron grasp!
Down went the Cumberland all a wrack,
  With a sudden shudder of death,
  And the cannon's breath
  For her dying gasp.

Next morn, as the sun rose over the bay,
  Still floated our flag at the mainmast head.
Lord, how beautiful was Thy day!
  Every waft of the air

Was a whisper of prayer,
Or a dirge for the dead.

Ho! brave hearts that went down in the seas!
 Ye are at peace in the troubled stream;
Ho! brave land! with hearts like these,
 Thy flag, that is rent in twain,
 Shall be one again,
 And without a seam!

SNOW-FLAKES

Out of the bosom of the Air,
 Out of the cloud-folds of her garments
  shaken,
Over the woodlands brown and bare,
 Over the harvest-fields forsaken,
 Silent, and soft, and slow
 Descends the snow.

Even as our cloudy fancies take
 Suddenly shape in some divine expression,
Even as the troubled heart doth make
 In the white countenance confession,
 The troubled sky reveals
 The grief it feels.

This is the poem of the air,
 Slowly in silent syllables recorded;
This is the secret of despair,
 Long in its cloudy bosom hoarded,

Now whispered and revealed
To wood and field.

A DAY OF SUNSHINE

O gift of God! O perfect day:
Whereon shall no man work, but play;
Whereon it is enough for me,
Not to be doing, but to be!

Through every fibre of my brain,
Through every nerve, through every vein,
I feel the electric thrill, the touch
Of life, that seems almost too much.

I hear the wind among the trees
Playing celestial symphonies;
I see the branches downward bent,
Like keys of some great instrument.

And over me unrolls on high
The splendid scenery of the sky,
Where through a sapphire sea the sun
Sails like a golden galleon,

Towards yonder cloud-land in the West,
Towards yonder Islands of the Blest,
Whose steep sierra far uplifts
Its craggy summits white with drifts.

Blow, winds! and waft through all the rooms

The snow-flakes of the cherry-blooms!
Blow, winds! and bend within my reach
The fiery blossoms of the peach!

O Life and Love! O happy throng
Of thoughts, whose only speech is song!
O heart of man! canst thou not be
Blithe as the air is, and as free?

SOMETHING LEFT UNDONE

Labor with what zeal we will,
  Something still remains undone,
Something uncompleted still
  Waits the rising of the sun.

By the bedside, on the stair,
  At the threshold, near the gates,
With its menace or its prayer,
  Like a mendicant it waits;

Waits, and will not go away;
  Waits, and will not be gainsaid;
By the cares of yesterday
  Each to-day is heavier made;

Till at length the burden seems
  Greater than our strength can bear,
Heavy as the weight of dreams,
  Pressing on us everywhere.

And we stand from day to day,
  Like the dwarfs of times gone by,
Who, as Northern legends say,
  On their shoulders held the sky.

WEARINESS

O little feet! that such long years
Must wander on through hopes and fears,
  Must ache and bleed beneath your load;
I, nearer to the wayside inn
Where toil shall cease and rest begin,
  Am weary, thinking of your road!

O little hands! that, weak or strong,
Have still to serve or rule so long,
  Have still so long to give or ask;
I, who so much with book and pen
Have toiled among my fellow-men,
  Am weary, thinking of your task.

O little hearts! that throb and beat
With such impatient, feverish heat,
  Such limitless and strong desires;
Mine, that so long has glowed and burned,
With passions into ashes turned,
  Now covers and conceals its fires.

O little souls! as pure and white
And crystalline as rays of light
  Direct from heaven, their source divine;

Refracted through the mist of years,
How red my setting sun appears,
  How lurid looks this soul of mine!

TALES OF A WAYSIDE INN

PART FIRST

PRELUDE

The Wayside Inn

One Autumn night, in Sudbury town,
Across the meadows bare and brown,
The windows of the wayside inn
Gleamed red with fire-light through the
    leaves
Of woodbine, hanging from the eaves
Their crimson curtains rent and thin.

As ancient is this hostelry
As any in the land may be,
Built in the old Colonial day,
When men lived in a grander way,
With ampler hospitality;
A kind of old Hobgoblin Hall,
Now somewhat fallen to decay,
With weather-stains upon the wall,

And stairways worn, and crazy doors,
And creaking and uneven floors,
And chimneys huge, and tiled and tall.

A region of repose it seems,
A place of slumber and of dreams,
Remote among the wooded hills!
For there no noisy railway speeds,
Its torch-race scattering smoke and gleeds;
But noon and night, the panting teams
Stop under the great oaks, that throw
Tangles of light and shade below,
On roofs and doors and window-sills.
Across the road the barns display
Their lines of stalls, their mows of hay,
Through the wide doors the breezes blow,
The wattled cocks strut to and fro,
And, half effaced by rain and shine,
The Red Horse prances on the sign.
Round this old-fashioned, quaint abode
Deep silence reigned, save when a gust
Went rushing down the county road,
And skeletons of leaves, and dust,
A moment quickened by its breath,
Shuddered and danced their dance of death,
And through the ancient oaks o'erhead
Mysterious voices moaned and fled.

But from the parlor of the inn
A pleasant murmur smote the ear,
Like water rushing through a weir:

Oft interrupted by the din
Of laughter and of loud applause,
And, in each intervening pause,
The music of a violin.
The fire-light, shedding over all
The splendor of its ruddy glow,
Filled the whole parlor large and low;
It gleamed on wainscot and on wall,
It touched with more than wonted grace
Fair Princess Mary's pictured face;
It bronzed the rafters overhead,
On the old spinet's ivory keys
It played inaudible melodies,
It crowned the sombre clock with flame,
The hands, the hours, the maker's name,
And painted with a livelier red
The Landlord's coat-of-arms again;
And, flashing on the window-pane,
Emblazoned with its light and shade
The jovial rhymes, that still remain,
Writ near a century ago,
By the great Major Molineaux,
Whom Hawthorne has immortal made.

Before the blazing fire of wood
Erect the rapt musician stood;
And ever and anon he bent
His head upon his instrument,
And seemed to listen, till he caught
Confessions of its secret thought, —
The joy, the triumph, the lament,
The exultation and the pain;

Then, by the magic of his art,
He soothed the throbbings of its heart,
And lulled it into peace again.

Around the fireside at their ease
There sat a group of friends, entranced
With the delicious melodies;
Who from the far-off noisy town
Had to the wayside inn come down,
To rest beneath its old oak trees.
The fire-light on their faces glanced,
Their shadows on the wainscot danced,
And, though of different lands and speech,
Each had his tale to tell, and each
Was anxious to be pleased and please.
And while the sweet musician plays,
Let me in outline sketch them all,
Perchance uncouthly as the blaze
With its uncertain touch portrays
Their shadowy semblance on the wall.

But first the Landlord will I trace;
Grave in his aspect and attire;
A man of ancient pedigree,
A Justice of the Peace was he,
Known in all Sudbury as "The Squire."
Proud was he of his name and race,
Of old Sir William and Sir Hugh,
And in the parlor, full in view,
His coat-of-arms, well framed and glazed,
Upon the wall in colors blazed;
He beareth gules upon his shield,

A chevron argent in the field,
With three wolf's heads, and for the crest
A Wyvern part-per-pale addressed
Upon a helmet barred; below
The scroll reads, "By the name of Howe."
And over this, no longer bright,
Though glimmering with a latent light,
Was hung the sword his grandsire bore
In the rebellious days of yore,
Down there at Concord in the fight.

A youth was there, of quiet ways,
A Student of old books and days,
To whom all tongues and lands were known,
And yet a lover of his own;
With many a social virtue graced,
And yet a friend of solitude;
A man of such a genial mood
The heart of all things he embraced,
And yet of such fastidious taste,
He never found the best too good.
Books were his passion and delight,
And in his upper room at home
Stood many a rare and sumptuous tome,
In vellum bound, with gold bedight,
Great volumes garmented in white,
Recalling Florence, Pisa, Rome.
He loved the twilight that surrounds
The border-land of old romance;
Where glitter hauberk, helm, and lance,
And banner waves, and trumpet sounds,
And ladies ride with hawk on wrist,

And mighty warriors sweep along,
Magnified by the purple mist,
The dusk of centuries and of song.
The chronicles of Charlemagne,
Of Merlin and the Mort d'Arthure,
Mingled together in his brain
With tales of Flores and Blanchefleur,
Sir Ferumbras, Sir Eglamour,
Sir Launcelot, Sir Morgadour,
Sir Guy, Sir Bevis, Sir Gawain.

A young Sicilian, too, was there;
In sight of Etna born and bred,
Some breath of its volcanic air
Was glowing in his heart and brain,
And, being rebellious to his liege,
After Palermo's fatal siege,
Across the western seas he fled,
In good King Bomba's happy reign.
His face was like a summer night,
All flooded with a dusky light;
His hands were small; his teeth shone white
As sea-shells, when he smiled or spoke;
His sinews supple and strong as oak;
Clean shaven was he as a priest,
Who at the mass on Sunday sings,
Save that upon his upper lip
His beard, a good palm's length at least,
Level and pointed at the tip,
Shot sideways, like a swallow's wings.
The poets read he o'er and o'er,
And most of all the Immortal Four

Of Italy; and next to those,
The story-telling bard of prose,
Who wrote the joyous Tuscan tales
Of the Decameron, that make
Fiesole's green hills and vales
Remembered for Boccaccio's sake.
Much too of music was his thought;
The melodies and measures fraught
With sunshine and the open air,
Of vineyards and the singing sea
Of his beloved Sicily;
And much it pleased him to peruse
The songs of the Sicilian muse, —
Bucolic songs by Meli sung
In the familiar peasant tongue,
That made men say, "Behold! once more
The pitying gods to earth restore
Theocritus of Syracuse!"

A Spanish Jew from Alicant
With aspect grand and grave was there;
Vender of silks and fabrics rare,
And attar of rose from the Levant.
Like an old Patriarch he appeared,
Abraham or Isaac, or at least
Some later Prophet or High-Priest;
With lustrous eyes, and olive skin,
And, wildly tossed from cheeks and chin,
The tumbling cataract of his beard.
His garments breathed a spicy scent
Of cinnamon and sandal blent,
Like the soft aromatic gales

That meet the mariner, who sails
Through the Moluccas, and the seas
That wash the shores of Celebes.
All stories that recorded are
By Pierre Alphonse he knew by heart,
And it was rumored he could say
The Parables of Sandabar,
And all the Fables of Pilpay,
Or if not all, the greater part!
Well versed was he in Hebrew books,
Talmud and Targum, and the lore
Of Kabala; and evermore
There was a mystery in his looks;
His eyes seemed gazing far away,
As if in vision or in trance
He heard the solemn sackbut play,
And saw the Jewish maidens dance.

A Theologian, from the school
Of Cambridge on the Charles, was there;
Skilful alike with tongue and pen,
He preached to all men everywhere
The Gospel of the Golden Rule,
The New Commandment given to men,
Thinking the deed, and not the creed,
Would help us in our utmost need.
With reverent feet the earth he trod,
Nor banished nature from his plan,
But studied still with deep research
To build the Universal Church,
Lofty as in the love of God,
And ample as the wants of man.

A Poet, too, was there, whose verse
Was tender, musical, and terse;
The inspiration, the delight,
The gleam, the glory, the swift flight,
Of thoughts so sudden, that they seem
The revelations of a dream,
All these were his; but with them came
No envy of another's fame;
He did not find his sleep less sweet
For music in some neighboring street,
Nor rustling hear in every breeze
The laurels of Miltiades.
Honor and blessings on his head
While living, good report when dead,
Who, not too eager for renown,
Accepts, but does not clutch, the crown!

Last the Musician, as he stood
Illumined by that fire of wood;
Fair-haired, blue-eyed, his aspect blithe,
His figure tall and straight and lithe,
And every feature of his face
Revealing his Norwegian race;
A radiance, streaming from within,
Around his eyes and forehead beamed,
The Angel with the violin,
Painted by Raphael, he seemed.
He lived in that ideal world
Whose language is not speech, but song;
Around him evermore the throng
Of elves and sprites their dances whirled;
The Strömkarl sang, the cataract hurled

Its headlong waters from the height;
And mingled in the wild delight
The scream of sea-birds in their flight,
The rumor of the forest trees,
The plunge of the implacable seas,
The tumult of the wind at night,
Voices of eld, like trumpets blowing,
Old ballads, and wild melodies
Through mist and darkness pouring forth,
Like Elivagar's river flowing
Out of the glaciers of the North.

The instrument on which he played
Was in Cremona's workshops made,
By a great master of the past,
Ere yet was lost the art divine;
Fashioned of maple and of pine,
That in Tyrolean forests vast
Had rocked and wrestled with the blast:
Exquisite was it in design,
Perfect in each minutest part,
A marvel of the lutist's art;
And in its hollow chamber, thus,
The maker from whose hands it came
Had written his unrivalled name, —
"Antonius Stradivarius."

And when he played, the atmosphere
Was filled with magic, and the ear
Caught echoes of that Harp of Gold,
Whose music had so weird a sound,
The hunted stag forgot to bound,

The leaping rivulet backward rolled,
The birds came down from bush and tree,
The dead came from beneath the sea,
The maiden to thc harper's knee!

The music ceased; the applause was loud,
The pleased musician smiled and bowed;
The wood-fire clapped its hands of flame,
The shadows on the wainscot stirred,
And from the harpsichord there came
A ghostly murmur of acclaim,
A sound like that sent down at night
By birds of passage in their flight,
From the remotest distance heard.

Then silence followed; then began
A clamor for the Landlord's tale, —
The story promised them of old,
They said, but always left untold;
And he, although a bashful man,
And all his courage seemed to fail,
Finding excuse of no avail,
Yielded; and thus the story ran.

THE LANDLORD'S TALE

Paul Revere's Ride

Listen, my children, and you shall hear
Of the midnight ride of Paul Revere,
On the eighteenth of April, in Seventy-five;

Hardly a man is now alive
Who remembers that famous day and year.

He said to his friend, "If the British march
By land or sea from the town to-night,
Hang a lantern aloft in the belfry arch
Of the North Church tower as a signal
   light, —
One, if by land, and two, if by sea;
And I on the opposite shore will be,
Ready to ride and spread the alarm
Through every Middlesex village and farm,
For the country folk to be up and to arm."
Then he said, "Good night!" and with
   muffled oar
Silently rowed to the Charlestown shore,
Just as the moon rose over the bay,
Where swinging wide at her moorings lay
The Somerset, British man-of-war;
A phantom ship, with each mast and spar
Across the moon like a prison bar,
And a huge black hulk, that was magnified
By its own reflection in the tide.

Meanwhile, his friend, through alley and
   street,
Wanders and watches with eager ears,
Till in the silence around him he hears
The muster of men at the barrack door,
The sound of arms, and the tramp of feet,
And the measured tread of the grenadiers,

Marching down to their boats on the shore.

Then he climbed the tower of the Old North
  Church,
By the wooden stairs, with stealthy tread,
To the belfry-chamber overhead,
And startled the pigeons from their perch
On the sombre rafters, that round him made
Masses and moving shapes of shade, —
By the trembling ladder, steep and tall,
To the highest window in the wall,
Where he paused to listen and look down
A moment on the roofs of the town,
And the moonlight flowing over all.
Beneath, in the churchyard, lay the dead,
In their night-encampment on the hill,
Wrapped in silence so deep and still
That he could hear, like a sentinel's tread,
The watchful night-wind, as it went
Creeping along from tent to tent,
And seeming to whisper, "All is well!"
A moment only he feels the spell
Of the place and the hour, and the secret
  dread
Of the lonely belfry and the dead;
For suddenly all his thoughts are bent
On a shadowy something far away,
Where the river widens to meet the bay, —
A line of black that bends and floats
On the rising tide, like a bridge of boats.

Meanwhile, impatient to mount and ride,

Booted and spurred, with a heavy stride
On the opposite shore walked Paul Revere.
Now he patted his horse's side,
Now gazed at the landscape far and near,
Then, impetuous, stamped the earth,
And turned and tightened his saddle girth;
But mostly he watched with eager search
The belfry-tower of the Old North Church,
As it rose above the graves on the hill,
Lonely and spectral and sombre and still.
And lo! as he looks, on the belfry's height
A glimmer, and then a gleam of light!
He springs to the saddle, the bridle he turns,
But lingers and gazes, till full on his sight
A second lamp in the belfry burns!

A hurry of hoofs in a village street,
A shape in the moonlight, a bulk in the dark,
And beneath, from the pebbles, in passing, a
    spark
Struck out by a steed flying fearless and fleet:
That was all! And yet, through the gloom
    and the light,
The fate of a nation was riding that night;
And the spark struck out by that steed, in his
    flight,
Kindled the land into flame with its heat.
He has left the village and mounted the steep,
And beneath him, tranquil and broad and
    deep,
Is the Mystic, meeting the ocean tides;
And under the alders, that skirt its edge,

Now soft on the sand, now loud on the ledge,
Is heard the tramp of his steed as he rides.

It was twelve by the village clock,
When he crossed the bridge into Medford
    town.
He heard the crowing of the cock,
And the barking of the farmer's dog,
And felt the damp of the river fog,
That rises after the sun goes down.

It was one by the village clock,
When he galloped into Lexington.
He saw the gilded weathercock
Swim in the moonlight as he passed,
And the meeting-house windows, blank and
    bare,
Gaze at him with a spectral glare,
As if they already stood aghast
At the bloody work they would look upon.

It was two by the village clock,
When he came to the bridge in Concord
    town.
He heard the bleating of the flock,
And the twitter of birds among the trees,
And felt the breath of the morning breeze
Blowing over the meadows brown.
And one was safe and asleep in his bed
Who at the bridge would be first to fall,
Who that day would be lying dead,
Pierced by a British musket-ball.

You know the rest. In the books you have
    read,
How the British Regulars fired and fled, —
How the farmers gave them ball for ball,
From behind each fence and farm-yard wall,
Chasing the red-coats down the lane,
Then crossing the fields to emerge again
Under the trees at the turn of the road,
And only pausing to fire and load.

So through the night rode Paul Revere;
And so through the night went his cry of
    alarm
To every Middlesex village and farm, —
A cry of defiance and not of fear,
A voice in the darkness, a knock at the door,
And a word that shall echo forevermore!
For, borne on the night-wind of the Past,
Through all our history, to the last,
In the hour of darkness and peril and need,
The people will waken and listen to hear
The hurrying hoof-beats of that steed,
And the midnight message of Paul Revere.

INTERLUDE

The Landlord ended thus his tale,
Then rising took down from its nail
The sword that hung there, dim with dust,
And cleaving to its sheath with rust,
And said, "This sword was in the fight."

The Poet seized it, and exclaimed,
"It is the sword of a good knight,
Though homespun was his coat-of-mail;
What matter if it be not named
Joyeuse, Colada, Durindale,
Excalibar, or Aroundight,
Or other name the books record?
Your ancestor, who bore this sword
As Colonel of the Volunteers,
Mounted upon his old gray mare,
Seen here and there and everywhere,
To me a grander shape appears
Than old Sir William, or what not,
Clinking about in foreign lands
With iron gauntlets on his hands,
And on his head an iron pot!"

All laughed; the Landlord's face grew red
As his escutcheon on the wall;
He could not comprehend at all
The drift of what the Poet said;
For those who had been longest dead
Were always greatest in his eyes;
And he was speechless with surprise
To see Sir William's plumed head
Brought to a level with the rest,
And made the subject of a jest.
And this perceiving, to appease
The Landlord's wrath, the others' fears,
The Student said, with careless ease,
"The ladies and the cavaliers,

The arms, the loves, the courtesies,
The deeds of high emprise, I sing!

Thus Ariosto says, in words
That have the stately stride and ring
Of armed knights and clashing swords.
Now listen to the tale I bring;
Listen! though not to me belong
The flowing draperies of his song,
The words that rouse, the voice that charms.
The Landlord's tale was one of arms,
Only a tale of love is mine,
Blending the human and divine,
A tale of the Decameron, told
In Palmieri's garden old,
By Fiametta, laurel-crowned,
While her companions lay around,
And heard the intermingled sound
Of airs that on their errands sped,
And wild birds gossiping overhead,
And lisp of leaves, and fountain's fall,
And her own voice more sweet than all,
Telling the tale, which, wanting these,
Perchance may lose its power to please."

THE STUDENT'S TALE

The Falcon of Ser Federigo

One summer morning, when the sun was hot,
Weary with labor in his garden-plot,

504

On a rude bench beneath his cottage eaves,
Ser Federigo sat among the leaves
Of a huge vine, that, with its arms outspread,
Hung its delicious clusters overhead.
Below him, through the lovely valley, flowed
The river Arno, like a winding road,
And from its banks were lifted high in air
The spires and roofs of Florence called the
    Fair;
To him a marble tomb, that rose above
His wasted fortunes and his buried love.
For there, in banquet and in tournament,
His wealth had lavished been, his substance
    spent,
To woo and lose, since ill his wooing sped,
Monna Giovanna, who his rival wed,
Yet ever in his fancy reigned supreme,
The ideal woman of a young man's dream.

Then he withdrew, in poverty and pain,
To this small farm, the last of his domain,
His only comfort and his only care
To prune his vines, and plant the fig and
    pear;
His only forester and only guest
His falcon, faithful to him, when the rest,
Whose willing hands had found so light of
    yore
The brazen knocker of his palace door,
Had now no strength to lift the wooden latch,
That entrance gave beneath a roof of thatch.

Companion of his solitary ways,
Purveyor of his feasts on holidays,
On him this melancholy man bestowed
The love with which his nature overflowed.

And so the empty-handed years went round,
Vacant, though voiceful with prophetic
　　sound,
And so, that summer morn, he sat and mused
With folded, patient hands, as he was used,
And dreamily before his half-closed sight
Floated the vision of his lost delight.
Beside him, motionless, the drowsy bird
Dreamed of the chase, and in his slumber
　　heard
The sudden, scythe-like sweep of wings, that
　　dare
The headlong plunge through eddying gulfs
　　of air,
Then, starting broad awake upon his perch,
Tinkled his bells, like mass-bells in a church,
And looking at his master, seemed to say,
"Ser Federigo, shall we hunt to-day?"

Ser Federigo thought not of the chase;
The tender vision of her lovely face,
I will not say he seems to see, he sees
In the leaf-shadows of the trellises,
Herself, yet not herself; a lovely child
With flowing tresses, and eyes wide and wild,
Coming undaunted up the garden walk,
And looking not at him, but at the hawk.

"Beautiful falcon!" said he, "would that I
Might hold thee on my wrist, or see thee fly!"
The voice was hers, and made strange echoes
    start
Through all the haunted chambers of his
    heart,
As an æolian harp through gusty doors
Of some old ruin its wild music pours.

"Who is thy mother, my fair boy?" he said,
His hand laid softly on that shining head.
"Monna Giovanna. Will you let me stay
A little while, and with your falcon play?
We live there, just beyond your garden wall,
In the great house behind the poplars tall."

So he spake on; and Federigo heard
As from afar each softly uttered word,
And drifted onward through the golden
    gleams
And shadows of the misty sea of dreams,
As mariners becalmed through vapors drift,
And feel the sea beneath them sink and lift,
And hear far off the mournful breakers roar,
And voices calling faintly from the shore!
Then waking from his pleasant reveries,
He took the little boy upon his knees,
And told him stories of his gallant bird,
Till in their friendship he became a third.

Monna Giovanna, widowed in her prime,

Had come with friends to pass the summer
    time
In her grand villa, half-way up the hill,
O'erlooking Florence, but retired and still;
With iron gates, that opened through long
    lines
Of sacred ilex and centennial pines,
And terraced gardens, and broad steps of
    stone,
And sylvan deities, with moss o'ergrown,
And fountains palpitating in the heat,
And all Val d'Arno stretched beneath its feet.
Here in seclusion, as a widow may,
The lovely lady whiled the hours away,
Pacing in sable robes the statued hall,
Herself the stateliest statue among all,
And seeing more and more, with secret joy,
Her husband risen and living in her boy,
Till the lost sense of life returned again,
Not as delight, but as relief from pain.
Meanwhile the boy, rejoicing in his strength,
Stormed down the terraces from length to
    length;
The screaming peacock chased in hot pur-
    suit,
And climbed the garden trellises for fruit.
But his chief pastime was to watch the flight
Of a gerfalcon, soaring into sight,
Beyond the trees that fringed the garden wall,
Then downward stooping at some distant
    call;
And as he gazed full often wondered he

Who might the master of the falcon be,
Until that happy morning, when he found
Master and falcon in the cottage ground.

And now a shadow and a terror fell
On the great house, as if a passing-bell
Tolled from the tower, and filled each spa-
    cious room
With secret awe and preternatural gloom;
The petted boy grew ill, and day by day
Pined with mysterious malady away.
The mother's heart would not be comforted;
Her darling seemed to her already dead,
And often, sitting by the sufferer's side,
"What can I do to comfort thee?" she cried.
At first the silent lips made no reply,
But, moved at length by her importunate cry,
"Give me," he answered, with imploring tone,
"Ser Federigo's falcon for my own!"

No answer could the astonished mother
    make;
How could she ask, e'en for her darling's
    sake,
Such favor at a luckless lover's hand,
Well knowing that to ask was to command?
Well knowing, what all falconers confessed,
In all the land that falcon was the best,
The master's pride and passion and delight,
And the sole pursuivant of this poor knight.
But yet, for her child's sake, she could no
    less

Than give assent, to soothe his restlessness,
So promised, and then promising to keep
Her promise sacred, saw him fall asleep.

The morrow was a bright September morn;
The earth was beautiful as if new-born;
There was that nameless splendor every-
    where,
That wild exhilaration in the air,
Which makes the passers in the city street
Congratulate each other as they meet.
Two lovely ladies, clothed in cloak and hood,
Passed through the garden gate into the
    wood,
Under the lustrous leaves, and through the
    sheen
Of dewy sunshine showering down between.
The one, close-hooded, had the attractive
    grace
Which sorrow sometimes lends a woman's
    face;
Her dark eyes moistened with the mists that
    roll
From the gulf-stream of passion in the soul;
The other with her hood thrown back, her
    hair
Making a golden glory in the air,
Her cheeks suffused with an auroral blush,
Her young heart singing louder than the
    thrush.
So walked, that morn, through mingled light
    and shade,

Each by the other's presence lovelier made,
Monna Giovanna and her bosom friend,
Intent upon their errand and its end.

They found Ser Federigo at his toil,
Like banished Adam, delving in the soil;
And when he looked and these fair women
  spied,
The garden suddenly was glorified;
His long-lost Eden was restored again,
And the strange river winding through the
  plain
No longer was the Arno to his eyes,
But the Euphrates watering Paradise!

Monna Giovanna raised her stately head,
And with fair words of salutation said:
"Ser Federigo, we come here as friends,
Hoping in this to make some poor amends
For past unkindness. I who ne'er before
Would even cross the threshold of your door,
I who in happier days such pride maintained,
Refused your banquets, and your gifts dis-
  dained,
This morning come, a self-invited guest,
To put your generous nature to the test,
And breakfast with you under your own
  vine."
To which he answered: "Poor desert of mine,
Not your unkindness call it, for if aught
Is good in me of feeling or of thought,

From you it comes, and this last grace out-
   weighs
All sorrows, all regrets of other days."

And after further compliment and talk,
Among the asters in the garden walk
He left his guests; and to his cottage turned,
And as he entered for a moment yearned
For the lost splendors of the days of old,
The ruby glass, the silver and the gold,
And felt how piercing is the sting of pride,
By want embittered and intensified.
He looked about him for some means or way
To keep this unexpected holiday;
Searched every cupboard, and then searched
   again,
Summoned the maid, who came, but came
   in vain;
"The Signor did not hunt to-day," she said,
"There's nothing in the house but wine and
   bread."
Then suddenly the drowsy falcon shook
His little bells, with that sagacious look,
Which said, as plain as language to the ear,
If anything is wanting, I am here!"
Yes, everything is wanting, gallant bird!
The master seized thee without further word.

Like thine own lure, he whirled thee round;
   ah me!
The pomp and flutter of brave falconry.
The bells, the jesses, the bright scarlet hood,

The flight and the pursuit o'er field and
    wood,
All these forevermore are ended now;
No longer victor, but the victim thou!

Then on the board a snow-white cloth he
    spread,
Laid on its wooden dish the loaf of bread,
Brought purple grapes with autumn sunshine
    hot,
The fragrant peach, the juicy bergamot;
Then in the midst a flask of wine he placed
And with autumnal flowers the banquet
    graced.
Ser Federigo, would not these suffice
Without thy falcon stuffed with cloves and
    spice?

When all was ready, and the courtly dame
With her companion to the cottage came,
Upon Ser Federigo's brain there fell
The wild enchantment of a magic spell!
The room they entered, mean and low and
    small,
Was changed into a sumptuous banquet-hall,
With fanfares by aerial trumpets blown;
The rustic chair she sat on was a throne;
He ate celestial food, and a divine
Flavor was given to his country wine,
And the poor falcon, fragrant with his spice,
A peacock was, or bird of paradise!

When the repast was ended, they arose
And passed again into the garden-close.
Then said the lady, "Far too well I know,
Remembering still the days of long ago,
Though you betray it not, with what surprise
You see me here in this familiar wise.
You have no children, and you cannot guess
What anguish, what unspeakable distress
A mother feels, whose child is lying ill,
Nor how her heart anticipates his will.
And yet for this, you see me lay aside
All womanly reserve and check of pride,
And ask the thing most precious in your
    sight,
Your falcon, your sole comfort and delight,
Which if you find it in your heart to give,
My poor, unhappy boy perchance may live."

Ser Federigo listens, and replies,
With tears of love and pity in his eyes:
"Alas, dear lady! there can be no task
So sweet to me, as giving when you ask.
One little hour ago, if I had known
This wish of yours, it would have been my
    own.
But thinking in what manner I could best
Do honor to the presence of my guest,
I deemed that nothing worthier could be
Than what most dear and precious was to
    me;
And so my gallant falcon breathed his last
To furnish forth this morning our repast."

In mute contrition, mingled with dismay,
The gentle lady turned her eyes away,
Grieving that he such sacrifice should make
And kill his falcon for a woman's sake,
Yet feeling in her heart a woman's pride,
That nothing she could ask for was denied;
Then took her leave, and passed out at the
    gate
With footstep slow and soul disconsolate.

Three days went by, and lo! a passing-bell
Tolled from the little chapel in the dell;
Ten strokes Ser Federigo heard, and said,
Breathing a prayer, "Alas! her child is dead!"
Three months went by; and lo! a merrier
    chime
Rang from the chapel bells at Christmas-
    time;
The cottage was deserted, and no more
Ser Federigo sat beside its door,
But now, with servitors to do his will,
In the grand villa, half-way up the hill,
Sat at the Christmas feast, and at his side
Monna Giovanna, his beloved bride,
Never so beautiful, so kind, so fair,
Enthroned once more in the old rustic chair,
High-perched upon the back of which there
    stood
The image of a falcon carved in wood,
And underneath the inscription, with a date,
"All things come round to him who will but
    wait."

INTERLUDE

Soon as the story reached its end,
One, over eager to commend,
Crowned it with injudicious praise;
And then the voice of blame found vent,
And fanned the embers of dissent
Into a somewhat lively blaze.

The Theologian shook his head;
"These old Italian tales," he said,
"From the much-praised Decameron down
Through all the rabble of the rest,
Are either trifling, dull, or lewd;
The gossip of a neighborhood
In some remote provincial town,
A scandalous chronicle at best!
They seem to me a stagnant fen,
Grown rank with rushes and with reeds,
Where a white lily, now and then,
Blooms in the midst of noxious weeds
And deadly nightshade on its banks!"

To this the Student straight replied,
"For the white lily, many thanks!
One should not say, with too much pride,
Fountain, I will not drink of thee!
Nor were it grateful to forget
That from these reservoirs and tanks
Even imperial Shakespeare drew
His Moor of Venice, and the Jew,

And Romeo and Juliet,
And many a famous comedy."

Then a long pause; till some one said,
"An Angel is flying overhead!"
At these words spake the Spanish Jew,
And murmured with an inward breath:
"God grant, if what you say be true,
It may not be the Angel of Death!"
And then another pause; and then,
Stroking his beard, he said again:
"This brings back to my memory
A story in the Talmud told,
That book of gems, that book of gold,
Of wonders many and manifold,
A tale that often comes to me,
And fills my heart, and haunts my brain,
And never wearies nor grows old."

THE SPANISH JEW'S TALE

The Legend of Rabbi Ben Levi

Rabbi Ben Levi, on the Sabbath, read
A volume of the Law, in which it said,
"No man shall look upon my face and live."
And as he read, he prayed that God would
    give
His faithful servant grace with mortal eye
To look upon His face and yet not die.

Then fell a sudden shadow on the page,
And, lifting up his eyes, grown dim with
   age,
He saw the Angel of Death before him stand,
Holding a naked sword in his right hand.
Rabbi Ben Levi was a righteous man,
Yet through his veins a chill of terror ran.
With trembling voice he said, "What wilt
   thou here?"
The angel answered, "Lo! the time draws
   near
When thou must die; yet first, by God's
   decree,
Whate'er thou askest shall be granted thee."
Replied the Rabbi, "Let these living eyes
First look upon my place in Paradise."

Then said the Angel, "Come with me and
   look."
Rabbi Ben Levi closed the sacred book,
And rising, and uplifting his gray head,
"Give me thy sword," he to the Angel said,
"Lest thou shouldst fall upon me by the way."
The angel smiled and hastened to obey,
Then led him forth to the Celestial Town,
And set him on the wall, whence, gazing
   down,
Rabbi Ben Levi, with his living eyes,
Might look upon his place in Paradise.

Then straight into the city of the Lord

The Rabbi leaped with the Death-Angel's
 sword,
And through the streets there swept a sud-
 den breath
Of something there unknown, which men call
 death.
Meanwhile the Angel stayed without, and
 cried,
"Come back!" To which the Rabbi's voice
 replied,
"No! in the name of God, whom I adore,
I swear that hence I will depart no more!"

Then all the Angels cried, "O Holy One,
See what the son of Levi here hath done!
The kingdom of Heaven he takes by violence,
And in Thy name refuses to go hence!"
The Lord replied, "My Angels, be not wroth;
Did e'er the son of Levi break his oath?
Let him remain; for he with mortal eye
Shall look upon my face and yet not die."

Beyond the outer wall the Angel of Death
Heard the great voice, and said, with panting
 breath,
"Give back the sword, and let me go my way."
Whereat the Rabbi paused, and answered,
 "Nay!
Anguish enough already hath it caused
Among the sons of men." And while he
 paused
He heard the awful mandate of the Lord

Resounding through the air, "Give back the
   sword!"

The Rabbi bowed his head in silent prayer;
Then said he to the dreadful Angel, "Swear
No human eye shall look on it again;
But when thou takest away the souls of men,
Thyself unseen, and with an unseen sword,
Thou wilt perform the bidding of the Lord."
The Angel took the sword again, and swore,
And walks on earth unseen forevermore.

INTERLUDE

He ended: and a kind of spell
Upon the silent listeners fell.
His solemn manner and his words
Had touched the deep, mysterious chords
That vibrate in each human breast
Alike, but not alike confessed.
The spiritual world seemed near;
And close above them, full of fear,
Its awful adumbration passed,
A luminous shadow, vague and vast.
They almost feared to look, lest there,
Embodied from the impalpable air,
They might behold the Angel stand,
Holding the sword in his right hand.

At last, but in a voice subdued,
Not to disturb their dreamy mood,

Said the Sicilian: "While you spoke,
Telling your legend marvellous,
Suddenly in my memory woke
The thought of one, now gone from us, —
An old Abate, meek and mild,
My friend and teacher, when a child,
Who sometimes in those days of old
The legend of an Angel told,
Which ran, as I remember, thus."

THE SICILIAN'S TALE

King Robert of Sicily

Robert of Sicily, brother of Pope Urbane
And Valmond, Emperor of Allemaine,
Apparelled in magnificent attire,
With retinue of many a knight and squire,
On St. John's eve, at vespers, proudly sat
And heard the priests chant the Magnificat.
And as he listened, o'er and o'er again
Repeated, like a burden or refrain,
He caught the words, *"Deposuit potentes
De sede, et exaltavit humiles,"*
And slowly lifting up his kingly head
He to a learned clerk beside him said,
"What mean these words?" The clerk made
     answer meet,
"He has put down the mighty from their seat,
And has exalted them of low degree."
Thereat King Robert muttered scornfully,

" 'T is well that such seditious words are sung
Only by priests and in the Latin tongue;
For unto priests and people be it known,
There is no power can push me from my
    throne!"
And leaning back, he yawned and fell asleep,
Lulled by the chant monotonous and deep.

When he awoke, it was already night;
The church was empty, and there was no
    light,
Save where the lamps, that glimmered few
    and faint,
Lighted a little space before some saint.
He started from his seat and gazed around,
But saw no living thing and heard no sound.
He groped towards the door, but it was
    locked;
He cried aloud, and listened, and then
    knocked,
And uttered awful threatenings and com-
    plaints,
And imprecations upon men and saints.
The sounds reëchoed from the roof and walls
As if dead priests were laughing in their stalls.

At length the sexton, hearing from without
The tumult of the knocking and the shout,
And thinking thieves were in the house of
    prayer,

Came with his lantern, asking, "Who is
    there?"
Half choked with rage, King Robert fiercely
    said,
"Open: 't is I, the King! Art thou afraid?"
The frightened sexton, muttering, with a
    curse,
"This is some drunken vagabond, or worse!"
Turned the great key and flung the portal
    wide;
A man rushed by him at a single stride,
Haggard, half naked, without hat or cloak,
Who neither turned, nor looked at him, nor
    spoke,
But leaped into the blackness of the night,
And vanished like a spectre from his sight.

Robert of Sicily, brother of Pope Urbane
And Valmond, Emperor of Allemaine,
Despoiled of his magnificent attire,
Bareheaded, breathless, and besprent with
    mire,
With sense of wrong and outrage desperate,
Strode on and thundered at the palace gate;
Rushed through the courtyard, thrusting in
    his rage
To right and left each seneschal and page,
And hurried up the broad and sounding stair,
His white face ghastly in the torches' glare.
From hall to hall he passed with breathless
    speed;
Voices and cries he heard, but did not heed,

Until at last he reached the banquet-room,
Blazing with light, and breathing with per-
 fume.

There on the dais sat another king,
Wearing his robes, his crown, his signet-ring,
King Robert's self in features, form, and
 height,
But all transfigured with angelic light!
It was an Angel; and his presence there
With a divine effulgence filled the air,
An exaltation, piercing the disguise,
Though none the hidden Angel recognize.

A moment speechless, motionless, amazed,
The throneless monarch on the Angel gazed,
Who met his look of anger and surprise
With the divine compassion of his eyes;
Then said, "Who art thou? and why com'st
 thou here?"
To which King Robert answered with a sneer,
"I am the King, and come to claim my own
From an impostor, who usurps my throne!"
And suddenly, at these audacious words,
Up sprang the angry guests, and drew their
 swords;
The Angel answered, with unruffled brow,
"Nay, not the King, but the King's Jester,
 thou
Henceforth shalt wear the bells and scalloped
 cape,
And for thy counsellor shalt lead an ape;

Thou shalt obey my servants when they call,
And wait upon my henchmen in the hall!"

Deaf to King Robert's threats and cries and
    prayers,
They thrust him from the hall and down the
    stairs;
A group of tittering pages ran before,
And as they opened wide the folding-door,
His heart failed, for he heard, with strange
    alarms,
The boisterous laughter of the men-at-arms,
And all the vaulted chamber roar and ring
With the mock plaudits of "Long live the
    King!"

Next morning, waking with the day's first
    beam,
He said within himself, "It was a dream!"
But the straw rustled as he turned his head,
There were the cap and bells beside his bed,
Around him rose the bare, discolored walls,
Close by, the steeds were champing in their
    stalls,
And in the corner, a revolting shape,
Shivering and chattering sat the wretched
    ape.
It was no dream; the world he loved so much
Had turned to dust and ashes at his touch!
Days came and went; and now returned again
To Sicily the old Saturnian reign;
Under the Angel's governance benign

The happy island danced with corn and wine,
And deep within the mountain's burning breast
Enceladus, the giant, was at rest.

Meanwhile King Robert yielded to his fate,
Sullen and silent and disconsolate.
Dressed in the motley garb that Jesters wear,
With look bewildered and a vacant stare,
Close shaven above the ears, as monks are shorn,
By courtiers mocked, by pages laughed to scorn,
His only friend the ape, his only food
What others left, — he still was unsubdued.
And when the Angel met him on his way,
And half in earnest, half in jest, would say,
Sternly, though tenderly, that he might feel
The velvet scabbard held a sword of steel,
"Art thou the King?" the passion of his woe
Burst from him in resistless overflow,
And, lifting high his forehead, he would fling
The haughty answer back, "I am, I am the King!"

Almost three years were ended; when there came
Ambassadors of great repute and name
From Valmond, Emperor of Allemaine,
Unto King Robert, saying that Pope Urbane
By letter summoned them forthwith to come
On Holy Thursday to his city of Rome.

The Angel with great joy received his guests,
And gave them presents of embroidered
    vests,
And velvet mantles with rich ermine lined,
And rings and jewels of the rarest kind.
Then he departed with them o'er the sea
Into the lovely land of Italy,
Whose loveliness was more resplendent made
By the mere passing of that cavalcade,
With plumes, and cloaks, and housings, and
    the stir
Of jewelled bridle and of golden spur.
And lo! among the menials, in mock state,
Upon a piebald steed, with shambling gait,
His cloak of fox-tails flapping in the wind,
The solemn ape demurely perched behind,
King Robert rode, making huge merriment
In all the country towns through which they
    went.

The Pope received them with great pomp
    and blare
Of bannered trumpets, on Saint Peter's
    square,
Giving his benediction and embrace,
Fervent, and full of apostolic grace.
While with congratulations and with prayers
He entertained the Angel unawares,
Robert, the Jester, bursting through the
    crowd,
Into their presence rushed, and cried aloud,
"I am the King! Look, and behold in me

Robert, your brother, King of Sicily!
This man, who wears my semblance to your
    eyes,
Is an impostor in a king's disguise.
Do you not know me? does no voice within
Answer my cry, and say we are akin?"
The Pope in silence, but with troubled mien,
Gazed at the Angel's countenance serene;
The Emperor, laughing, said, "It is strange
    sport
To keep a madman for thy Fool at court!"
And the poor, baffled Jester in disgrace
Was hustled back among the populace.

In solemn state the Holy Week went by,
And Easter Sunday gleamed upon the sky;
The presence of the Angel, with its light,
Before the sun rose, made the city bright,
And with new fervor filled the hearts of men,
Who felt that Christ indeed had risen again.
Even the Jester, on his bed of straw,
With haggard eyes the unwonted splendor
    saw,
He felt within a power unfelt before,
And, kneeling humbly on his chamber floor,
He heard the rushing garments of the Lord
Sweep through the silent air, ascending heav-
    enward.
And now the visit ending, and once more
Valmond returning to the Danube's shore,
Homeward the Angel journeyed, and again

528

The land was made resplendent with his
    train,
Flashing along the towns of Italy
Unto Salerno, and from thence by sea.
And when once more within Palermo's wall,
And, seated on the throne in his great hall,
He heard the Angelus from convent towers,
As if the better world conversed with ours,
He beckoned to King Robert to draw nigher,
And with a gesture bade the rest retire;
And when they were alone, the Angel said,
"Art thou the King?" Then, bowing down his
    head,
King Robert crossed both hands upon his
    breast,
And meekly answered him: "Thou knowest
    best!
My sins as scarlet are; let me go hence,
And in some cloister's school of penitence,
Across those stones, that pave the way to
    heaven,
Walk barefoot, till my guilty soul be shriven!"

The Angel smiled, and from his radiant face
A holy light illumined all the place,
And through the open window, loud and
    clear,
They heard the monks chant in the chapel
    near,
Above the stir and tumult of the street:
"He has put down the mighty from their seat,
And has exalted them of low degree!"

And through the chant a second melody
Rose like the throbbing of a single string:
"I am an Angel, and thou art the King!"

King Robert, who was standing near the
  throne,
Lifted his eyes, and lo! he was alone!
But all apparelled as in days of old,
With ermined mantle and with cloth of gold;
And when his courtiers came, they found
  him there
Kneeling upon the floor, absorbed in silent
  prayer.

INTERLUDE

And then the blue-eyed Norseman told
A Saga of the days of old.
"There is," said he, "a wondrous book
Of Legends in the old Norse tongue,
Of the dead kings of Norroway, —
Legends that once were told or sung
In many a smoky fireside nook
Of Iceland, in the ancient day,
By wandering Saga-man or Scald;
'Heimskringla' is the volume called;
And he who looks may find therein
The story that I now begin."

And in each pause the story made
Upon his violin he played,

As an appropriate interlude,
Fragments of old Norwegian tunes
That bound in one the separate runes,
And held the mind in perfect mood,
Entwining and encircling all
The strange and antiquated rhymes
With melodies of olden times;
As over some half-ruined wall,
Disjointed and about to fall,
Fresh woodbines climb and interlace,
And keep the loosened stones in place.

THE MUSICIAN'S TALE

The Saga of King Olaf

I
The Challenge of Thor

I am the God Thor,
I am the War God,
I am the Thunderer!
Here in my Northland,
My fastness and fortress,
Reign I forever!

Here amid icebergs
Rule I the nations;
This is my hammer,
Miölner the mighty;
Giants and sorcerers

Cannot withstand it!

These are the gauntlets
Wherewith I wield it,
And hurl it afar off,
This is my girdle;
Whenever I brace it,
Strength is redoubled!

The light thou beholdest
Stream through the heavens,
In flashes of crimson,
Is but my red beard
Blown by the night-wind,
Affrighting the nations!

Jove is my brother;
Mine eyes are the lightning;
The wheels of my chariot
Roll in the thunder,
The blows of my hammer
Ring in the earthquake!

Force rules the world still,
Has ruled it, shall rule it;
Meekness is weakness,
Strength is triumphant,
Over the whole earth
Still is it Thor's-Day!

Thou art a God too,

O Galilean!
And thus single-handed
Unto the combat,
Gauntlet or Gospel,
Here I defy thee!

II
King Olaf's Return

And King Olaf heard the cry,
Saw the red light in the sky,
  Laid his hand upon his sword,
As he leaned upon the railing,
And his ships went sailing, sailing
  Northward into Drontheim fiord.

There he stood as one who dreamed;
And the red light glanced and gleamed
  On the armor that he wore;
And he shouted, as the rifted
Streamers o'er him shook and shifted,
  "I accept thy challenge, Thor!"

To avenge his father slain,
And reconquer realm and reign,
  Came the youthful Olaf home,
Through the midnight sailing, sailing,
Listening to the wild wind's wailing,
  And the dashing of the foam.

To his thoughts the sacred name
Of his mother Astrid came,

And the tale she oft had told
Of her flight by secret passes
Through the mountains and morasses,
  To the home of Hakon old.

Then strange memories crowded back
Of Queen Gunhild's wrath and wrack,
  And a hurried flight by sea;
Of grim Vikings, and the rapture
Of the sea-fight, and the capture,
  And the life of slavery.

How a stranger watched his face
In the Esthonian market-place,
  Scanned his features one by one,
Saying, "We should know each other;
I am Sigurd, Astrid's brother,
  Thou art Olaf, Astrid's son!"

Then as Queen Allogia's page,
Old in honors, young in age,
  Chief of all her men-at-arms;
Till vague whispers, and mysterious,
Reached King Valdemar, the imperious,
  Filling him with strange alarms.

Then his cruisings o'er the seas,
Westward to the Hebrides
  And to Scilly's rocky shore;
And the hermit's cavern dismal,
Christ's great name and rites baptismal
  In the ocean's rush and roar.

All these thoughts of love and strife
Glimmered through his lurid life,
  As the stars' intenser light
Through the red flames o'er him trailing,
As his ships went sailing, sailing
  Northward in the summer night.

Trained for either camp or court,
Skilful in each manly sport,
  Young and beautiful and tall;
Art of warfare, craft of chases,
Swimming, skating, snow-shoe races,
  Excellent alike in all.

When at sea, with all his rowers,
He along the bending oars
  Outside of his ship could run.
He the Smalsor Horn ascended,
And his shining shield suspended
  On its summit, like a sun.

On the ship-rails he could stand,
Wield his sword with either hand,
  And at once two javelins throw;
At all feasts where ale was strongest
Sat the merry monarch longest,
  First to come and last to go.

Norway never yet had seen
One so beautiful of mien,
  One so royal in attire,
When in arms completely furnished,

Harness gold-inlaid and burnished,
  Mantle like a flame of fire.

Thus came Olaf to his own,
When upon the night-wind blown
  Passed that cry along the shore;
And he answered, while the rifted
Streamers o'er him shook and shifted,
  "I accept thy challenge, Thor!"

III
Thora of Rimol

"Thora of Rimol! hide me! hide me!
Danger and shame and death betide me!
For Olaf the King is hunting me down
Through field and forest, through thorp and
    town!"
  Thus cried Jarl Hakon
  To Thora, the fairest of women.

"Hakon Jarl! for the love I bear thee
Neither shall shame nor death come near
    thee!
But the hiding-place wherein thou must lie
Is the cave underneath the swine in the sty."
  Thus to Jarl Hakon
  Said Thora, the fairest of women.

So Hakon Jarl and his base thrall Karker
Crouched in the cave, than a dungeon darker,
As Olaf came riding, with men in mail,

Through the forest roads into Orkadale,
  Demanding Jarl Hakon
  Of Thora, the fairest of women.

"Rich and honored shall be whoever
The head of Hakon Jarl shall dissever!"
Hakon heard him, and Karker the slave,
Through the breathing-holes of the darksome
    cave.
  Alone in her chamber
  Wept Thora, the fairest of women.

Said Karker, the crafty, "I will not slay thee!
For all the king's gold I will never betray
    thee!"
"Then why dost thou turn so pale, O churl,
And then again black as the earth?" said the
    Earl.
  More pale and more faithful
  Was Thora, the fairest of women.

From a dream in the night the thrall started,
    saying,
"Round my neck a gold ring King Olaf was
    laying!"
And Hakon answered, "Beware of the king!
He will lay round thy neck a blood-red ring."
  At the ring on her finger
  Gazed Thora, the fairest of women.

At daybreak slept Hakon, with sorrows en-
    cumbered,

But screamed and drew up his feet as he
    slumbered;
The thrall in the darkness plunged with his
    knife,
And the Earl awakened no more in this life.
    But wakeful and weeping
    Sat Thora, the fairest of women.

At Nidarholm the priests are all singing,
Two ghastly heads on the gibbet are swing-
    ing;
One is Jarl Hakon's and one is his thrall's,
And the people are shouting from windows
    and walls;
    While alone in her chamber
    Swoons Thora, the fairest of women.

IV
Queen Sigrid the Haughty

Queen Sigrid the Haughty sat proud and
    aloft
In her chamber, that looked over meadow
    and croft.
    Heart's dearest,
    Why dost thou sorrow so?

The floor with tassels of fir was besprent,
Filling the room with their fragrant scent.

She heard the birds sing, she saw the sun
    shine,

The air of summer was sweeter than wine.

Like a sword without scabbard the bright
    river lay
Between her own kingdom and Norroway.

But Olaf the King had sued for her hand,
The sword would be sheathed, the river be
    spanned.

Her maidens were seated around her knee,
Working bright figures in tapestry.

And one was singing the ancient rune
Of Brynhilda's love and the wrath of Gu-
    drun.

And through it, and round it, and over it all
Sounded incessant the waterfall.

The Queen in her hand held a ring of gold,
From the door of Ladé's Temple old.

King Olaf had sent her this wedding gift,
But her thoughts as arrows were keen and
    swift.

She had given the ring to her goldsmiths
    twain,
Who smiled, as they handed it back again.

And Sigrid the Queen, in her haughty way,

Said, "Why do you smile, my goldsmiths,
    say?"

And they answered: "O Queen! if the truth
    must be told,
The ring is of copper, and not of gold!"

The lightning flashed o'er her forehead and
    cheek,
She only murmured, she did not speak:

"If in his gifts he can faithless be,
There will be no gold in his love to me."

A footstep was heard on the outer stair,
And in strode King Olaf with royal air.

He kissed the Queen's hand, and he whis-
    pered of love,
And swore to be true as the stars are above.

But she smiled with contempt as she an-
    swered: "O King,
Will you swear it, as Odin once swore, on the
    ring?"

And the King: "Oh speak not of Odin to me,
The wife of King Olaf a Christian must be."

Looking straight at the King, with her level
    brows,

She said, "I keep true to my faith and my
   vows."

Then the face of King Olaf was darkened
   with gloom,
He rose in his anger and strode through the
   room.

"Why, then, should I care to have thee?" he
   said, —
"A faded old woman, a heathenish jade!"

His zeal was stronger than fear or love,
And he struck the Queen in the face with his
   glove.

Then forth from the chamber in anger he
   fled,
And the wooden stairway shook with his
   tread.

Queen Sigrid the Haughty said under her
   breath,
"This insult, King Olaf, shall be thy death!"
   Heart's dearest,
   Why dost thou sorrow so?

V
The Skerry of Shrieks

Now from all King Olaf's farms
   His men-at-arms

Gathered on the Eve of Easter;
To his house at Angvalds-ness
  Fast they press,
Drinking with the royal feaster.

Loudly through the wide-flung door
  Came the roar
Of the sea upon the Skerry;
And its thunder loud and near
  Reached the ear,
Mingling with their voices merry.

"Hark!" said Olaf to his Scald,
  Halfred the Bald,
"Listen to that song, and learn it!
Half my kingdom would I give,
  As I live,
If by such songs you would earn it!

"For of all the runes and rhymes
  Of all times,
Best I like the ocean's dirges,
When the old harper heaves and rocks,
  His hoary locks
Flowing and flashing in the surges!"

Halfred answered: "I am called
  The Unappalled!
Nothing hinders me or daunts me.
Hearken to me, then, O King,
  While I sing
The great Ocean Song that haunts me."

"I will hear your song sublime
   Some other time,"
Says the drowsy monarch, yawning,
And retires; each laughing guest
   Applauds the jest;
Then they sleep till day is dawning.

Pacing up and down the yard,
   King Olaf's guard
Saw the sea-mist slowly creeping
O'er the sands, and up the hill,
   Gathering still
Round the house where they were sleeping.

It was not the fog he saw,
   Nor misty flaw,
That above the landscape brooded;
It was Eyvind Kallda's crew
   Of warlocks blue
With their caps of darkness hooded!

Round and round the house they go,
   Weaving slow
Magic circles to encumber
And imprison in their ring
   Olaf the King,
As he helpless lies in slumber.

Then athwart the vapors dun
   The Easter sun
Streamed with one broad track of splendor!
In their real forms appeared

The warlocks weird,
Awful as the Witch of Endor.

Blinded by the light that glared,
  They groped and stared,
Round about with steps unsteady;
From his window Olaf gazed,
  And, amazed,
"Who are these strange people?" said he.

"Eyvind Kallda and his men!"
  Answered then
From the yard a sturdy farmer;
While the men-at-arms apace
  Filled the place,
Busily buckling on their armor.

From the gates they sallied forth,
  South and north,
Scoured the island coast around them,
Seizing all the warlock band,
  Foot and hand
On the Skerry's rocks they bound them.

And at eve the king again
  Called his train,
And, with all the candles burning,
Silent sat and heard once more
  The sullen roar
Of the ocean tides returning.

Shrieks and cries of wild despair

Filled the air,
Growing fainter as they listened;
Then the bursting surge alone
    Sounded on; —
Thus the sorcerers were christened!

"Sing, O Scald, your song sublime,
    Your ocean-rhyme,"
Cried King Olaf: "it will cheer me!"
Said the Scald, with pallid cheeks,
    "The Skerry of Shrieks
Sings too loud for you to hear me!"

VI
The Wraith of Odin

The guests were loud, the ale was strong,
King Olaf feasted late and long;
The hoary Scalds together sang;
O'erhead the smoky rafters rang.
    Dead rides Sir Morten of Fogelsang.

The door swung wide, with creak and din;
A blast of cold night-air came in,
And on the threshold shivering stood
A one-eyed guest, with cloak and hood.
    Dead rides Sir Morten of Fogelsang.

The King exclaimed, "O graybeard pale!
Come warm thee with this cup of ale."
The foaming draught the old man quaffed,
The noisy guests looked on and laughed.

Dead rides Sir Morten of Fogelsang.

Then spake the King: "Be not afraid:
Sit here by me." The guest obeyed,
And, seated at the table, told
Tales of the sea, and Sagas old.
    Dead rides Sir Morten of Fogelsang.

And ever, when the tale was o'er,
The King demanded yet one more;
Till Sigurd the Bishop smiling said,
" 'T is late, O King, and time for bed."
    Dead rides Sir Morten of Fogelsang.

The King retired; the stranger guest
Followed and entered with the rest;
The lights were out, the pages gone,
But still the garrulous guest spake on.
    Dead rides Sir Morten of Fogelsang.

As one who from a volume reads,
He spake of heroes and their deeds,
Of lands and cities he had seen,
And stormy gulfs that tossed between.
    Dead rides Sir Morten of Fogelsang.

Then from his lips in music rolled
The Havamal of Odin old,
With sounds mysterious as the roar
Of billows on a distant shore.
    Dead rides Sir Morten of Fogelsang.

"Do we not learn from runes and rhymes
Made by the gods in elder times,
And do not still the great Scalds teach
That silence better is than speech?"
    Dead rides Sir Morten of Fogelsang.

Smiling at this, the King replied,
"Thy lore is by thy tongue belied;
For never was I so enthralled
Either by Saga-man or Scald."
    Dead rides Sir Morten of Fogelsang.

The Bishop said, "Late hours we keep!
Night wanes, O King! 't is time for sleep!"
Then slept the King, and when he woke
The guest was gone, the morning broke.
    Dead rides Sir Morten of Fogelsang.

They found the doors securely barred,
They found the watch-dog in the yard,
There was no footprint in the grass,
And none had seen the stranger pass.
    Dead rides Sir Morten of Fogelsang.

King Olaf crossed himself and said:
"I know that Odin the Great is dead;
Sure is the triumph of our Faith,
The one-eyed stranger was his wraith."
    Dead rides Sir Morten of Fogelsang.

Olaf the King, one summer morn,
Blew a blast on his bugle-horn,
Sending his signal through the land of
   Drontheim.

And to the Hus-Ting held at Mere
Gathered the farmers far and near,
With their war weapons ready to confront
   him.

Ploughing under the morning star,
Old Iron-Beard in Yriar
Heard the summons, chuckling with a low
   laugh.

He wiped the sweat-drops from his brow,
Unharnessed his horses from the plough,
And clattering came on horseback to King
   Olaf.

He was the churliest of the churls;
Little he cared for king or earls;
Bitter as home-brewed ale were his foaming
   passions.

Hodden-gray was the garb he wore,
And by the Hammer of Thor he swore;
He hated the narrow town, and all its fash-
   ions.

But he loved the freedom of his farm,
His ale at night, by the fireside warm,
Gudrun his daughter, with her flaxen tresses.

He loved his horses and his herds,
The smell of the earth, and the song of
  birds,
His well-filled barns, his brook with its wa-
  tercresses.

Huge and cumbersome was his frame;
His beard, from which he took his name,
Frosty and fierce, like that of Hymer the Gi-
  ant.

So at the Hus-Ting he appeared,
The farmer of Yriar, Iron-Beard,
On horseback, in an attitude defiant.

And to King Olaf he cried aloud,
Out of the middle of the crowd,
That tossed about him like a stormy ocean:

"Such sacrifices shalt thou bring
To Odin and to Thor, O King,
As other kings have done in their devotion!"

King Olaf answered: "I command
This land to be a Christian land;
Here is my Bishop who the folk baptizes!

"But if you ask me to restore

Your sacrifices, stained with gore,
Then will I offer human sacrifices!

"Not slaves and peasants shall they be,
But men of note and high degree,
Such men as Orm of Lyra and Kar of Gryt-
  ing!"

Then to their Temple strode he in,
And loud behind him heard the din
Of his men-at-arms and the peasants fiercely
  fighting.

There in the Temple, carved in wood,
The image of great Odin stood,
And other gods, with Thor supreme among
  them.

King Olaf smote them with the blade
Of his huge war-axe, gold inlaid,
And downward shattered to the pavement
  flung them.

At the same moment rose without,
From the contending crowd, a shout,
A mingled sound of triumph and of wailing.

And there upon the trampled plain
The farmer Iron-Beard lay slain,
Midway between the assailed and the assail-
  ing.

King Olaf from the doorway spoke:
"Choose ye between two things, my folk,
To be baptized or given up to slaughter!"

And seeing their leader stark and dead,
The people with a murmur said,
"O King, baptize us with thy holy water."

So all the Drontheim land became
A Christian land in name and fame,
In the old gods no more believing and trust-
    ing.

And as a blood-atonement, soon
King Olaf wed the fair Gudrun;
And thus in peace ended the Drontheim
    Hus-Ting!

VIII
Gudrun

On King Olaf's bridal night
Shines the moon with tender light,
And across the chamber streams
    Its tide of dreams.

At the fatal midnight hour,
When all evil things have power,
In the glimmer of the moon
    Stands Gudrun.

Close against her heaving breast

Something in her hand is pressed;
Like an icicle, its sheen
  Is cold and keen.

On the cairn are fixed her eyes
Where her murdered father lies,
And a voice remote and drear
  She seems to hear.

What a bridal night is this!
Cold will be the dagger's kiss;
Laden with the chill of death
  Is its breath.

Like the drifting snow she sweeps
To the couch where Olaf sleeps;
Suddenly he wakes and stirs,
  His eyes meet hers.

"What is that," King Olaf said,
"Gleams so bright above my head?
Wherefore standest thou so white
  In pale moonlight?"

" 'T is the bodkin that I wear
When at night I bind my hair;
It woke me falling on the floor;
  'T is nothing more."

"Forests have ears, and fields have eyes;
Often treachery lurking lies
Underneath the fairest hair!

Gudrun beware!"

Ere the earliest peep of morn
Blew King Olaf's bugle-horn;
And forever sundered ride
  Bridegroom and bride!

IX
Thangbrand the Priest

Short of stature, large of limb,
  Burly face and russet beard,
All the women stared at him,
  When in Iceland he appeared.
  "Look!" they said,
  With nodding head,
"There goes Thangbrand, Olaf's Priest."

All the prayers he knew by rote,
  He could preach like Chrysostom,
From the Fathers he could quote,
  He had even been at Rome.
  A learned clerk,
  A man of mark,
Was this Thangbrand, Olaf's Priest.

He was quarrelsome and loud,
  And impatient of control,
Boisterous in the market crowd,
  Boisterous at the wassail-bowl,
  Everywhere
  Would drink and swear,

Swaggering Thangbrand, Olaf's Priest.

In his house this malcontent
  Could the King no longer bear,
So to Iceland he was sent
  To convert the heathen there,
    And away
    One summer day
Sailed this Thangbrand, Olaf's Priest.

There in Iceland, o'er their books
  Pored the people day and night,
But he did not like their looks,
  Nor the songs they used to write.
    "All this rhyme
    Is waste of time!"
Grumbled Thangbrand, Olaf's Priest.

To the alehouse, where he sat,
  Came the Scalds and Saga-men;
Is it to be wondered at
  That they quarrelled now and then,
    When o'er his beer
    Began to leer
Drunken Thangbrand, Olaf's Priest?

All the folk in Altafiord
  Boasted of their island grand;
Saying in a single word,
  "Iceland is the finest land
    That the sun
    Doth shine upon!"

Loud laughed Thangbrand, Olaf's Priest.

And he answered: "What's the use
  Of this bragging up and down,
When three women and one goose
  Make a market in your town!"
  Every Scald
  Satires scrawled
On poor Thangbrand, Olaf's Priest.

Something worse they did than that;
  And what vexed him most of all
Was a figure in shovel hat,
  Drawn in charcoal on the wall;
  With words that go
  Sprawling below,
"This is Thangbrand, Olaf's Priest."

Hardly knowing what he did,
  Then he smote them might and main,
Thorvald Veile and Veterlid
  Lay there in the alehouse slain.
  "To-day we are gold,
  To-morrow mould!"
Muttered Thangbrand, Olaf's Priest.

Much in fear of axe and rope,
  Back to Norway sailed he then.
"O King Olaf! little hope
  Is there of these Iceland men!"
  Meekly said,
  With bending head,

X
Raud the Strong

"All the old gods are dead,
All the wild warlocks fled;
But the White Christ lives and reigns,
And throughout my wide domains
His Gospel shall be spread!"
  On the Evangelists
  Thus swore King Olaf.

But still in dreams of the night
Beheld he the crimson light,
And heard the voice that defied
Him who was crucified,
And challenged him to the fight.
  To Sigurd the Bishop
  King Olaf confessed it.

And Sigurd the Bishop said,
"The old gods are not dead,
For the great Thor still reigns,
And among the Jarls and Thanes
The old witchcraft still is spread."
  Thus to King Olaf
  Said Sigurd the Bishop.

"Far north in the Salten Fiord,
By rapine, fire, and sword,
Lives the Viking, Raud the Strong;

All the Godoe Isles belong
To him and his heathen horde."
  Thus went on speaking
  Sigurd the Bishop.

"A warlock, a wizard is he,
And lord of the wind and the sea;
And whichever way he sails,
He has ever favoring gales,
By his craft in sorcery."
  Here the sign of the cross
  Made devoutly King Olaf.

"With rites that we both abhor,
He worships Odin and Thor;
So it cannot yet be said,
That all the old gods are dead,
And the warlocks are no more,"
  Flushing with anger
  Said Sigurd the Bishop.

Then King Olaf cried aloud:
"I will talk with this mighty Raud,
And along the Salten Fiord
Preach the Gospel with my sword,
Or be brought back in my shroud!"
  So northward from Drontheim
  Sailed King Olaf!

Bishop Sigurd of Salten Fiord

Loud the angry wind was wailing
As King Olaf's ships came sailing
Northward out of Drontheim haven
  To the mouth of Salten Fiord.

Though the flying sea-spray drenches
Fore and aft the rowers' benches,
Not a single heart is craven
  Of the champions there on board.

All without the Fiord was quiet,
But within it storm and riot,
Such as on his Viking cruises
  Raud the Strong was wont to ride.

And the sea through all its tide-ways
Swept the reeling vessels sideways,
As the leaves are swept through sluices,
  When the flood-gates open wide.

" 'T is the warlock! 't is the demon
Raud!" cried Sigurd to the seamen;
"But the Lord is not affrighted
  By the witchcraft of his foes."

To the ship's bow he ascended,
By his choristers attended,
Round him were the tapers lighted,
  And the sacred incense rose.

On the bow stood Bishop Sigurd,
In his robes, as one transfigured,
And the Crucifix he planted
  High amid the rain and mist.

Then with holy water sprinkled
All the ship; the mass-bells tinkled:
Loud the monks around him chanted,
  Loud he read the Evangelist.

As into the Fiord they darted,
On each side the water parted;
Down a path like silver molten
  Steadily rowed King Olaf's ships;

Steadily burned all night the tapers,
And the White Christ through the vapors
Gleamed across the Fiord of Salten,
  As through John's Apocalypse, —

Till at last they reached Raud's dwelling
On the little isle of Gelling;
Not a guard was at the doorway,
  Not a glimmer of light was seen.

But at anchor, carved and gilded,
Lay the dragon-ship he builded;
'T was the grandest ship in Norway,
  With its crest and scales of green.

Up the stairway, softly creeping,
To the loft where Raud was sleeping,

With their fists they burst asunder
  Bolt and bar that held the door.

Drunken with sleep and ale they found him,
Dragged him from his bed and bound him,
While he stared with stupid wonder
  At the look and garb they wore.

Then King Olaf said: "O Sea-King!
Little time have we for speaking,
Choose between the good and evil;
  Be baptized! or thou shalt die!"

But in scorn the heathen scoffer
Answered: "I disdain thine offer;
Neither fear I God nor Devil;
  Thee and thy Gospel I defy!"

Then between his jaws distended,
When his frantic struggles ended,
Through King Olaf's horn an adder,
  Touched by fire, they forced to glide.

Sharp his tooth was as an arrow,
As he gnawed through bone and marrow;
But without a groan or shudder,
  Raud the Strong blaspheming died.

Then baptized they all that region,
Swarthy Lap and fair Norwegian,
Far as swims the salmon, leaping,
  Up the streams of Salten Fiord.

In their temples Thor and Odin
Lay in dust and ashes trodden,
As King Olaf, onward sweeping,
   Preached the Gospel with his sword.

Then he took the carved and gilded
Dragon-ship that Raud had builded,
And the tiller single-handed
   Grasping, steered into the main.

Southward sailed the sea-gulls o'er him,
Southward sailed the ship that bore him,
Till at Drontheim haven landed
   Olaf and his crew again.

XII
King Olaf's Christmas

At Drontheim, Olaf the King
Heard the bells of Yule-tide ring,
   As he sat in his banquet-hall,
Drinking the nut-brown ale,
With his bearded Berserks hale
   And tall.

Three days his Yule-tide feasts
He held with Bishops and Priests,
   And his horn filled up to the brim;
But the ale was never too strong,
Nor the Saga-man's tale too long,
   For him.

O'er his drinking-horn, the sign
He made of the cross divine,
  As he drank, and muttered his prayers;
But the Berserks evermore
Made the sign of the Hammer of Thor
  Over theirs.

The gleams of the fire-light dance
Upon helmet and hauberk and lance,
  And laugh in the eyes of the King;
And he cries to Halfred the Scald,
Gray-bearded, wrinkled, and bald,
  "Sing!"

"Sing me a song divine,
With a sword in every line,
  And this shall be thy reward."
And he loosened the belt at his waist,
And in front of the singer placed
  His sword.

"Quern-biter of Hakon the Good,
Wherewith at a stroke he hewed
  The millstone through and through,
And Foot-breadth of Thoralf the Strong,
Were neither so broad nor so long,
  Nor so true."

Then the Scald took his harp and sang,
And loud through the music rang
  The sound of that shining word;
And the harp-strings a clangor made,

As if they were struck with the blade
  Of a sword.

And the Berserks round about
Broke forth into a shout
  That made the rafters ring:
They smote with their fists on the board,
And shouted, "Long live the Sword,
  And the King!"

But the King said, "O my son,
I miss the bright word in one
  Of thy measures and thy rhymes."
And Halfred the Scald replied,
"In another 't was multiplied
  Three times."

Then King Olaf raised the hilt
Of iron, cross-shaped and gilt,
  And said, "Do not refuse;
Count well the gain and the loss,
Thor's hammer or Christ's cross:
  Choose!"

And Halfred the Scald said, "This
In the name of the Lord I kiss,
  Who on it was crucified!"
And a shout went round the board,
"In the name of Christ the Lord,
  Who died!"

Then over the waste of snows

The noonday sun uprose,
  Through the driving mists revealed,
Like the lifting of the Host,
By incense-clouds almost
  Concealed.

On the shining wall a vast
And shadowy cross was cast
  From the hilt of the lifted sword,
And in foaming cups of ale
The Berserks drank "Was-hael!
  To the Lord!"

XIII
The Building of the Long Serpent

Thorberg Skafting, master-builder,
  In his ship-yard by the sea,
Whistling, said, "It would bewilder
Any man but Thorberg Skafting,
  Any man but me!"

Near him lay the Dragon stranded,
  Built of old by Raud the Strong,
And King Olaf had commanded
He should build another Dragon,
  Twice as large and long.

Therefore whistled Thorberg Skafting,
  As he sat with half-closed eyes,
And his head turned sideways, drafting
That new vessel for King Olaf

Twice the Dragon's size.

Round him busily hewed and hammered
  Mallet huge and heavy axe;
Workmen laughed and sang and clamored;
Whirred the wheels, that into rigging
  Spun the shining flax!

All this tumult heard the master, —
  It was music to his ear;
Fancy whispered all the faster,
"Men shall hear of Thorberg Skafting
  For a hundred year!"

Workmen sweating at the forges
  Fashioned iron bolt and bar,
Like a warlock's midnight orgies
Smoked and bubbled the black caldron
  With the boiling tar.

Did the warlocks mingle in it,
  Thorberg Skafting, any curse?
Could you not be gone a minute
But some mischief must be doing,
  Turning bad to worse?

'T was an ill wind that came wafting
  From his homestead words of woe;
To his farm went Thorberg Skafting,
Oft repeating to his workmen,
  Build ye thus and so.

After long delays returning
  Came the master back by night;
To his ship-yard longing, yearning,
Hurried he, and did not leave it
  Till the morning's light.

"Come and see my ship, my darling!"
  On the morrow said the King;
"Finished now from keel to carling;
Never yet was seen in Norway
  Such a wondrous thing!"

In the ship-yard, idly talking,
  At the ship the workmen stared:
Some one, all their labor balking,
Down her sides had cut deep gashes,
  Not a plank was spared!

"Death be to the evil-doer!"
  With an oath King Olaf spoke;
"But rewards to his pursuer!"
And with wrath his face grew redder
  Than his scarlet cloak.

Straight the master-builder, smiling,
  Answered thus the angry King:
"Cease blaspheming and reviling,
Olaf, it was Thorberg Skafting
  Who has done this thing!"

Then he chipped and smoothed the plank-
  ing,

Till the King, delighted, swore,
With much lauding and much thanking,
"Handsomer is now my Dragon
    Than she was before!"

Seventy ells and four extended
    On the grass the vessel's keel;
High above it, gilt and splendid,
Rose the figure-head ferocious
    With its crest of steel.

Then they launched her from the tressels,
    In the ship-yard by the sea;
She was the grandest of all vessels,
Never ship was built in Norway
    Half so fine as she!

The Long Serpent was she christened,
    'Mid the roar of cheer on cheer!
They who to the Saga listened
Heard the name of Thorberg Skafting
    For a hundred year!

XIV
The Crew of the Long Serpent

Safe at anchor in Drontheim bay
King Olaf's fleet assembled lay,
    And, striped with white and blue,
Downward fluttered sail and banner,
As alights the screaming lanner;
Lustily cheered, in their wild manner,

The Long Serpent's crew.

Her forecastle man was Ulf the Red;
Like a wolf's was his shaggy head,
  His teeth as large and white;
His beard, of gray and russet blended,
Round as a swallow's nest descended;
As standard-bearer he defended
  Olaf's flag in the fight.

Near him Kolbiorn had his place,
Like the King in garb and face,
  So gallant and so hale;
Every cabin-boy and varlet
Wondered at his cloak of scarlet;
Like a river, frozen and star-lit,
  Gleamed his coat of mail.

By the bulkhead, tall and dark,
Stood Thrand Rame of Thelemark,
  A figure gaunt and grand;
On his hairy arm imprinted
Was an anchor, azure-tinted;
Like Thor's hammer, huge and dinted
  Was his brawny hand.

Einar Tamberskelver, bare
To the winds his golden hair,
  By the mainmast stood;
Graceful was his form, and slender,
And his eyes were deep and tender
As a woman's, in the splendor

Of her maidenhood.

In the fore-hold Biorn and Bork
Watched the sailors at their work:
  Heavens! how they swore!
Thirty men they each commanded,
Iron-sinewed, horny handed,
Shoulders broad, and chests expanded,
  Tugging at the oar.

These, and many more like these,
With King Olaf sailed the seas,
  Till the waters vast
Filled them with a vague devotion,
With the freedom and the motion,
With the roll and roar of ocean
  And the sounding blast.

When they landed from the fleet,
How they roared through Drontheim's street,
  Boisterous as the gale!
How they laughed and stamped and
  pounded,
Till the tavern roof resounded,
And the host looked on astounded
  As they drank the ale!

Never saw the wild North Sea
Such a gallant company
  Sail its billows blue!
Never, while they cruised and quarrelled,
Old King Gorm, or Blue-Tooth Harald,

Owned a ship so well apparelled,
    Boasted such a crew!

XV
A Little Bird in the Air

A little bird in the air
Is singing of Thyri the fair,
    The sister of Svend the Dane;
And the song of the garrulous bird
In the streets of the town is heard,
    And repeated again and again.
    Hoist up your sails of silk,
    And flee away from each other.

To King Burislaf, it is said,
Was the beautiful Thyri wed,
    And a sorrowful bride went she;
And after a week and a day
She has fled away and away
    From his town by the stormy sea.
    Hoist up your sails of silk,
    And flee away from each other.

They say, that through heat and through cold,
Through weald, they say, and through wold,
    By day and by night, they say,
She has fled; and the gossips report
She has come to King Olaf's court,
    And the town is all in dismay.
    Hoist up your sails of silk,
    And flee away from each other.

It is whispered King Olaf has seen,
Has talked with the beautiful Queen;
  And they wonder how it will end;
For surely, if here she remain,
It is war with King Svend the Dane,
  And King Burislaf the Vend!
    Hoist up your sails of silk,
    And flee away from each other.

Oh, greatest wonder of all!
It is published in hamlet and hall,
  It roars like a flame that is fanned!
The King — yes, Olaf the King —
Has wedded her with his ring,
  And Thyri is Queen in the land!
    Hoist up your sails of silk,
    And flee away from each other.

XVI
Queen Thyri and the Angelica Stalks

Northward over Drontheim,
Flew the clamorous sea-gulls,
Sang the lark and linnet
  From the meadows green;

Weeping in her chamber,
Lonely and unhappy,
Sat the Drottning Thyri,
  Sat King Olaf's Queen.

In at all the windows

Streamed the pleasant sunshine,
On the roof above her
  Softly cooed the dove;

But the sound she heard not,
Nor the sunshine heeded,
For the thoughts of Thyri
  Were not thoughts of love.

Then King Olaf entered,
Beautiful as morning,
Like the sun at Easter
  Shone his happy face;

In his hand he carried
Angelicas uprooted,
With delicious fragrance
  Filling all the place.

Like a rainy midnight
Sat the Drottning Thyri,
Even the smile of Olaf
  Could not cheer her gloom;

Nor the stalks he gave her
With a gracious gesture,
And with words as pleasant
  As their own perfume.

In her hands he placed them,
And her jewelled fingers
Through the green leaves glistened

Like the dews of morn;

But she cast them from her,
Haughty and indignant,
On the floor she threw them
  With a look of scorn.

"Richer presents," said she,
"Gave King Harald Gormson
To the Queen, my mother,
  Than such worthless weeds;

"When he ravaged Norway,
Laying waste the kingdom,
Seizing scatt and treasure
  For her royal needs.

"But thou darest not venture
Through the Sound to Vendland,
My domains to rescue
  From King Burislaf,

"Lest King Svend of Denmark,
Forked Beard, my brother,
Scatter all thy vessels
  As the wind the chaff."

Then up sprang King Olaf,
Like a reindeer bounding,
With an oath he answered
  Thus the luckless Queen:

"Never yet did Olaf
Fear King Svend of Denmark;
This right hand shall hale him
  By his forked chin!"

Then he left the chamber,
Thundering through the doorway,
Loud his steps resounded
  Down the outer stair.

Smarting with the insult,
Through the streets of Drontheim
Strode he red and wrathful,
  With his stately air.

All his ships he gathered,
Summoned all his forces,
Making his war levy
  In the region round.

Down the coast of Norway,
Like a flock of sea-gulls,
Sailed the fleet of Olaf
  Through the Danish Sound.

With his own hand fearless
Steered he the Long Serpent,
Strained the creaking cordage,
  Bent each boom and gaff;

Till in Vendland landing,
The domains of Thyri

He redeemed and rescued
  From King Burislaf.

Then said Olaf, laughing,
"Not ten yoke of oxen
Have the power to draw us
  Like a woman's hair!

"Now will I confess it,
Better things are jewels
Than angelica stalks are
  For a queen to wear."

XVII
King Svend of the Forked Beard

Loudly the sailors cheered
Svend of the Forked Beard,
As with his fleet he steered
  Southward to Vendland;
Where with their courses hauled
All were together called,
Under the Isle of Svald
  Near to the mainland.

After Queen Gunhild's death,
So the old Saga saith,
Plighted King Svend his faith
  To Sigrid the Haughty;
And to avenge his bride,
Soothing her wounded pride,
Over the waters wide

King Olaf sought he.

Still on her scornful face,
Blushing with deep disgrace,
Bore she the crimson trace
  Of Olaf's gauntlet;
Like a malignant star,
Blazing in heaven afar,
Red shone the angry scar
  Under her frontlet.

Oft to King Svend she spake,
"For thine own honor's sake
Shalt thou swift vengeance take
  On the vile coward!"
Until the King at last,
Gusty and overcast,
Like a tempestuous blast
  Threatened and lowered.

Soon as the Spring appeared,
Svend of the Forked Beard
High his red standard reared,
  Eager for battle;
While every warlike Dane,
Seizing his arms again,
Left all unsown the grain,
  Unhoused the cattle.

Likewise the Swedish King
Summoned in haste a Thing,
Weapons and men to bring

In aid of Denmark;
Eric the Norseman, too,
As the war-tidings flew,
Sailed with a chosen crew
  From Lapland and Finmark.

So upon Easter day
Sailed the three kings away,
Out of the sheltered bay,
  In the bright season;
With them Earl Sigvald came,
Eager for spoil and fame;
Pity that such a name
  Stooped to such treason!

Safe under Svald at last,
Now were their anchors cast,
Safe from the sea and blast,
  Plotted the three kings;
While, with a base intent,
Southward Earl Sigvald went,
On a foul errand bent,
  Unto the Sea-kings.

Thence to hold on his course
Unto King Olaf's force,
Lying within the hoarse
  Mouths of Stet-haven;
Him to ensnare and bring
Unto the Danish king,
Who his dead corse would fling
  Forth to the raven!

XVIII

King Olaf and Earl Sigvald

On the gray sea-sands
King Olaf stands,
Northward and seaward
He points with his hands.

With eddy and whirl
The sea-tides curl,
Washing the sandals
Of Sigvald the Earl.

The mariners shout,
The ships swing about,
The yards are all hoisted,
The sails flutter out.

The war-horns are played,
The anchors are weighed,
Like moths in the distance
The sails flit and fade.

The sea is like lead,
The harbor lies dead,
As a corse on the sea-shore,
Whose spirit has fled!

On that fatal day,
The histories say,
Seventy vessels
Sailed out of the bay.

But soon scattered wide
O'er the billows they ride,
While Sigvald and Olaf
Sail side by side.

Cried the Earl: "Follow me!
I your pilot will be,
For I know all the channels
Where flows the deep sea!"

So into the strait
Where his foes lie in wait,
Gallant King Olaf
Sails to his fate!

Then the sea-fog veils
The ships and their sails;
Queen Sigrid the Haughty,
Thy vengeance prevails!

XIX
King Olaf's War-Horns

"Strike the sails!" King Olaf said;
"Never shall men of mine take flight;
Never away from battle I fled,
Never away from my foes!
  Let God dispose
Of my life in the fight!"

"Sound the horns!" said Olaf the King;
And suddenly through the drifting brume

The blare of the horns began to ring,
Like the terrible trumpet shock
  Of Regnarock,
On the Day of Doom!

Louder and louder the war-horns sang
Over the level floor of the flood;
All the sails came down with a clang,
And there in the midst overhead
  The sun hung red
As a drop of blood.

Drifting down on the Danish fleet
Three together the ships were lashed,
So that neither should turn and retreat;
In the midst, but in front of the rest,
  The burnished crest
Of the Serpent flashed.

King Olaf stood on the quarter-deck,
With bow of ash and arrows of oak,
His gilded shield was without a fleck,
His helmet inlaid with gold,
  And in many a fold
Hung his crimson cloak.

On the forecastle Ulf the Red
Watched the lashing of the ships;
"If the Serpent lie so far ahead,
We shall have hard work of it here,"
  Said he with a sneer
On his bearded lips.

King Olaf laid an arrow on string,
"Have I a coward on board?" said he.
"Shoot it another way, O King!"
Sullenly answered Ulf,
  The old sea-wolf;
"You have need of me!"

In front came Svend, the King of the Danes;
Sweeping down with his fifty rowers;
To the right, the Swedish king with his
    thanes;
And on board of the Iron Beard
  Earl Eric steered
To the left with his oars.

"These soft Danes and Swedes," said the
    King,
"At home with their wives had better stay,
Than come within reach of my Serpent's
    sting:
But where Eric the Norseman leads
  Heroic deeds
Will be done to-day!"

Then as together the vessels crashed,
Eric severed the cables of hide,
With which King Olaf's ships were lashed,
And left them to drive and drift
  With the currents swift
Of the outward tide.

Louder the war-horns growl and snarl,

Sharper the dragons bite and sting!
Eric the son of Hakon Jarl
A death-drink salt as the sea
    Pledges to thee,
Olaf the King!

XX
Einar Tamberskelver

It was Einar Tamberskelver
    Stood beside the mast;
From his yew-bow, tipped with silver,
    Flew the arrows fast;
Aimed at Eric unavailing,
    As he sat concealed,
Half behind the quarter-railing,
    Half behind his shield.

First an arrow struck the tiller,
    Just above his head;
"Sing, O Eyvind Skaldaspiller,"
    Then Earl Eric said.
"Sing the song of Hakon dying,
    Sing his funeral wail!"
And another arrow flying
    Grazed his coat of mail.

Turning to a Lapland yeoman,
    As the arrow passed,
Said Earl Eric, "Shoot that bowman
    Standing by the mast."
Sooner than the word was spoken

Flew the yeoman's shaft;
Einar's bow in twain was broken,
  Einar only laughed.

"What was that?" said Olaf, standing
  On the quarter-deck.
"Something heard I like the stranding
  Of a shattered wreck."
Einar then, the arrow taking
  From the loosened string,
Answered, "That was Norway breaking
  From thy hand, O King!"

"Thou art but a poor diviner,"
  Straightway Olaf said;
"Take my bow, and swifter, Einar,
  Let thy shafts be sped."
Of his bows the fairest choosing,
  Reached he from above;
Einar saw the blood-drops oozing
  Through his iron glove.

But the bow was thin and narrow;
  At the first assay,
O'er its head he drew the arrow,
  Flung the bow away;
Said, with hot and angry temper
  Flushing in his cheek,
"Olaf! for so great a Kämper
  Are thy bows too weak!"

Then, with smile of joy defiant

On his beardless lip,
Scaled he, light and self-reliant,
  Eric's dragon-ship.
Loose his golden locks were flowing,
  Bright his armor gleamed;
Like Saint Michael overthrowing
  Lucifer he seemed.

XXI
King Olaf's Death-Drink

All day has the battle raged,
All day have the ships engaged,
But not yet is assuaged
  The vengeance of Eric the Earl.

The decks with blood are red,
The arrows of death are sped,
The ships are filled with the dead,
  And the spears the champions hurl.

They drift as wrecks on the tide,
The grappling-irons are plied,
The boarders climb up the side,
  The shouts are feeble and few.

Ah! never shall Norway again
See her sailors come back o'er the main;
They all lie wounded or slain,
  Or asleep in the billows blue!

On the deck stands Olaf the King,

Around him whistle and sing
The spears that the foemen fling,
  And the stones they hurl with their hands.

In the midst of the stones and the spears,
Kolbiorn, the marshal, appears,
His shield in the air he uprears,
  By the side of King Olaf he stands.

Over the slippery wreck
Of the Long Serpent's deck
Sweeps Eric with hardly a check,
  His lips with anger are pale;

He hews with his axe at the mast,
Till it falls, with the sails overcast,
Like a snow-covered pine in the vast
  Dim forests of Orkadale.

Seeking King Olaf then,
He rushes aft with his men,
As a hunter into the den
  Of the bear, when he stands at bay.

"Remember Jarl Hakon!" he cries;
When lo! on his wondering eyes,
Two kingly figures arise,
  Two Olafs in warlike array!

Then Kolbiorn speaks in the ear
Of King Olaf a word of cheer,
In a whisper that none may hear,

With a smile on his tremulous lip;

Two shields raised high in the air,
Two flashes of golden hair,
Two scarlet meteors' glare,
   And both have leaped from the ship.

Earl Eric's men in the boats
Seize Kolbiorn's shield as it floats,
And cry, from their hairy throats,
   "See! it is Olaf the King!"

While far on the opposite side
Floats another shield on the tide,
Like a jewel set in the wide
   Sea-current's eddying ring.

There is told a wonderful tale,
How the King stripped off his mail,
Like leaves of the brown sea-kale,
   As he swam beneath the main;

But the young grew old and gray,
And never, by night or by day,
In his kingdom of Norroway
   Was King Olaf seen again!

XXII
The Nun of Nidaros

In the convent of Drontheim,
Alone in her chamber

Knelt Astrid the Abbess,
At midnight, adoring,
Beseeching, entreating
The Virgin and Mother.

She heard in the silence
The voice of one speaking,
Without in the darkness,
In gusts of the night-wind,
Now louder, now nearer,
Now lost in the distance.

The voice of a stranger
It seemed as she listened,
Of some one who answered
Beseeching, imploring,
A cry from afar off
She could not distinguish.

The voice of Saint John,
The beloved disciple,
Who wandered and waited
The Master's appearance,
Alone in the darkness,
Unsheltered and friendless.

"It is accepted,
The angry defiance,
The challenge of battle!
It is accepted,
But not with the weapons
Of war that thou wieldest!

"Cross against corselet,
Love against hatred,
Peace-cry for war-cry!
Patience is powerful;
He that o'ercometh
Hath power o'er the nations!

"As torrents in summer,
Half dried in their channels,
Suddenly rise, though the
Sky is still cloudless,
For rain has been falling
Far off at their fountains;

"So hearts that are fainting
Grow full to o'erflowing,
And they that behold it
Marvel, and know not
That God at their fountains
Far off has been raining!

"Stronger than steel
Is the sword of the Spirit;
Swifter than arrows
The light of the truth is,
Greater than anger
Is love, and subdueth!

"Thou art a phantom,
A shape of the sea-mist,
A shape of the brumal
Rain, and the darkness

Fearful and formless;
Day dawns and thou art not!

"The dawn is not distant,
Nor is the night starless;
Love is eternal!
God is still God, and
His faith shall not fail us;
Christ is eternal!"

INTERLUDE

A strain of music closed the tale,
A low, monotonous, funeral wail,
That with its cadence, wild and sweet,
Made the long Saga more complete.

"Thank God," the Theologian said,
"The reign of violence is dead,
Or dying surely from the world;
While Love triumphant reigns instead,
And in a brighter sky o'erhead
His blessed banners are unfurled.
And most of all thank God for this:
The war and waste of clashing creeds
Now end in words, and not in deeds,
And no one suffers loss, or bleeds,
For thoughts that men call heresies.

"I stand without here in the porch,
I hear the bell's melodious din,

I hear the organ peal within,
I hear the prayer, with words that scorch
Like sparks from an inverted torch,
I hear the sermon upon sin,
With threatenings of the last account.
And all, translated in the air,
Reach me but as our dear Lord's Prayer,
And as the Sermon on the Mount.

"Must it be Calvin, and not Christ?
Must it be Athanasian creeds,
Or holy water, books, and beads?
Must struggling souls remain content
With councils and decrees of Trent?
And can it be enough for these
The Christian Church the year embalms
With evergreens and boughs of palms,
And fills the air with litanies?
"I know that yonder Pharisee
Thanks God that he is not like me;
In my humiliation dressed,
I only stand and beat my breast,
And pray for human charity.

"Not to one church alone, but seven,
The voice prophetic spake from heaven;
And unto each the promise came,
Diversified, but still the same;
For him that overcometh are
The new name written on the stone,
The raiment white, the crown, the throne,

And I will give him the Morning Star!

"Ah! to how many Faith has been
No evidence of things unseen,
But a dim shadow, that recasts
The creed of the Phantasiasts,
For whom no Man of Sorrows died,
For whom the Tragedy Divine
Was but a symbol and a sign,
And Christ a phantom crucified!

"For others a diviner creed
Is living in the life they lead.
The passing of their beautiful feet
Blesses the pavement of the street,
And all their looks and words repeat
Old Fuller's saying, wise and sweet,
Not as a vulture, but a dove,
The Holy Ghost came from above.

"And this brings back to me a tale
So sad the hearer well may quail,
And question if such things can be;
Yet in the chronicles of Spain
Down the dark pages runs this stain,
And naught can wash them white again,
So fearful is the tragedy."

THE THEOLOGIAN'S TALE

Torquemada

In the heroic days when Ferdinand
And Isabella ruled the Spanish land,
And Torquemada, with his subtle brain,
Ruled them, as Grand Inquisitor of Spain,
In a great castle near Valladolid,
Moated and high and by fair woodlands hid,
There dwelt, as from the chronicles we learn,
An old Hidalgo proud and taciturn,
Whose name has perished, with his towers of
    stone,
And all his actions save this one alone;
This one, so terrible, perhaps 't were best
If it, too, were forgotten with the rest;
Unless, perchance, our eyes can see therein
The martyrdom triumphant o'er the sin;
A double picture, with its gloom and glow,
The splendor overhead, the death below.

This sombre man counted each day as lost
On which his feet no sacred threshold
    crossed;
And when he chanced the passing Host to
    meet,
He knelt and prayed devoutly in the street;
Oft he confessed; and with each mutinous
    thought,
As with wild beasts at Ephesus, he fought.

In deep contrition scourged himself in Lent,
Walked in processions, with his head down
    bent,
At plays of Corpus Christi oft was seen,
And on Palm Sunday bore his bough of
    green.
His sole diversion was to hunt the boar
Through tangled thickets of the forest hoar,
Or with his jingling mules to hurry down
To some grand bull-fight in the neighboring
    town,
Or in the crowd with lighted taper stand,
When Jews were burned, or banished from
    the land.
Then stirred within him a tumultuous joy;
The demon whose delight is to destroy
Shook him, and shouted with a trumpet tone,
"Kill! kill! and let the Lord find out his own!"
And now, in that old castle in the wood,
His daughters, in the dawn of womanhood,
Returning from their convent school, had
    made
Resplendent with their bloom the forest
    shade,
Reminding him of their dead mother's face,
When first she came into that gloomy
    place, —
A memory in his heart as dim and sweet
As moonlight in a solitary street,
Where the same rays, that lift the sea, are
    thrown
Lovely but powerless upon walls of stone.

These two fair daughters of a mother dead
Were all the dream had left him as it fled.
A joy at first, and then a growing care,
As if a voice within him cried, "Beware!"
A vague presentiment of impending doom,
Like ghostly footsteps in a vacant room,
Haunted him day and night; a formless fear
That death to some one of his house was
    near,
With dark surmises of a hidden crime,
Made life itself a death before its time.
Jealous, suspicious, with no sense of shame,
A spy upon his daughters he became;
With velvet slippers, noiseless on the floors,
He glided softly through half-open doors;
Now in the room, and now upon the stair,
He stood beside them ere they were aware;
He listened in the passage when they talked,
He watched them from the casement when
    they walked,
He saw the gypsy haunt the river's side,
He saw the monk among the cork-trees glide;
And, tortured by the mystery and the doubt
Of some dark secret, past his finding out,
Baffled he paused; then reassured again
Pursued the flying phantom of his brain.
He watched them even when they knelt in
    church;
And then, descending lower in his search,
Questioned the servants, and with eager eyes
Listened incredulous to their replies;
The gypsy? none had seen her in the wood!

The monk? a mendicant in search of food!
At length the awful revelation came,
Crushing at once his pride of birth and name;
The hopes his yearning bosom forward cast
And the ancestral glories of the past,
All fell together, crumbling in disgrace,
A turret rent from battlement to base.
His daughters talking in the dead of night
In their own chamber, and without a light,
Listening, as he was wont, he overheard,
And learned the dreadful secret, word by
    word;
And hurrying from his castle, with a cry
He raised his hands to the unpitying sky,
Repeating one dread word, till bush and tree
Caught it, and shuddering answered, "Her-
    esy!"

Wrapped in his cloak, his hat drawn o'er his
    face,
Now hurrying forward, now with lingering
    pace,
He walked all night the alleys of his park,
With one unseen companion in the dark,
The Demon who within him lay in wait
And by his presence turned his love to hate,
Forever muttering in an undertone,
"Kill! kill! and let the Lord find out his own!"

Upon the morrow, after early Mass,
While yet the dew was glistening on the grass,
And all the woods were musical with birds,

The old Hidalgo, uttering fearful words,
Walked homeward with the Priest, and in his
    room
Summoned his trembling daughters to their
    doom.
When questioned, with brief answers they
    replied,
Nor when accused evaded or denied;
Expostulations, passionate appeals,
All that the human heart most fears or feels,
In vain the Priest with earnest voice essayed;
In vain the father threatened, wept, and
    prayed;
Until at last he said, with haughty mien,
"The Holy Office, then, must intervene!"
And now the Grand Inquisitor of Spain,
With all the fifty horsemen of his train,
His awful name resounding, like the blast
Of funeral trumpets, as he onward passed,
Came to Valladolid, and there began
To harry the rich Jews with fire and ban.
To him the Hidalgo went, and at the gate
Demanded audience on affairs of state,
And in a secret chamber stood before
A venerable graybeard of fourscore,
Dressed in the hood and habit of a friar;
Out of his eyes flashed a consuming fire,
And in his hand the mystic horn he held,
Which poison and all noxious charms dis-
    pelled.
He heard in silence the Hidalgo's tale,

Then answered in a voice that made him
    quail:
"Son of the Church! when Abraham of old
To sacrifice his only son was told,
He did not pause to parley nor protest,
But hastened to obey the Lord's behest.
In him it was accounted righteousness;
The Holy Church expects of thee no less!"

A sacred frenzy seized the father's brain,
And Mercy from that hour implored in vain.
Ah! who will e'er believe the words I say?
His daughters he accused, and the same day
They both were cast into the dungeon's
    gloom,
That dismal antechamber of the tomb,
Arraigned, condemned, and sentenced to the
    flame,
The secret torture and the public shame.

Then to the Grand Inquisitor once more
The Hidalgo went more eager than before,
And said: "When Abraham offered up his
    son,
He clave the wood wherewith it might be
    done.
By his example taught, let me too bring
Wood from the forest for my offering!"
And the deep voice, without a pause, replied:
"Son of the Church! by faith now justified,
Complete thy sacrifice, even as thou wilt;

The Church absolves thy conscience from all
   guilt!"

Then this most wretched father went his way
Into the woods, that round his castle lay,
Where once his daughters in their childhood
   played
With their young mother in the sun and
   shade.
Now all the leaves had fallen; the branches
   bare
Made a perpetual moaning in the air,
And screaming from their eyries overhead
The ravens sailed athwart the sky of lead.
With his own hands he lopped the boughs
   and bound
Fagots, that crackled with foreboding sound,
And on his mules, caparisoned and gay
With bells and tassels, sent them on their
   way.

Then with his mind on one dark purpose
   bent,
Again to the Inquisitor he went,
And said: "Behold, the fagots I have brought,
And now, lest my atonement be as naught,
Grant me one more request, one last
   desire, —
With my own hand to light the funeral fire!"
And Torquemada answered from his seat,
"Son of the Church! Thine offering is com-
   plete;

Her servants through all ages shall not cease
To magnify thy deed. Depart in peace!"

Upon the market-place, builded of stone
The scaffold rose, whereon Death claimed
   his own.
At the four corners, in stern attitude,
Four statues of the Hebrew Prophets stood,
Gazing with calm indifference in their eyes
Upon this place of human sacrifice,
Round which was gathering fast the eager
   crowd,
With clamor of voices dissonant and loud,
And every roof and window was alive
With restless gazers, swarming like a hive.

The church-bells tolled, the chant of monks
   drew near,
Loud trumpets stammered forth their notes
   of fear,
A line of torches smoked along the street,
There was a stir, a rush, a tramp of feet,
And, with its banners floating in the air,
Slowly the long procession crossed the
   square,
And, to the statues of the Prophets bound,
The victims stood, with fagots piled around.
Then all the air a blast of trumpets shook,
And louder sang the monks with bell and
   book,
And the Hidalgo, lofty, stern, and proud,

Lifted his torch, and, bursting through the
    crowd,
Lighted in haste the fagots, and then fled,
Lest those imploring eyes should strike him
    dead!

O pitiless skies! why did your clouds retain
For peasants' fields their floods of hoarded
    rain?
O pitiless earth! why open no abyss
To bury in its chasm a crime like this?

That night, a mingled column of fire and
    smoke
From the dark thickets of the forest broke,
And, glaring o'er the landscape leagues away,
Made all the fields and hamlets bright as day.
Wrapped in a sheet of flame the castle blazed,
And as the villagers in terror gazed,
They saw the figure of that cruel knight
Lean from a window in the turret's height,
His ghastly face illumined with the glare,
His hands upraised above his head in prayer,
Till the floor sank beneath him, and he fell
Down the black hollow of that burning well.

Three centuries and more above his bones
Have piled the oblivious years like funeral
    stones;
His name has perished with him, and no trace
Remains on earth of his afflicted race;
But Torquemada's name, with clouds

o'ercast,
Looms in the distant landscape of the Past,
Like a burnt tower upon a blackened heath,
Lit by the fires of burning woods beneath!

INTERLUDE

Thus closed the tale of guilt and gloom,
That cast upon each listener's face
Its shadow, and for some brief space
Unbroken silence filled the room.
The Jew was thoughtful and distressed;
Upon his memory thronged and pressed
The persecution of his race,
Their wrongs and sufferings and disgrace;
His head was sunk upon his breast,
And from his eyes alternate came
Flashes of wrath and tears of shame.

The Student first the silence broke,
As one who long has lain in wait,
With purpose to retaliate,
And thus he dealt the avenging stroke.
"In such a company as this,
A tale so tragic seems amiss,
That by its terrible control
O'ermasters and drags down the soul
Into a fathomless abyss.
The Italian Tales that you disdain,
Some merry Night of Straparole,
Or Machiavelli's Belphagor,

Would cheer us and delight us more,
Give greater pleasure and less pain
Than your grim tragedies of Spain!"

And here the Poet raised his hand,
With such entreaty and command,
It stopped discussion at its birth,
And said: "The story I shall tell
Has meaning in it, if not mirth;
Listen, and hear what once befell
The merry birds of Killingworth!"

THE POET'S TALE

The Birds of Killingworth

It was the season, when through all the land
  The merle and mavis build, and building
  sing
Those lovely lyrics, written by His hand,
  Whom Saxon Cædmon calls the Blithe-
  heart King;
When on the boughs the purple buds expand,
  The banners of the vanguard of the Spring,
And rivulets, rejoicing, rush and leap,
And wave their fluttering signals from the
  steep.

The robin and the bluebird, piping loud,
  Filled all the blossoming orchards with
  their glee;

The sparrows chirped as if they still were
   proud
  Their race in Holy Writ should mentioned
   be;
And hungry crows, assembled in a crowd,
  Clamored their piteous prayer incessantly,
Knowing who hears the ravens cry, and said:
  "Give us, O Lord, this day, our daily
   bread!"

Across the Sound the birds of passage sailed,
  Speaking some unknown language strange
   and sweet
Of tropic isle remote, and passing hailed
  The village with the cheers of all their fleet;
Or quarrelling together, laughed and railed
  Like foreign sailors, landed in the street
Of seaport town, and with outlandish noise
Of oaths and gibberish frightening girls and
   boys.

Thus came the jocund Spring in Killing-
   worth,
  In fabulous days, some hundred years ago;
And thrifty farmers, as they tilled the earth,
  Heard with alarm the cawing of the crow,
That mingled with the universal mirth,
  Cassandra-like, prognosticating woe;
They shook their heads, and doomed with
   dreadful words
To swift destruction the whole race of birds.

And a town-meeting was convened straight-
  way
  To set a price upon the guilty heads
Of these marauders, who, in lieu of pay,
  Levied black-mail upon the garden beds
And cornfields, and beheld without dismay
  The awful scarecrow, with his fluttering
    shreds;
The skeleton that waited at their feast,
Whereby their sinful pleasure was increased.

Then from his house, a temple painted white,
  With fluted columns, and a roof of red,
The Squire came forth, august and splendid
    sight!
  Slowly descending, with majestic tread,
Three flights of steps, nor looking left nor
    right,
  Down the long street he walked, as one
    who said,
"A town that boasts inhabitants like me
Can have no lack of good society!"

The Parson, too, appeared, a man austere,
  The instinct of whose nature was to kill;
The wrath of God he preached from year to
    year,
  And read, with fervor, Edwards on the Will;
His favorite pastime was to slay the deer
  In summer on some Adirondac hill;
E'en now, while walking down the rural lane,
He lopped the wayside lilies with his cane.

From the Academy, whose belfry crowned
  The hill of Science with its vane of brass,
Came the Preceptor, gazing idly round,
  Now at the clouds, and now at the green
    grass,
And all absorbed in reveries profound
  Of fair Almira in the upper class,
Who was, as in a sonnet he had said,
As pure as water, and as good as bread.

And next the Deacon issued from his door,
  In his voluminous neck-cloth, white as
    snow;
A suit of sable bombazine he wore;
  His form was ponderous, and his step was
    slow;
There never was so wise a man before;
  He seemed the incarnate "Well, I told you
    so!"
And to perpetuate his great renown
There was a street named after him in town.

These came together in the new town-hall,
  With sundry farmers from the region
    round.
The Squire presided, dignified and tall,
  His air impressive and his reasoning sound;
Ill fared it with the birds, both great and
    small;
  Hardly a friend in all that crowd they
    found,
But enemies enough, who every one

Charged them with all the crimes beneath
  the sun.

When they had ended, from his place apart
  Rose the Preceptor, to redress the wrong,
And, trembling like a steed before the start,
  Looked round bewildered on the expectant
    throng;
Then thought of fair Almira, and took heart
  To speak out what was in him, clear and
    strong,
Alike regardless of their smile or frown,
And quite determined not to be laughed
  down.

"Plato, anticipating the Reviewers,
  From his Republic banished without pity
The Poets; in this little town of yours,
  You put to death, by means of a Commit-
    tee,
The ballad-singers and the Troubadours,
  The street-musicians of the heavenly city,
The birds, who make sweet music for us all
  In our dark hours, as David did for Saul.

"The thrush that carols at the dawn of day
  From the green steeples of the piny wood;
The oriole in the elm; the noisy jay,
  Jargoning like a foreigner at his food;
The bluebird balanced on some topmost
    spray,
  Flooding with melody the neighborhood;

Linnet and meadow-lark, and all the throng
That dwell in nests, and have the gift of song.

"You slay them all! and wherefore? for the
    gain
  Of a scant handful more or less of wheat,
Or rye, or barley, or some other grain,
  Scratched up at random by industrious feet,
Searching for worm or weevil after rain!
  Or a few cherries, that are not so sweet
As are the songs these uninvited guests
Sing at their feast with comfortable breasts.

"Do you ne'er think what wondrous beings
    these?
  Do you ne'er think who made them, and
    who taught
The dialect they speak, where melodies
  Alone are the interpreters of thought?
Whose household words are songs in many
    keys,
  Sweeter than instrument of man e'er
    caught!
Whose habitations in the tree-tops even
Are half-way houses on the road to heaven!

"Think, every morning when the sun peeps
    through
  The dim, leaf-latticed windows of the grove,
How jubilant the happy birds renew
  Their old, melodious madrigals of love!
And when you think of this, remember too

'T is always morning somewhere, and above
The awakening continents, from shore to
    shore,
Somewhere the birds are singing evermore.

"Think of your woods and orchards without
    birds!
    Of empty nests that cling to boughs and
    beams
As in an idiot's brain remembered words
    Hang empty 'mid the cobwebs of his
    dreams!
Will bleat of flocks or bellowing of herds
    Make up for the lost music, when your
    teams
Drag home the stingy harvest, and no more
The feathered gleaners follow to your door?

"What! would you rather see the incessant
    stir
    Of insects in the windrows of the hay,
And hear the locust and the grasshopper
    Their melancholy hurdy-gurdies play?
Is this more pleasant to you than the whir
    Of meadow-lark, and her sweet roundelay,
Or twitter of little field-fares, as you take
Your nooning in the shade of bush and brake?

"You call them thieves and pillagers; but
    know,
    They are the winged wardens of your farms,

Who from the cornfields drive the insidious
   foe,
  And from your harvests keep a hundred
   harms;
Even the blackest of them all, the crow,
  Renders good service as your man-at-arms,
Crushing the beetle in his coat of mail,
And crying havoc on the slug and snail.

"How can I teach your children gentleness,
  And mercy to the weak, and reverence
For Life, which, in its weakness or excess,
  Is still a gleam of God's omnipotence,
Or Death, which, seeming darkness, is no
   less
  The selfsame light, although averted hence,
When by your laws, your actions, and your
   speech,
You contradict the very things I teach?"

With this he closed; and through the audi-
   ence went
  A murmur, like the rustle of dead leaves;
The farmers laughed and nodded, and some
   bent
  Their yellow heads together like their
   sheaves;
Men have no faith in fine-spun sentiment
  Who put their trust in bullocks and in
   beeves.
The birds were doomed; and, as the record
   shows,

A bounty offered for the heads of crows.

There was another audience out of reach,
  Who had no voice nor vote in making laws,
But in the papers read his little speech,
  And crowned his modest temples with ap-
    plause;
They made him conscious, each one more
    than each,
  He still was victor, vanquished in their
    cause.
Sweetest of all the applause he won from
    thee,
O fair Almira at the Academy!

And so the dreadful massacre began;
  O'er fields and orchards, and o'er woodland
    crests,
The ceaseless fusillade of terror ran.
  Dead fell the birds, with blood-stains on
    their breasts,
Or wounded crept away from sight of man,
  While the young died of famine in their
    nests;
A slaughter to be told in groans, not words,
The very St. Bartholomew of Birds!

The Summer came, and all the birds were
    dead;
  The days were like hot coals; the very
    ground
Was burned to ashes; in the orchards fed

Myriads of caterpillars, and around
The cultivated fields and garden beds
  Hosts of devouring insects crawled, and
    found
No foe to check their march, till they had
    made
The land a desert without leaf or shade.

Devoured by worms, like Herod, was the
    town,
  Because, like Herod, it had ruthlessly
Slaughtered the Innocents. From the trees
    spun down
  The canker-worms upon the passers-by,
Upon each woman's bonnet, shawl, and
    gown,
  Who shook them off with just a little cry;
They were the terror of each favorite walk,
The endless theme of all the village talk.

The farmers grew impatient, but a few
  Confessed their error, and would not com-
    plain,
For after all, the best thing one can do
  When it is raining, is to let it rain.
Then they repealed the law, although they
    knew
  It would not call the dead to life again;
As school-boys, finding their mistake too late,
Draw a wet sponge across the accusing slate.

That year in Killingworth the Autumn came

Without the light of his majestic look,
The wonder of the falling tongues of flame,
  The illumined pages of his Doom's-Day
  book.
A few lost leaves blushed crimson with their
  shame,
  And drowned themselves despairing in the
  brook,
While the wild wind went moaning every-
  where,
Lamenting the dead children of the air!

But the next Spring a stranger sight was seen,
  A sight that never yet by bard was sung,
As great a wonder as it would have been
  If some dumb animal had found a tongue!
A wagon, overarched with evergreen,
  Upon whose boughs were wicker cages
  hung,
All full of singing birds, came down the
  street,
Filling the air with music wild and sweet.

From all the country round these birds were
  brought,
  By order of the town, with anxious quest,
And, loosened from their wicker prisons,
  sought
  In woods and fields the places they loved
  best,
Singing loud canticles, which many thought
  Were satires to the authorities addressed,

While others, listening in green lanes, averred
Such lovely music never had been heard!

But blither still and louder carolled they
   Upon the morrow, for they seemed to know
It was the fair Almira's wedding-day,
   And everywhere, around, above, below,
When the Preceptor bore his bride away,
   Their songs burst forth in joyous overflow,
And a new heaven bent over a new earth
Amid the sunny farms of Killingworth.

FINALE

The hour was late; the fire burned low,
The Landlord's eyes were closed in sleep,
And near the story's end a deep
Sonorous sound at times was heard,
As when the distant bagpipes blow.
At this all laughed; the Landlord stirred,
As one awaking from a swound,
And, gazing anxiously around,
Protested that he had not slept,
But only shut his eyes, and kept
His ears attentive to each word.

Then all arose, and said "Good Night."
Alone remained the drowsy Squire
To rake the embers of the fire,
And quench the waning parlor light;
While from the windows, here and there,

The scattered lamps a moment gleamed,
And the illumined hostel seemed
The constellation of the Bear,
Downward, athwart the misty air,
Sinking and setting toward the sun.
Far off the village clock struck one.

from
PART SECOND

THE SPANISH JEW'S TALE

Kambalu

Into the city of Kambalu,
By the road that leadeth to Ispahan,
At the head of his dusty caravan,
Laden with treasure from realms afar,
Baldacca and Kelat and Kandahar,
Rode the great captain Alau.

The Khan from his palace-window gazed,
And saw in the thronging street beneath,
In the light of the setting sun, that blazed
Through the clouds of dust by the caravan
    raised,
The flash of harness and jewelled sheath,
And the shining scimitars of the guard,
And the weary camels that bared their teeth,
As they passed and passed through the gates
    unbarred
Into the shade of the palace-yard.

Thus into the city of Kambalu
Rode the great captain Alau;
And he stood before the Khan, and said:
"The enemies of my lord are dead;
All the Kalifs of all the West
Bow and obey thy least behest;
The plains are dark with the mulberry-trees,
The weavers are busy in Samarcand,
The miners are sifting the golden sand,
The divers plunging for pearls in the seas,
And peace and plenty are in the land.

"Baldacca's Kalif, and he alone,
Rose in revolt against thy throne:
His treasures are at thy palace-door,
With the swords and the shawls and the
    jewels he wore;
His body is dust o'er the desert blown.

"A mile outside of Baldacca's gate
I left my forces to lie in wait,
Concealed by forests and hillocks of sand,
And forward dashed with a handful of men,
To lure the old tiger from his den
Into the ambush I had planned.
Ere we reached the town the alarm was
    spread,
For we heard the sound of gongs from within;
And with clash of cymbals and warlike din
The gates swung wide; and we turned and
    fled;

615

And the garrison sallied forth and pursued,
With the gray old Kalif at their head,
And above them the banner of Mohammed:
So we snared them all, and the town was
  subdued.

"As in at the gate we rode, behold,
A tower that is called the Tower of Gold!
For there the Kalif had hidden his wealth,
Heaped and hoarded and piled on high,
Like sacks of wheat in a granary;
And thither the miser crept by stealth
To feel of the gold that gave him health,
And to gaze and gloat with his hungry eye
On jewels that gleamed like a glow-worm's
  spark,
Or the eyes of a panther in the dark.

"I said to the Kalif: 'Thou art old,
Thou hast no need of so much gold.
Thou shouldst not have heaped and hidden
  it here,
Till the breath of battle was hot and near,
But have sown through the land these use-
  less hoards
To spring into shining blades of swords,
And keep thine honor sweet and clear.
These grains of gold are not grains of wheat;
These bars of silver thou canst not eat;
These jewels and pearls and precious stones
Cannot cure the aches in thy bones,
Nor keep the feet of Death one hour

From climbing the stairways of thy tower!'

"Then into his dungeon I locked the drone,
And left him to feed there all alone
In the honey-cells of his golden hive;
Never a prayer, nor a cry, nor a groan
Was heard from those massive walls of stone,
Nor again was the Kalif seen alive!

"When at last we unlocked the door,
We found him dead upon the floor;
The rings had dropped from his withered
    hands,
His teeth were like bones in the desert sands:
Still clutching his treasure he had died;
And as he lay there, he appeared
A statue of gold with a silver beard,
His arms outstretched as if crucified."
This is the story, strange and true,
That the great captain Alau
Told to his brother the Tartar Khan,
When he rode that day into Kambalu
By the road that leadeth to Ispahan.

THE STUDENT'S TALE

The Cobbler of Hagenau

I trust that somewhere and somehow
You all have heard of Hagenau,
A quiet, quaint, and ancient town

617

Among the green Alsatian hills,
A place of valleys, streams, and mills,
Where Barbarossa's castle, brown
With rust of centuries, still looks down
On the broad, drowsy land below, —
On shadowy forests filled with game,
And the blue river winding slow
Through meadows, where the hedges grow
That give this little town its name.

It happened in the good old times,
While yet the Master-singers filled
The noisy workshop and the guild
With various melodies and rhymes,
That here in Hagenau there dwelt
A cobbler, — one who loved debate,
And, arguing from a postulate,
Would say what others only felt;
A man of forecast and of thrift,
And of a shrewd and careful mind
In this world's business, but inclined
Somewhat to let the next world drift.

Hans Sachs with vast delight he read,
And Regenbogen's rhymes of love,
For their poetic fame had spread
Even to the town of Hagenau;
And some Quick Melody of the Plough,
Or Double Harmony of the Dove
Was always running in his head.
He kept, moreover, at his side,

Among his leathers and his tools,
Reynard the Fox, the Ship of Fools,
Or Eulenspiegel, open wide;
With these he was much edified:
He thought them wiser than the Schools.

His good wife, full of godly fear,
Liked not these worldly themes to hear;
The Psalter was her book of songs;
The only music to her ear
Was that which to the Church belongs,
When the loud choir on Sunday chanted,
And the two angels carved in wood,
That by the windy organ stood,
Blew on their trumpets loud and clear,
And all the echoes, far and near,
Gibbered as if the church were haunted.

Outside his door, one afternoon,
This humble votary of the muse
Sat in the narrow strip of shade
By a projecting cornice made,
Mending the Burgomaster's shoes,
And singing a familiar tune: —

"Our ingress into the world
    Was naked and bare;
Our progress through the world
    Is trouble and care;
Our egress from the world
    Will be nobody knows where:
But if we do well here

We shall do well there;
And I could tell you no more,
  Should I preach a whole year!"

Thus sang the cobbler at his work;
And with his gestures marked the time,
Closing together with a jerk
Of his waxed thread the stitch and rhyme.

Meanwhile his quiet little dame
Was leaning o'er the window-sill,
Eager, excited, but mouse-still,
Gazing impatiently to see
What the great throng of folk might be
That onward in procession came,
Along the unfrequented street,
With horns that blew, and drums that beat,
And banners flying, and the flame
Of tapers, and, at times, the sweet
Voices of nuns; and as they sang
Suddenly all the church-bells rang.

In a gay coach, above the crowd,
There sat a monk in ample hood,
Who with his right hand held aloft
A red and ponderous cross of wood,
To which at times he meekly bowed.
In front three horsemen rode, and oft,
With voice and air importunate,
A boisterous herald cried aloud:
"The grace of God is at your gate!"
So onward to the church they passed.

The cobbler slowly turned his last,
And, wagging his sagacious head,
Unto his kneeling housewife said:
" 'T is the monk Tetzel. I have heard
The cawings of that reverend bird.
Don't let him cheat you of your gold;
Indulgence is not bought and sold."

The church of Hagenau, that night,
Was full of people, full of light;
An odor of incense filled the air,
The priest intoned, the organ groaned
Its inarticulate despair;
The candles on the altar blazed,
And full in front of it upraised
The red cross stood against the glare.
Below, upon the altar-rail
Indulgences were set to sale,
Like ballads at a country fair.
A heavy strong-box, iron-bound
And carved with many a quaint device,
Received, with a melodious sound,
The coin that purchased Paradise.

Then from the pulpit overhead,
Tetzel the monk, with fiery glow,
Thundered upon the crowd below.
"Good people all, draw near!" he said;
"Purchase these letters, signed and sealed,
By which all sins, though unrevealed
And unrepented, are forgiven!
Count but the gain, count not the loss!

Your gold and silver are but dross,
And yet they pave the way to heaven.
I hear your mothers and your sires
Cry from their purgatorial fires,
And will ye not their ransom pay?
O senseless people! when the gate
Of heaven is open, will ye wait?
Will ye not enter in to-day?
To-morrow it will be too late;
I shall be gone upon my way.
Make haste! bring money while ye may!"

The women shuddered, and turned pale;
Allured by hope or driven by fear,
With many a sob and many a tear,
All crowded to the altar-rail.
Pieces of silver and of gold
Into the tinkling strong-box fell
Like pebbles dropped into a well;
And soon the ballads were all sold.
The cobbler's wife among the rest
Slipped into the capacious chest
A golden florin; then withdrew,
Hiding the paper in her breast;
And homeward through the darkness went
Comforted, quieted, content;
She did not walk, she rather flew,
A dove that settles to her nest,
When some appalling bird of prey
That scared her has been driven away.

The days went by, the monk was gone,

The summer passed, the winter came;
Though seasons changed, yet still the same
The daily round of life went on;
The daily round of household care,
The narrow life of toil and prayer.
But in her heart the cobbler's dame
Had now a treasure beyond price,
A secret joy without a name,
The certainty of Paradise.
Alas, alas! Dust unto dust!
Before the winter wore away,
Her body in the churchyard lay,
Her patient soul was with the Just!
After her death, among the things
That even the poor preserve with care, —
Some little trinkets and cheap rings,
A locket with her mother's hair,
Her wedding gown, the faded flowers
She wore upon her wedding day, —
Among these memories of past hours,
That so much of the heart reveal,
Carefully kept and put away,
The Letter of Indulgence lay
Folded, with signature and seal.

Meanwhile the Priest, aggrieved and pained,
Waited and wondered that no word
Of mass or requiem he heard,
As by the Holy Church ordained:
Then to the Magistrate complained,
That as this woman had been dead
A week or more, and no mass said,

It was rank heresy, or at least
Contempt of Church; thus said the Priest;
And straight the cobbler was arraigned.

He came, confiding in his cause,
But rather doubtful of the laws.
The Justice from his elbow-chair
Gave him a look that seemed to say:
"Thou standest before a Magistrate,
Therefore do not prevaricate!"
Then asked him in a business way,
Kindly but cold: "Is thy wife dead?"
The cobbler meekly bowed his head;
"She is," came struggling from his throat
Scarce audibly. The Justice wrote
The words down in a book, and then
Continued, as he raised his pen;
"She is; and hath a mass been said
For the salvation of her soul?
Come, speak the truth! confess the whole!"
The cobbler without pause replied:
"Of mass or prayer there was no need;
For at the moment when she died
Her soul was with the glorified!"
And from his pocket with all speed
He drew the priestly title-deed,
And prayed the Justice he would read.

The Justice read, amused, amazed;
And as he read his mirth increased;
At times his shaggy brows he raised,
Now wondering at the cobbler gazed,

Now archly at the angry Priest.
"From all excesses, sins, and crimes
Thou hast committed in past times
Thee I absolve! And furthermore,
Purified from all earthly taints,
To the communion of the Saints
And to the sacraments restore!
All stains of weakness, and all trace
Of shame and censure I efface;
Remit the pains thou shouldst endure,
And make thee innocent and pure,
So that in dying, unto thee
The gates of heaven shall open be!
Though long thou livest, yet this grace
Until the moment of thy death
Unchangeable continueth!"

Then said he to the Priest: "I find
This document is duly signed
Brother John Tetzel, his own hand.
At all tribunals in the land
In evidence it may be used;
Therefore acquitted is the accused."
Then to the cobbler turned: "My friend,
Pray tell me, didst thou ever read
Reynard the Fox?" — "Oh yes, indeed!" —
"I thought so. Don't forget the end."

The Legend Beautiful

"Hadst thou stayed, I must have fled!"
That is what the Vision said.

In his chamber all alone,
Kneeling on the floor of stone,
Prayed the Monk in deep contrition
For his sins of indecision,
Prayed for greater self-denial
In temptation and in trial;
It was noonday by the dial,
And the Monk was all alone.

Suddenly, as if it lightened,
An unwonted splendor brightened
All within him and without him
In that narrow cell of stone;
And he saw the Blessed Vision
Of our Lord, with light Elysian
Like a vesture wrapped about Him,
Like a garment round Him thrown.

Not as crucified and slain,
Not in agonies of pain,
Not with bleeding hands and feet,
Did the Monk his Master see;
But as in the village street,
In the house or harvest-field,

Halt and lame and blind He healed,
When He walked in Galilee.

In an attitude imploring,
Hands upon his bosom crossed,
Wondering, worshipping, adoring,
Knelt the Monk in rapture lost.
Lord, he thought, in heaven that reignest,
Who am I, that thus thou deignest
To reveal thyself to me?
Who am I, that from the centre
Of thy glory thou shouldst enter
This poor cell, my guest to be?

Then amid his exaltation,
Loud the convent bell appalling,
From its belfry calling, calling,
Rang through court and corridor
With persistent iteration
He had never heard before.
It was now the appointed hour
When alike in shine or shower,
Winter's cold or summer's heat,
To the convent portals came
All the blind and halt and lame,
All the beggars of the street,
For their daily dole of food
Dealt them by the brotherhood;
And their almoner was he
Who upon his bended knee,
Rapt in silent ecstasy
Of divinest self-surrender,

Saw the Vision and the Splendor.
Deep distress and hesitation
Mingled with his adoration;
Should he go or should he stay?
Should he leave the poor to wait
Hungry at the convent gate,
Till the Vision passed away?
Should he slight his radiant guest,
Slight this visitant celestial,
For a crowd of ragged, bestial
Beggars at the convent gate?
Would the Vision there remain?
Would the Vision come again?
Then a voice within his breast
Whispered, audible and clear
As if to the outward ear:
"Do thy duty; that is best;
Leave unto thy Lord the rest!"

Straightway to his feet he started,
And with longing look intent
On the Blessed Vision bent,
Slowly from his cell departed,
Slowly on his errand went.

At the gate the poor were waiting,
Looking through the iron grating,
With that terror in the eye
That is only seen in those
Who amid their wants and woes
Hear the sound of doors that close,
And of feet that pass them by;

Grown familiar with disfavor,
Grown familiar with the savor
Of the bread by which men die!
But to-day, they knew not why,
Like the gate of Paradise
Seemed the convent gate to rise,
Like a sacrament divine
Seemed to them the bread and wine.
In his heart the Monk was praying,
Thinking of the homeless poor,
What they suffer and endure;
What we see not, what we see;
And the inward voice was saying:
"Whatsoever thing thou doest
To the least of mine and lowest,
That thou doest unto me!"

Unto me! but had the Vision
Come to him in beggar's clothing,
Come a mendicant imploring,
Would he then have knelt adoring,
Or have listened with derision,
And have turned away with loathing?

Thus his conscience put the question,
Full of troublesome suggestion,
As at length, with hurried pace,
Towards his cell he turned his face,
And beheld the convent bright
With a supernatural light,
Like a luminous cloud expanding
Over floor and wall and ceiling.

But he paused with awe-struck feeling
At the threshold of his door,
For the Vision still was standing
As he left it there before,
When the convent bell appalling,
From its belfry calling, calling,
Summoned him to feed the poor.
Through the long hour intervening
It had waited his return,
And he felt his bosom burn,
Comprehending all the meaning,
When the Blessed Vision said,
"Hadst thou stayed, I must have fled!"

from
PART THIRD

THE SPANISH JEW'S TALE

Azrael

King Solomon, before his palace gate
At evening, on the pavement tessellate
Was walking with a stranger from the East,
Arrayed in rich attire as for a feast,
The mighty Runjeet-Sing, a learned man,
And Rajah of the realms of Hindostan.
And as they walked the guest became aware
Of a white figure in the twilight air,
Gazing intent, as one who with surprise
His form and features seemed to recognize;
And in a whisper to the king he said:

"What is yon shape, that, pallid as the dead,
Is watching me, as if he sought to trace
In the dim light the features of my face?"

The king looked, and replied: "I know him
    well;
It is the Angel men call Azrael,
'T is the Death Angel; what hast thou to
    fear?"
And the guest answered: "Lest he should
    come near,
And speak to me, and take away my breath!
Save me from Azrael, save me from death!
O king, that hast dominion o'er the wind,
Bid it arise and bear me hence to Ind."

The king gazed upward at the cloudless sky,
Whispered a word, and raised his hand on
    high,
And lo! the signet-ring of chrysoprase
On his uplifted finger seemed to blaze
With hidden fire, and rushing from the west
There came a mighty wind, and seized the
    guest
And lifted him from earth, and on they
    passed,
His shining garments streaming in the blast,
A silken banner o'er the walls upreared,
A purple cloud, that gleamed and dis-
    appeared.
Then said the Angel, smiling: "If this man

Be Rajah Runjeet-Sing of Hindostan,
Thou hast done well in listening to his prayer;
I was upon my way to seek him there."

THE SICILIAN'S TALE

The Monk of Casal-Maggiore

Once on a time, some centuries ago,
  In the hot sunshine two Franciscan friars
Wended their weary way, with footsteps slow,
  Back to their convent, whose white walls
    and spires
Gleamed on the hillside like a patch of snow;
  Covered with dust they were, and torn by
    briers,
And bore like sumpter-mules upon their
    backs
  The badge of poverty, their beggar's sacks.

The first was Brother Anthony, a spare
  And silent man, with pallid cheeks and thin,
Much given to vigils, penance, fasting, prayer,
  Solemn and gray, and worn with discipline,
As if his body but white ashes were,
  Heaped on the living coals that glowed
    within;
A simple monk, like many of his day,
Whose instinct was to listen and obey.

A different man was Brother Timothy,

Of larger mould and of a coarser paste;
A rubicund and stalwart monk was he,
  Broad in the shoulders, broader in the
    waist,
Who often filled the dull refectory
  With noise by which the convent was dis-
    graced,
But to the mass-book gave but little heed,
By reason he had never learned to read.

Now, as they passed the outskirts of a wood,
  They saw, with mingled pleasure and sur-
    prise,
Fast tethered to a tree an ass, that stood
  Lazily winking his large, limpid eyes.
The farmer Gilbert, of that neighborhood,
  His owner was, who, looking for supplies
Of fagots, deeper in the wood had strayed,
Leaving his beast to ponder in the shade.

As soon as Brother Timothy espied
  The patient animal, he said: "Good-lack!
Thus for our needs doth Providence provide;
  We 'll lay our wallets on the creature's
    back."
This being done, he leisurely untied
  From head and neck the halter of the jack,
And put it round his own, and to the tree
Stood tethered fast as if the ass were he.

And, bursting forth into a merry laugh,

He cried to Brother Anthony: "Away!
And drive the ass before you with your staff;
  And when you reach the convent you may
    say
You left me at a farm, half tired and half
  Ill with a fever, for a night and day,
And that the farmer lent this ass to bear
Our wallets, that are heavy with good fare."

Now Brother Anthony, who knew the pranks
  Of Brother Timothy, would not persuade
Or reason with him on his quirks and cranks,
  But, being obedient, silently obeyed;
And, smiting with his staff the ass's flanks,
  Drove him before him over hill and glade,
Safe with his provend to the convent gate,
Leaving poor Brother Timothy to his fate.

Then Gilbert, laden with fagots for his fire,
  Forth issued from the wood, and stood
    aghast
To see the ponderous body of the friar
  Standing where he had left his donkey last.
Trembling he stood, and dared not venture
    nigher,
  But stared, and gaped, and crossed himself
    full fast;
For, being credulous and of little wit,
He thought it was some demon from the pit.

While speechless and bewildered thus he
  gazed,

And dropped his load of fagots on the
  ground,
Quoth Brother Timothy: "Be not amazed
  That where you left a donkey should be
  found
A poor Franciscan friar, half-starved and
  crazed,
  Standing demure and with a halter bound;
But set me free, and hear the piteous story
Of Brother Timothy of Casal-Maggiore.

"I am a sinful man, although you see
  I wear the consecrated cowl and cape;
You never owned an ass, but you owned me,
  Changed and transformed from my own
  natural shape
All for the deadly sin of gluttony,
  From which I could not otherwise escape,
Than by this penance, dieting on grass,
And being worked and beaten as an ass.

"Think of the ignominy I endured;
  Think of the miserable life I led,
The toil and blows to which I was inured,
  My wretched lodging in a windy shed,
My scanty fare so grudgingly procured,
  The damp and musty straw that formed
  my bed!
But, having done this penance for my sins,
My life as man and monk again begins."

The simple Gilbert, hearing words like these,

Was conscience-stricken, and fell down
  apace
Before the friar upon his bended knees,
  And with a suppliant voice implored his
  grace;
And the good monk, now very much at ease,
  Granted him pardon with a smiling face,
Nor could refuse to be that night his guest,
It being late, and he in need of rest.

Upon a hillside, where the olive thrives,
  With figures painted on its whitewashed
  walls,
The cottage stood; and near the humming
  hives
  Made murmurs as of far-off waterfalls;
A place where those who love secluded lives
  Might live content, and, free from noise
  and brawls,
Like Claudian's Old Man of Verona here
Measure by fruits the slow-revolving year.

And, coming to this cottage of content,
  They found his children, and the buxom
  wench
His wife, Dame Cicely, and his father, bent
  With years and labor, seated on a bench,
Repeating over some obscure event
  In the old wars of Milanese and French;
All welcomed the Franciscan, with a sense
Of sacred awe and humble reverence.

When Gilbert told them what had come to
    pass,
  How beyond question, cavil, or surmise,
Good Brother Timothy had been their ass,
    You should have seen the wonder in their
    eyes;
You should have heard them cry "Alas! alas!"
    Have heard their lamentations and their
    sighs!
For all believed the story, and began
To see a saint in this afflicted man.

Forthwith there was prepared a grand repast,
  To satisfy the craving of the friar
After so rigid and prolonged a fast;
    The bustling housewife stirred the kitchen
    fire;
Then her two barn-yard fowls, her best and
    last
    Were put to death, at her express desire,
And served up with a salad in a bowl,
And flasks of country wine to crown the
    whole.

It would not be believed should I repeat
  How hungry Brother Timothy appeared;
It was a pleasure but to see him eat,
    His white teeth flashing through his russet
    beard,
His face aglow and flushed with wine and
    meat,
    His roguish eyes that rolled and laughed

and leered!
Lord! how he drank the blood-red country
    wine
As if the village vintage were divine!

And all the while he talked without surcease,
    And told his merry tales with jovial glee
That never flagged, but rather did increase,
    And laughed aloud as if insane were he,
And wagged his red beard, matted like a
    fleece,
    And cast such glances at Dame Cicely
That Gilbert now grew angry with his guest,
And thus in words his rising wrath expressed.

"Good father," said he, "easily we see
    How needful in some persons, and how
    right,
Mortification of the flesh may be.
    The indulgence you have given it to-night,
After long penance, clearly proves to me
    Your strength against temptation is but
    slight,
And shows the dreadful peril you are in
Of a relapse into your deadly sin.

"To-morrow morning, with the rising sun,
    Go back unto your convent, nor refrain
From fasting and from scourging, for you
    run
    Great danger to become an ass again,
Since monkish flesh and asinine are one;

Therefore be wise, nor longer here remain,
Unless you wish the scourge should be ap-
  plied
By other hands, that will not spare your
  hide."

When this the monk had heard, his color fled
  And then returned, like lightning in the air,
Till he was all one blush from foot to head,
  And even the bald spot in his russet hair
Turned from its usual pallor to bright red!
  The old man was asleep upon his chair.
Then all retired, and sank into the deep
And helpless imbecility of sleep.

They slept until the dawn of day drew near,
  Till the cock should have crowed, but did
    not crow,
For they had slain the shining chanticleer
  And eaten him for supper, as you know.
The monk was up betimes and of good cheer,
  And, having breakfasted, made haste to go,
As if he heard the distant matin bell,
And had but little time to say farewell.

Fresh was the morning as the breath of kine;
  Odors of herbs commingled with the sweet
Balsamic exhalations of the pine;
  A haze was in the air presaging heat;
Uprose the sun above the Apennine,
  And all the misty valleys at its feet
Were full of the delirious song of birds,

Voices of men, and bells, and low of herds.

All this to Brother Timothy was naught;
  He did not care for scenery, nor here
His busy fancy found the thing it sought;
  But when he saw the convent walls appear,
And smoke from kitchen chimneys upward
    caught
  And whirled aloft into the atmosphere,
He quickened his slow footsteps, like a beast
That scents the stable a league off at least.

And as he entered through the convent gate
  He saw there in the court the ass, who stood
Twirling his ears about, and seemed to wait,
  Just as he found him waiting in the wood;
And told the Prior that, to alleviate
  The daily labors of the brotherhood,
The owner, being a man of means and thrift,
  Bestowed him on the convent as a gift.

And thereupon the Prior for many days
  Revolved this serious matter in his mind,
And turned it over many different ways,
  Hoping that some safe issue he might find;
But stood in fear of what the world would
    say,
  If he accepted presents of this kind,
Employing beasts of burden for the packs
That lazy monks should carry on their backs.

Then, to avoid all scandal of the sort,

And stop the mouth of cavil, he decreed
That he would cut the tedious matter short,
  And sell the ass with all convenient speed,
Thus saving the expense of his support,
  And hoarding something for a time of need.
So he despatched him to the neighboring
    Fair,
And freed himself from cumber and from
    care.

It happened now by chance, as some might
    say,
  Others perhaps would call it destiny,
Gilbert was at the Fair; and heard a bray,
  And nearer came, and saw that it was he,
And whispered in his ear, "Ah, lackaday!
  Good father, the rebellious flesh, I see,
Has changed you back into an ass again,
And all my admonitions were in vain."

The ass, who felt this breathing in his ear,
  Did not turn round to look, but shook his
    head,
As if he were not pleased these words to hear,
  And contradicted all that had been said.
And this made Gilbert cry in voice more
    clear,
  "I know you well; your hair is russet-red;
Do not deny it; for you are the same
Franciscan friar, and Timothy by name."

The ass, though now the secret had come
    out,
  Was obstinate, and shook his head again;
Until a crowd was gathered round about
  To hear this dialogue between the twain;
And raised their voices in a noisy shout
  When Gilbert tried to make the matter
    plain,
And flouted him and mocked him all day
    long
With laughter and with jibes and scraps of
    song.

"If this be Brother Timothy," they cried,
  "Buy him, and feed him on the tenderest
    grass;
Thou canst not do too much for one so tried
  As to be twice transformed into an ass."
So simple Gilbert bought him, and untied
  His halter, and o'er mountain and morass
He led him homeward, talking as he went
Of good behavior and a mind content.

The children saw them coming, and ad-
    vanced,
  Shouting with joy, and hung about his
    neck, —
Not Gilbert's, but the ass's, — round him
    danced,
  And wove green garlands wherewithal to
    deck
His sacred person; for again it chanced

Their childish feelings, without rein or
    check,
Could not discriminate in any way
A donkey from a friar of Orders Gray.

"O Brother Timothy," the children said,
    "You have come back to us just as before;
We were afraid, and thought that you were
    dead,
    And we should never see you any more."
And then they kissed the white star on his
    head,
    That like a birth-mark or a badge he wore,
And patted him upon the neck and face,
And said a thousand things with childish
    grace.

Thenceforward and forever he was known
    As Brother Timothy, and led alway
A life of luxury, till he had grown
    Ungrateful, being stuffed with corn and
    hay,
And very vicious. Then in angry tone,
    Rousing himself, poor Gilbert said one day,
"When simple kindness is misunderstood
A little flagellation may do good."

His many vices need not here be told;
    Among them was a habit that he had
Of flinging up his heels at young and old,
    Breaking his halter, running off like mad

O'er pasture-lands and meadow, wood and
   wold,
   And other misdemeanors quite as bad;
But worst of all was breaking from his shed
At night, and ravaging the cabbage-bed.

So Brother Timothy went back once more
   To his old life of labor and distress;
Was beaten worse than he had been before;
   And now, instead of comfort and caress,
Came labors manifold and trials sore;
   And as his toils increased his food grew
   less,
Until at last the great consoler, Death,
Ended his many sufferings with his breath.

Great was the lamentation when he died;
   And mainly that he died impenitent;
Dame Cicely bewailed, the children cried,
   The old man still remembered the event
In the French war, and Gilbert magnified
   His many virtues, as he came and went,
And said: "Heaven pardon Brother Timothy,
And keep us from the sin of gluttony."